Disembodying Narrative

DISPATCHES FROM THE NEW DIASPORA

Series Editors: Marc H. Ellis and Susanne Scholz

"New Diaspora" evokes the biblical theme of exile, as developed in Marc H. Ellis's many writings, to describe the intellectual's posture as an "exile" from established and dominant communities of religious and political orthodoxy, and to highlight the practices of inquiry and solidarity across boundaries that constitute the critical work of scholarship in biblical, theological, and religious-studies disciplines. The serviceability of scholarship to constellations of power, especially destructive power, is a target of Dispatches, but the series also seeks to describe and present the positive practices that are already establishing a new and more humane social reality.

Titles in this series

Disembodying Narrative: A Postcolonial Subversion of Genesis, by Jeremiah Cataldo

The New Diaspora and the Global Prophetic: Engaging the Scholarship of Marc H. Ellis, edited by Susanne Scholz and Santiago Slabodsky

Disembodying Narrative

A Postcolonial Subversion of Genesis

Jeremiah Cataldo

LEXINGTON BOOKS/FORTRESS ACADEMIC

Lanham • Boulder • New York • London

Published by Lexington Books/Fortress Academic
Lexington Books is an imprint of The Rowman & Littlefield Publishing Group, Inc.
4501 Forbes Boulevard, Suite 200, Lanham, Maryland 20706
www.rowman.com

86-90 Paul Street, London EC2A 4NE, United Kingdom

Copyright © 2024 by The Rowman & Littlefield Publishing Group, Inc.

All rights reserved. No part of this book may be reproduced in any form or by any electronic or mechanical means, including information storage and retrieval systems, without written permission from the publisher, except by a reviewer who may quote passages in a review.

British Library Cataloguing in Publication Information Available

Library of Congress Cataloging-in-Publication Data

Names: Cataldo, Jeremiah W., author.
Title: Disembodying narrative : a postcolonial subversion of genesis / Jeremiah Cataldo.
Description: Lanham : Lexington Books/Fortress Academic, [2024] | Series: Dispatches from the new diaspora | Includes bibliographical references and index. | Summary: "In this book, Jeremiah Cataldo subjects the Book of Genesis to postcolonial analysis. He explores the continuing impact that ideological colonialism has not only on dominant traditions of biblical interpretation but also on human social and political relationships touched by assumptions about the Bible, God, power, and human identity"— Provided by publisher.
Identifiers: LCCN 2023040480 (print) | LCCN 2023040481 (ebook) | ISBN 9781978714977 (cloth) | ISBN 9781978714984 (epub)
Subjects: LCSH: Bible. Genesis—Postcolonial criticism.
Classification: LCC BS1235.52 .C38 2024 (print) | LCC BS1235.52 (ebook) | DDC 222/.1106—dc23/eng/20231016
LC record available at https://lccn.loc.gov/2023040480
LC ebook record available at https://lccn.loc.gov/2023040481

♾™ The paper used in this publication meets the minimum requirements of American National Standard for Information Sciences—Permanence of Paper for Printed Library Materials, ANSI/NISO Z39.48-1992.

For David Clines, whose work influenced me when I was a student and whose later friendship helped me find the confidence as a scholar to say what needed to be said.

Contents

Acknowledgments   ix

Abbreviations   xi

Chapter 1: Introduction   1

Chapter 2: Adam, Eve, and Steve's Serpent   29

Chapter 3: Colonizing Cain   51

Chapter 4: Highbrow Hamitic Hypothesis   71

Chapter 5: Flooding the World and Saving a Few   83

Chapter 6: Inverting the Tower of Babel   97

Chapter 7: Father Abraham Sentenced a Son, or Two   117

Chapter 8: A(n Incestual, Pedophilic) Cave-Dwelling Lot   137

Chapter 9: Sarah's (Colonizing) Laughter and Hagar's (Colonized) Tears   151

Chapter 10: Jacob and Esau   163

Chapter 11: Joseph from Lowly Status into Authoritative Body   175

Conclusion: Taking Stock of the Trajectory of Genesis   187

Bibliography   195

Index   207

About the Author   211

Acknowledgments

No project is truly completed alone. There are many influences, some major and some minor, some obvious and some subtle, that have an impact upon what an author says, or how it is said. For that reason, I am thankful to Susanne Scholz who saw the potential of this project. In addition, both Susanne and Marc Ellis guided me away from potential landmines in some of the arguments I was making. Repeated conversations with Heather McKay on related themes helped me revise and refine my analysis. Likewise, Ehud ben Zvi took the time to read through projects impacted by this research and talk about main themes over Zoom. Dwayne Tunstall graciously helped me work through and rephrase some potentially problematic areas. Maria Cimitile provided feedback on portions of an early draft. Lastly, my family suffered through "another book" which took me away, if not physically then mentally, for repeated long periods of time. To all, thank you.

Abbreviations

Abraham	"Abraham's faith and obedience," in *Works of Menno Simon, volume 1.*
Ant.	Josephus, *Antiquities of the Jews,* William Whiston, trans.
Ap. John	*Apocryphon of John*
Ber. Rab.	*Bereishit Rabbah*
Cain	Ambrose, "Cain and Abel," in *Hexameron, Paradise, and Cain and Abel,* trans. John J. Savage (Washington, DC: Catholic University of America Press, 1961)
City	Augustine, *City of God* (Schaff, Philip, ed. *A Select Library of the Nicene and Post-Nicene Fathers of the Christian Church: St. Augustin's City of God and Christian Doctrine.* Translated by Marcus Dods and J. F. Shaw. Vol. 2. London: T&T Clark, 1886)
Com. Bible	Matthew Henry, *Commentary on the Whole of the Bible, Volume I (Genesis to Deuteronomy)*
Com. Gen.	John Calvin, *Commentary on the First Book of Moses Called Genesis,* trans. John King. Christian Classics Ethereal Library
Confusion	Philo, *On the Confusion of Tongues*
Dum diversas	Latin text published in Levy Maria Jordao, ed., *Bullarium patronoatus Portugalliae regum in ecclesiis Africae, Asiae atque Oceaniae: bullas, brevia, epistolas, decreta actaque sancte sedis ab Alexandro III ad hoc usque tempus amplectens* (Olisipone: Ex typographia nationalia, 1868).

Duties	Ambrose, *On the Duties of the Clergy: Book I,* trans. Philip Schaff. *The Complete Church Fathers.*
Ei. Rab.	*Eikhah Rabba.* Vilna, 1899.
Gen.	Augustine, *De Genesi ad litteram libri duodecim* (J.-P. Migne, *Patrologia Cursus Completus [Patrologia Latina],* vol. 34 [Paris, 1845]; English translation by John Hammon, S. J. *St. Augustine, The Literal Meaning of Genesis* [Ancient Christian Writers; Ramsey, NJ: Paulist, 1982]).
Good Marr.	Augustine, *Of the Good of Marriage* (translated by C.L. Cornish. *From Nicene and Post-Nicene Fathers,* First Series, Vol. 3. Edited by Philip Schaff. [Buffalo, NY: Christian Literature Publishing Co., 1887.] Revised and edited for New Advent by Kevin Knight).
Gov.	Aristotle, *A Treatise on Government* (translated by William Ellis, 1928).
Hero	Ignatius (attributed). Epistle.
Hist. Church	Joseph Smith, *History of the Church*
Histories	Herodotus
Looking Back	Jonathan Edwards, "Sermon IV: The Folly of Looking Back in Fleeing Out of Sodom," in *Works of Jonathan Edwards, Volume Two*
Notes	John Wesley, *Notes on the Bible*
Studies	John Fletcher, *Studies on Slavery* (Charleston: McCarter & Allen, 1852)
Summa	Thomas Aquinas, *Summa Theologiae* (translated by the Fathers of the English Dominican Province, 1920)
Sup. Greg. Dom.	*Super gregum dominicum in Monumenta Henricina,* volume V, doc. 49, pp. 113–115
Ten Comm.	Martin Luther, *Sermon on the Ten Commandments,* 1516, WA I

Chapter 1

Introduction

Listen, then speak.
Usually in that order.
Shout in the face of oppression.

Staring at disfigured faces marred by lost histories, identities, values, and dignities, but reconstructed through forced foreign replacements of those things lost, imposed upon now subordinated bodies, postcolonialism, with its unwavering gaze, challenges oppressive legacies rooted in preserved histories, cultures, concepts of land, politics, economics, and ethnicities.[1] It demands an accounting. It demands a bearing of responsibility. It *demands* an exposure of the hidden and disfigured body of the "other" whose attributes a dominating subject has defined as its own antithesis. After all, in interpretation and the preservation of meaning there is a dangerous power in its acceptance or rejection, in who can demand that marginalized others accept meaning defined according to an external and dominating cultural framework, and punish in public display those who do not. Concerned about these things, postcolonialism *demands* recognition that translation is simultaneously an act of embodiment *and* disembodiment. It must expose that in translation, the essence of who "I" am radiates while the essence of who "you" are is disfigured, deconstructed, and re-figured. It challenges those situations in which "I" have defined "you" according to the categories of meaning codified in and by the cultural frameworks and institutions in which the radiating echoes of who "I" am are joyously passed on from one boundary to another. But "you" are the sum of what I reject. And if, to borrow from Northrop Frye generally and Vico's axiom in particular, *verum factum*, what is true in criticism (and interpretation) we have made true, we can also say that translation is the act of doing just that by mapping out the relations of meaning to the structures and ideologies that are the objects of philosophy, history, and communication on political, social, religious, and economic grounds.[2] It is an act of deconstructing and remaking bodies that *already are* in static form, frozen

2   *Chapter 1*

in a foreign process of becoming. *"You" become the body that "I" see.* And the colonized face that stares back are the contours of a disfigured form that no longer represents what its body knows it used to be.

If you are expecting a book chock-full of feel-good stories and emotion-laden pleas about "colonized cultures," you've picked up the wrong book. Postcolonialism shouldn't entail third-person stories alone. It is not those stories. It is a disconcerting method of critique, of subversion, of challenge. It begins from the constructivist position that (translating the quote) "colonialism was condemned, a priori, to its disappearance" and that (translating the quote) "the imposition of an external dominion over any population generates resistance, and this ends up being costly . . ."[3] That is what you will get with this book.

Initially, I wanted to use "neo-postcolonialism" in the title to signal that this work was doing something more than that what currently passes for postcolonial analysis in biblical studies. But titles should invoke a sense of recognition, and neo-postcolonialism is not something that has yet asserted its own identity in academic discourse. So I opted to keep "postcolonialism" without the "neo" preformative. Not only that, but the prefix "neo" suggests a something *beyond* postcolonialism. I am not sure we are at a point where we could even identify what that is. So, again, I kept the title as it is now trusting that this discussion will provide some sense of my approach to postcolonialism as a method. I believe it is a tool belt capable of adapting other methods in pursuit of its overall aim: dismantling oppressive power structures and networks that thrive on erasure. That dismantled "beyond" of postcolonialism is a world in which there is no need for subversion. But as an intelligent young man, Eli, pointed out that "beyond" is ideal because, as postcolonialism reminds us, we must be always diligent about preserving space for the humanity of others. In that, postcolonialism is not just a reaction to the fabricated dichotomies of colonialism, or even to the historical realities of colonialism. It challenges the cultural systems and institutions that continue to preserve inequalities between power centers and their margins.

Postcolonialism's position is humanitarian because it seeks to reclaim the bastions of self-preservation, which were colonized by others, that are fundamental to "peoplehood." One must not lose that fundamental strategy and focus when adopting postcolonialism as a lens to interpret texts. In its subversive need, it must deconstruct the fabricated body of the "other," which it rejects as itself, because a dominating culture constructed that body through an application of prostheses that transform the body into one culturally acceptable. To fail to do so, to be "civil" and "polite," which are concepts and categories around acceptable behavior themselves defined by a dominant culture, is to legitimate the very institutions and assumptions that

Introduction 3

bolster the division between subjects binarily opposed in structures of power. Those, we must acknowledge, are themselves legacies of colonialism that also claim the authority of translation and its privatization of meaning and "truth." Such expectations also tend to allow for the raw truth to be softened, if not obscured, within the conventionally accepted vocabulary and values of a dominant tradition not looking to condemn itself.

In applying postcolonial studies to the Bible, a pitfall we must avoid is hastily finding proof of postcolonial subjects or foci in binaries of empires and defeated peoples. Too often, biblical scholars adopt the vocabulary and motifs of postcolonialism without challenging the normalized traditions and interpretations rooted in colonized histories from which they benefit as scholars. *Look, everyone! I found a new minority! Let "me" tell "you" what "it" is using the dominant theories and "authoritative" works.* Biblical references to empire vis-à-vis Israel, imperial politics voiced by Judean prophets, and even Israel's military losses to Near Eastern empires are the joy of interpreters promoting Israel to be a postcolonial subject, or in more theological terms, the "suffering servant." While not always consciously so, and I want to be attentive to the everyday relevance of what I'm addressing, such views tend to build the framework for an anti-Palestinian perspective among Jews and Christians.[4] Of all the monotheistic traditions claiming its legion of biblical scholars, Christianity may be the most guilty of culturally appropriating the sufferings of colonized bodies to privatize the qualities and attributes of its Suffering Servant, Jesus, and by extension the Body of Christ, as the inverted image of the fetishized object of the "other." *Join with us and we will show you how Christ will save those who conform to his image; all others are Satan's fodder!*

This re-appropriation prevails within US Christian culture. According to the National Association of Evangelicals, 76 percent of church leaders in the United States, surveyed in 2016, expect they will be persecuted for their faith.[5] Is *real* persecution on the rise? Not in the United States. But two main beliefs support that expectation: Christianity's cultural stranglehold is loosening, and the eschatological expectations at the core of Christianity—*the establishment of a divine "empire"*—prime Christians to find evidence of the body suffering.

With that in mind, we must be wary of how dominant traditions of interpretation are rooted in the vocabularies of empire. Empires, as physical entities and as metaphors of ideological oppression, the latter upon which this work will focus, are guilty of imposing singularity and universalism in meaning and interpretation in an act of subordinating others. *You are who I say you are.* The potential to deconstruct that is pressing. To ignore it is to reinforce the legacies of colonialism that have given birth to modern theological and biblical discourse. One of the most astonishing examples is justification for

4 *Chapter 1*

segregation and slavery, the former being an attempt to cling to the ideological assumption that bolstered the latter. While most countries of the modern world, such as the United States, outlaw slavery, minoritized cultural agents can still feel how prejudiced inequalities have shaped dominant cultural traditions and traditions of interpretation. One need not be consciously prejudiced to benefit from ideas and meanings constructed through a prejudice of values. Take the example of Humphrey Ezell,

> The most robust effort to apply Noah's curse to American segregation appeared in 1959 in Humphrey K. Ezell's *The Christian Problem of Racial Segregation.* Claiming to engage in a "careful study of the Bible passages that relate to this subject," Ezell offered a gloss on the curse specifically adapted to the needs of the Christian segregationist. In a chapter titled "The Old Testament Teaches Racial Segregation," Ezell quoted Genesis 9:20–27 in its entirety, calling it "an important passage on racial segregation."[6]

The ease with which monotheistic traditions perpetuate prejudice, reinforcing insider-outsider distinctions, and what modern individuals might refer to as a transgression of human rights and dignities is reason enough to demand a full accounting of how those traditions and their cultures interpret sacred texts.[7] *Everybody's standing in silence / and I'm still gazing / a human inside me is calling / who sympathizes with me?*[8] Not the history of the dominant majority, if that "me" is a minority, an accusation that can be leveled at religious traditions as well. The history of religion is rooted in the political, in the exchange and protection of power and access to it. Among religion's familial traditions, monotheisms are the biggest charlatans. Despite their claims to altruism, underneath their colorful and enticing outfits, draped upon the mutantized bodies of the colonized and converted "other," they are strategies of empire building.[9] *My God and his plan will rule. The eventual reality of Heaven, or restoration, confirms that.* Understanding that underlying strategy reveals their emphases upon conversion, upon control over public morality, upon defining "family," gender, upon control over education, through how they justify wars, segregation, colonization, and even slavery. Control over these areas is to claim the power to define the dominant attributes (a means to enculturate) of a collective identity that defines a people. It is power to define who others are in relation to the dominant self and what the bodies of insiders in contrast to outsiders represent. That these issues continue to be present even after the political and material commonness of empires and colonization is one reason postcolonial scholars have referred to concepts such as "ideological colonialism" and the "Global South."[10] Used appropriately, these concepts help expose the multi-centered nature of power and periphery

Introduction 5

and move postcolonialism past the historical (and frequently material) binary (colonizer-colonized) assumptions that first defined it as a methodology.

Moreover, those concepts reinforce the understanding that unequally yoked or imbalanced power structures that favor a specific community are not the consequences of physical empires alone. One finds inequality perpetuated also in ideology. The first concept, ideological colonialism, refers to the perpetuation of those institutions, frameworks, value systems, moralities, concepts of citizenship, preservation of histories, and vocabularies that reinforce a dichotomy between a dominant culture and those marginalized or outright rejected. An example of a community marginalized is the African American community in the United States. An example of one rejected is LGBTQIA communities in Uganda. The second concept, Global South, refers to disenfranchised peoples and cultures suffering under shared subjugation to a "transnational political Other."

I maintain unless we are content to remain stuck in ossified categories of postcolonial analysis, mired in rigid, elementary binary assumptions about power, a contentedness which is part of the reason postcolonialism has remained on the margins of academic discourse, we must see postcoloniality as something more diverse. "Colonized" subjects, whose "reborn" bodies are the fetish of foreign aims, must be seen as those who negotiate their losses and identities through a process of triangulation: "unstable, ambivalent, and relational positions between a coerced centre, a desired centre, and an alternative periphery."[11] To recognize that means one also recognizes that postcolonial concerns of the twentieth and twenty-first centuries are bigger than what most scholars have historically associated with postcolonialism. They call, as Bogdan Ştefănescu writes, for recognition that postcoloniality is "multi-centric and poly-peripheral," which sees "a different, more complex geo-cultural and historical portrayal than the one provided by mainstream postcolonialism."[12] In this sense of what it must become, as though a type of *neo*-postcolonialism (but recall my earlier discussion of this term), it must be adopted as an intersectional method that seeks to deconstruct demonized bodies of the "other" by incorporating liberationist thinking, empire-colony binaries (but we should not limit it there), Neo-Marxist criticisms, feminist criticism, queer methodologies, affect theory, prosthetic criticisms, and more. When we recognize that, we can move beyond, but not abandon, the older empire-colony binary and address the pervasive ideological colonialisms that exist in the present world. Only by doing that will it bring us closer to being able to unpack the role of ideology in stitching together its colonized subjects. Because, as Althusser notes, ideology "bends to the interests of the times, but without any apparent reason, being content for collective historical changes which is its mission to assimilate and master by some perceptual modification of its peculiar internal relations."[13] Whose interests are being served by the non-disrupted status quo? Postcolonialism pulls back the scab of sociopolitical and religious ideologies to show us that those interests are not those of the marginalized and minoritized.

To understand how resistance to change can be reified, one must understand the nature of ideology, which Althusser describes as moving with culture and seeking always to remain static. It reflects the essence of its time. Put better, a prevailing cultural ideology reflects the essence of a dominant or dominating culture. When dominant cultures include minority perspectives in ideological change, they typically do so within the containment of prevailing dominant and linguistic and meaning frameworks.[14] That situation forces the marginalized body to conform to imposed expectations, reinforced by dominating institutions and systems of power, on behavior and ideology to be accepted as an insider. Real change that breaks down center-periphery dichotomies, postcolonialism reminds us, breaks those expectations as well.

The girth of academic studies on postcolonialism, however, does not focus on most of what I've described, which is itself a small aspect of postcolonial concern. Most studies, rather, tend to cherry-pick aspects of postcolonial method that don't threaten the scholarly normative while also appealing to softhearted liberal concerns. While I share the liberal concern for the status of minorities, I find the lack of internal criticism and subversion in scholarly activities to be little more than saying the right things while also not challenging the institutions that created the need for those things to be said. *My scholarship claims that minority concerns are important! Yes, but have you cited accepted works to prove that?* There's too much in the way, perhaps, for most scholars. Either they fear challenging the faith traditions to which they still keep some connection, to whatever degree, or they crave acceptance and legitimation by their peers. The latter is an unavoidable evil in Academia. Careers live and die based on peer legitimation and acceptance. But that fear often translates into diminished risk-taking, which serves to reinforce the traditional institutions, values, and systems fashioned in an imperial context in which things like Orientalism were en vogue. *The very things postcolonialism seeks to subvert!*

There is a third option, an either-or-*or* paradigm that takes over for an "and-then" one.[15] Faced with two options that reflect presupposed aims, "The body falls back on desiring-production, attracts it, and appropriates it for its own."[16] Forced to choose whether to be what a dominant power says it is, the marginalized body liberates itself when it rejects the restraints of that choice, "You've said I can be that or thus, but I'll be this." It comes in the expectation of postcolonialism's demand that academics revise their bibliographies, which have relied upon works written by and published for cultures rooted in colonial pasts. It is too easy, however, to adopt superficial ideas into one's already defined academic enterprise. Doing so, paying lip service to postcolonialism,

Introduction 7

only neuters it. Where one might see references to empire, imperial politics, and imperial conquest, it is tempting to attach postcolonialism as an optic through which to interpret biblical passages, as though they needed "rescued from a strange and perilous situation" and "restored to life."[17] This so-called third option creates space for the expanded understanding of postcolonialism that Ştefănescu called for.[18] And it addresses the concern voiced by Mishra and Hodges, "History is not some contingent, endlessly deferred, and non-foundational language game; it has real, foundational value in the lives of the recently emancipated. The trouble is that the historical center has been too sweepingly invoked even in postcolonial theory, where very often 'pedagogical expediency' triumphs over localized and rigorous 'political and economic scrutiny.'"[19] That scrutiny must attend to the complex of intersections that increasingly define the disfigured body of the postcolonial position. In biblical studies, it must frequently resist the monotheistic paradigm of theological expediency that has marginalized if not obscured the multiplicity of meaning, value, and identity. Biblical interpretation has been one area of guilt that has frequently dodged such scrutiny. With theological sleight of hand, dominant Christian interpretive traditions highlight an empire-imperialized binary as the root of a metaphor for the "suffering servant" *and* the Body of Christ that must take up Christ's example. With that binary assumption about Christ's rule/domain throughout history, those traditions have solidified the framework through which to justify social, political, economic and ethnic inequalities—a point that I will discuss throughout this work.

Take, for additional example, the biblical prophets. Most of them focus on some element of imperial conflict or reality either with the Assyrian Empire, the Babylonian Empire, or even the Persian Empire sometimes, such as Third Isaiah. For the most part, their concerns were the relationship between the Israelites, or Judeans, the decline in national power, and the imperial power that ruled the land. In other words, they were general social and political concerns one can find in all societies and cultures in which foreign empires had established themselves over conquered peoples. Most societies don't celebrate or desire foreign imperial overrule, which is an external institution that diminishes the subjugated's potential. As Mitri Raheb writes, "Empires are always about control."[20] Control includes the ability to define the dominant narrative, politics, and ideologies that govern a geo-political territory or context. In that context, colonized or imperialized cultures are those that are expected to fit themselves within a dominating framework. But as I noted earlier, this subjugated existence is not definable as a simple binary. It includes ideological conflicts over where subjugated peoples are, where they want to be, and the other "peripheries" that emerge in their continued attempts to navigate their uprooted, colonized statuses. At the same time, the prophets, despite their historically contingent, multi-periphery, and prejudiced

8   *Chapter 1*

concerns, are interpreted as being universally relevant, knowable through a singular binary by which the world is categorized, and almost always anticipating, for Christians, Christ's rule.

It is a well-known, to those with any real historical and sociological awareness, that all conquered or subject peoples eventually resist the weight of imperial rule, whether through preserved cultural narratives or embodied in physical and revolutionary action depends on the people, context, and access to material resources. The desire to make decisions for one's own body, independent of the control of outside forces, is innate within human beings—which can be seen in the tension of continual self-subjection in religions to a divine Other while denying desires of the self, social protests for equality that highlight the divide between the religious ideal of the body and self and who a person is in their entirety, and more. At the same time, human beings also desire the power to restrict the potential and identity of others to conform them to our own social-political image.

Put differently, we have a tendency as human beings in the world dominated by governments to chafe against demands by ruling bodies that we do not feel have our best interests in mind. The lack of national or collective autonomy that results from being subjected to foreign (over)rule reinforces internal concerns for stability. Communities seek the freedom and power to define and categorize for themselves institutions and systems and values upon which they thrive. For groups and individuals, social acceptance is rooted in clearly defined places within the dominant normative. That sense of place may come in a variety of ways but is confirmed in the narratives of self that communities and individuals tell. As Deborah Shiffrin put it, "The stories we tell about or own and others' lives are a pervasive form of text through which we construct, interpret, and share experience . . . "[21] And Elinor Ochs and Lisa Capps write, "Adherence to a dominant narrative is also community-building in that it presumes that each member ascribes to a common story."[22] In various ways, it is *that presumption* that postcolonialism challenges because the "common story" is the story of a dominant culture and its institutions. To connect this to the Bible, let me propose here that the dominant traditions of biblical interpretation are attempts to colonize the world fueled by a common story that burgeoned in the communities of Western European Christians, who historically, radically shook off Christianity's Jewish heritage and celebrated Christianity's compatibility with imperial rule.

That is why biblical interpretations must avoid hasty correlations between reference to empire and imperial defeat as evidence of colonization. There is more at stake than mere vocabulary. Postcolonialism is an attempt to expose aspects of colonization, namely, those aspects in which a subject or colonized people lose something about themselves and are forced to define themselves vis-à-vis imposed categories consistent with the common story of a foreign

Introduction 9

and dominating culture.[23] If I must define or understand who I am according to how you define me, then I must cease those traditions, meanings, and values that defined me and adopt yours. That is the very expectation of colonialism. In response, postcolonialism seeks to liberate human dignities, persons, cultures, and traditions from *all* of the centers of influence and power that force them to adopt ideas, values, and physical realities that are the attributes of a dominating culture. It seeks the return of the marginalized body to a space in which it ceases to exist as marginal, and to where it has the unchained freedom to voice its own narrative.

After all, conscientiousness demands that we avoid the simplistic dichotomy of empire-defeated peoples as evidence of colonialism.[24] It does not bear the expectation of postcolonial theory. While some may say that the death toll has sounded for postcolonialism, it is because they miss its expanded potential. Clinging to the assumption of a single binary of power-periphery, such individuals miss its evolution into something more powerful as it deconstructs the image a dominating power has forced upon a colonized body. In that process, it has taken on aspects of critical analyses that are consistent with Neo-Marxist, queer, prosthetic, ideological, feminist, and liberation criticisms.[25] Missing that larger complexity, many biblical scholars claiming to practice postcolonial theory in biblical analyses, specifically of the prophets, have found comfort in the dichotomy of empire and defeated peoples, while failing to challenge the institutions and values bolstering legacies of colonialism within traditions of biblical interpretations. In that oversight, they miss the more aggressive "bite" of what postcolonialism in its evolving form attempts to accomplish. The weight of Western Capitalism, an ideological force imposing constraints often unacknowledged, has already constrained the intended audiences of such studies to those who already share a common story. *Scholars representing a dominant majority tend to write for scholars representing a dominant majority.*

That speaks to another issue that postcolonialism must free itself from, having been cast there originally by colonial definitions of knowledge about its own beleaguered circumstances. The method is not solely that of an archaeologist uncovering the relics of historical cultures and identities covered over by power hierarchies and the institutional systems characteristic of a dominant culture. That *is* part of its job, but it isn't *only* that. It must become more self-aware. It must take on the task of undoing translations imposed and seeking what it gleans from the past as a meaningful commentary, even accusation, for the present. Because translation involves awareness of the translator's positionality, translations are the outcomes of networks of affects.[26] In that, postcolonialism may challenge present oppressions and struggles driven by ideological colonialism.[27] It is by focusing there that postcolonialism may be effective at addressing present struggles of minority communities chafing

10   *Chapter 1*

against dominant narratives that demand conformity to cultural ideals, values, commitments, and mores.

If postcolonialism does not do that, if it embraces its imposed limitations of simply an archaeologist of the past, then it will continue to be shackled to the margins, as Rasiah Sugirtharajah has already bemoaned.[28] And in this moment of reckoning, I can't help but be reminded of what Malcolm X championed, that the struggle for civil rights must become the struggle for human rights.[29] Denial of human rights and freedoms is simultaneously a rejection of any possibility of a more universal morality. *That* is a concern postcolonialism shares.

While the methodological transition I describe is one being adopted by some postcolonial theorists, it is less known within biblical studies. Contrary to trends in biblical studies to treat postcolonialism as such, it is *more* than just reading response. It is a strategy, a protest, a hermeneutic of interpretation that focuses on the past, not only in what the biblical text says but in how major traditions have limited its meanings. By exposing those elements, it *subverts* them and offers new strategies of interpretation attentive to the liberation and recognition of an oppressed or minoritized or marginalized minority. It shares some concerns, in that regard, with liberation theology. Its goal is to challenge the dominant traditions of biblical interpretation in ways that expose the prejudices and exclusivist tendencies that bolster them. It seeks from the biblical texts strategies for creating space for the unregulated expression of a community's own sense of self. It does not pursue the codification of vocabulary, theological or otherwise, about its subjects that subjects them to a foreign linguistic and meaning system.

In that sense, postcolonialism should aspire to write itself out of existence, to consider itself a tool with which to deconstruct or "undo" the Frankensteinian image of its defendant's colonized body. No longer needed, it would be buried under the sands of time, awaiting archaeologists of the future to find it and speculate on why people of the past oppressed and mutantized others to conform to the self-image and narratives of dominating powers. Certainly, that's ideal and may likely never happen. That does not mean, however, we should stop pursuing its aims. Humans love to hate each other and to divide themselves based on differences. So much so that we, as human beings, developed religious traditions alongside empires, after all, to legitimate, and make permanent, colonizing actions—a point this work will address throughout. While the passing (should I say "ascension"?) of postcolonialism as I refer to it is ideal, the intent behind its conduct should be to change the nature of discourse and awareness to the extent it is no longer needed. Regarding biblical studies, it should change those things in the dominant discourses around interpretation so much that the perspectives of minority groups are heard and embraced within the larger dialogue, not

Introduction 11

simply as the expression of a minority but of someone who is engaged within the larger conversation.

In that sense, postcolonialism as a methodological approach facilitates a change in how what someone says is valued and heard. In doing that, it subverts the dominant traditions and ideological assumptions that reinforce them. And, it does this to unmake the institutional and systematic inequalities that oppress. Such inequalities are also found in religious traditions, biblical interpretations, theologies, and doctrines rooted in the belief that a dichotomy—of insider-outsider, center-margin, or good-evil—is foundational for defining the people of God. Postcolonialism must be, in other words, even if only temporarily, anti-monotheistic. It must seek to fragment the monotheistic body, which is the core of monotheistic identities (those manifest in different traditions).[30]

Postcolonialism challenges the imperial and colonial foundations upon which Western religions have matured. It *must* challenge those legacies. After all, they are preserved in the histories told, the cultures ascending to dominance, concepts of land defined by biblical interpretations (of Genesis, nonetheless!), the definition of community and land as relevant to the Middle East, and international politics about it.[31] It must pay attention to, among many other things, ideological claims supporting Israel's political claim over Palestinian territories, as well as the extent of the military, economic, among other, actions taken by Israel to claim that land.[32] Individuals and communities who hold to the view that God gave the land to a specific ethnicity have mired their ideological positions in the interpretive tradition of a theologically romanticized vision of a biblical Israel and its past. A vision that monotheism makes highly exclusive.

With its privatization of God, much of Western Christianity is rooted in the belief that God's revelation entailed the election of a particular people group, and that Christians are the descendants of that people. The basis of that is also the root of belief that Israel belongs to the Jews. I will address why that is a politically problematic assertion, but one that Western Christians support because of their own theological and eschatological aspirations: the land must be under Jewish occupation for the eschaton to occur.[33] We can wrap all of that in as much feel-good theology as we like. *God loves us, we can be certain, even though many of his ways are beyond human comprehension.* But we must come to terms with the fact that those theologies are rooted in the dominant cultural concerns of a majority group benefiting from colonial and imperial foundations. *The ultimate gain of Jewish occupation of Israel is Christian rule with the second coming of Christ.* That is the dirty underbelly of Christian support "for the Jews"—the goal of Heaven and co-rule with Christ. I will explain this at greater length within this book. But let me say here that how we engage in politics is shaped by how we understand the

12   *Chapter 1*

nature of power, community, morals, ethics, and how those things have been defined in terms of economics and ethnicities, *and* that understanding stems from one's own perspective. In biblical studies, then, postcolonialism should challenge the dominant hold those legacies have had on dominant traditions of interpretation, especially those that provide the basis for assumptions about morality, ethics, the nature of good, and human obligation to the divine.

As postcolonialism challenges, it subverts; and it does so by drawing critical question to those traditions. Subversion changes institutions and systems from within. A challenge without a subversive element can be ignored, like the lone knight outside the city walls throwing rocks, issuing challenges. He can be ignored, and his challenge will go nowhere. But the propaganda, the conspiracy, the changing of a narrative facilitated by rebels within the walls heighten the impact of the knight's rocks cast. Postcolonialism must behave somewhat like that. Not that we want to fall into the trap of saying that the dominant normative is the ideal against which postcolonialism must define itself and replace the essence of its form. Claiming that is very much part of a colonial enterprise. It must subvert within while challenging from without.

That is also why postcolonial theory must challenge dominant conceptions of morality, civility, and identity. It must be intentionally rude, and sometimes angry, when that is necessary to disrupt the status quo without bending to the status quo's own terms. Moreover, it must subvert the dominant hold that colonial and imperialist legacies have on traditions of biblical interpretation, as well as cultural values and norms that biblical interpretation reinforces. It must do so not simply for the sake of deconstruction, or to challenge only the conclusions of interpretations. For me, postcolonialism isn't about just undermining or subverting for no greater purpose. Its greater purpose is noble. It is a struggle for human rights and an increased awareness of the diversity of human cultures. It aims to liberate those suffering beneath ideological colonialism. In this expanded definition, postcolonialism is a method that seeks to emphasize and liberate human individuals and communities and their concerns by dismantling "multi-centers" and "poly-peripheries," an oppressive type of intersectionality, that subject them to the ideals and values of a dominating "other." It does so by recognizing there are human individuals at the end of theories whose cultures and identities are being erased beneath the oppressive weight of a dominant culture.

GENESIS AS A POSTCOLONIAL CASE STUDY IN THE SEARCH FOR HUMAN DIVERSITY

From among all the books in the Bible, Bible readers frequently cite Genesis for the archetypes of marriage, gender, family, right to the Promised Land,

Introduction 13

and more. It provides, in the minds of some, support for imposed ideals, values, and institutions that constitute a blueprint for some of the foundational aspects of the social world. It is used, in other words, as support for ideological colonialism rather than a challenge of it. Those tendencies should be challenged to expose the rootedness of assumptions about meaning, power, and identity in cultures motivated by ideological colonialism. A rather bold claim that antagonizes conservative assumptions about Genesis and the Bible as a whole, to be sure, but let my reader be assured that supporting that claim will be my aim in this project. I will argue that Genesis is not very "postcolonial" in part because it is not obviously about liberating a subject from a dominant power. Instead, its interpretations are frequently tools of ideological colonialism. Exodus, in contrast, discusses the liberation of the Hebrews from the foreign empire of Egypt. That exposes part of the problem because postcolonial interpretations of Exodus rest upon a binary of center and periphery in terms of power. As I discussed earlier, this simplistic binary is one that continues to be championed by some biblical scholars who are more content to discuss postcolonialism but not suffer any action for it. Moreover, this binary is limited because it risks reinforcing the dominant assumptions, even within dominant cultures, about the divine-human relationship and who benefits.

As I alluded, Genesis is frequently cited for a defense of marriage,[34] gender,[35] family,[36] the right to the Promised Land,[37] and more. It is often interpreted in support of "civilized" constructs of body, restricted to the image of communities in power over monotheistic traditions, in terms of role, gender, freedoms, and more. For many in the United States, how one defines and understands marriage, how one defines and understands gender, family, and Promised Land is rooted in a "proper" biblical understanding. Yet, does it really convey a singular, objective meaning? Even if that meaning discriminates against minorities and shows unabashed favor for a majority community? As I already described but will explain in greater detail throughout this work, the tradition that frames dominant interpretations and assumptions about Genesis is rooted in the colonial Western traditions that are also reinforced by the legacies of colonialism and imperialism expressed in the articulation of history, culture, land, politics, economics, and ethnicity. Unpacking that will be a focus of much of my discussion. I seek to expose how interpretation facilitates oppression, discrimination, and prejudice, and to do so by adopting methods of analysis that subvert dominant traditions. These include postcolonial, queer, Neo-Marxist, prosthetic, ideological, feminist, among others. Each of these contributes to a criticism of different power centers against peripheries are defined.

The correlation and the connection of all of that, I will discuss at length in the rest of this book. Suffice to say here that marriage and family are, within Western biblical tradition, considered the core of society. And that is not specific to biblical tradition, as one can also see it in the works of Aristotle (cf. *Gov.* 1.2–3). *What indeed has Athens to do with Jerusalem? Perhaps a great deal, Tertullian.* The definition of family and how it is discussed exposes numerous assumptions about the Bible, about God, about morality, about gender, about politics, about ethnicities, and so forth. In most modern arguments that stem from a conservative ideological position, marriage is an extension of family, as also are sexuality and gender. One motivation for an emphasis on family within biblical interpretation has been an attempt to define the nature of empire within Western Europe as the church sought to consolidate its hold over a significantly large political realm.[38] By controlling family and by extension marriage, one could control political relationships, political alliances, and be able to define the nature of who and what a citizen was.[39] But so that one does not accuse me of leaving unresolved issues, I will explain such concepts in fuller detail in the length of this work. That said, as I mentioned before, postcolonialism can't stop there. It must identify and recognize those legacies and challenge them. What, for instance, does the concept of family as it has been defined in the historical West mean for marginalized or colonized people? How does, if at all, the marginalized or colonized people group use that concept of family to say something about it without submitting themselves to a dominant culture's meaning and value system? I'm not sure they can. While families may be similar between cultures, what defines their social function and meaning is rooted in the particularities of culture.

The narratives of Genesis, foundational not only for Jewish and Christian traditions, also have become foundational in the modern context—if not "foundational," in some cases, then highly influential—for defining dominant attributes and contours of society. Where those interpretations become the framework by which the cultural milieu is regulated, they must be subjected to postcolonial analysis in order to deconstruct the restrictive and foreign identities imposed upon marginalized bodies. Therefore, in order to protest the repressive tendencies inherent within traditions of biblical interpretation, we must resist any interpretations upholding Genesis as a revelation that reinforces the dichotomy between center and periphery, or citizen and marginalized.

Toward that goal, part of my intent in this work is to challenge Genesis as a defense of conservative positions on marriage, gender, family, right to the so-called Promised Land, which are cornerstones for the very ideas and institutions on which Western societies are founded. *The people who will be saved by God are people like me, not you. But you can convert and become **one of us.*** The reading strategy is subversive. It poses a challenge. I want to recognize that and to emphasize that this subversive practice isn't an attempt to undermine the Bible or religion. It is an attempt to challenge the assumptions

Introduction 15

about society, or ideologies, traditions, and assumptions about what a society should *be* in productive ways to highlight areas of needed conversation. Because those traditions and interpretations are rooted in Western colonial fields of knowledge, this analysis will include a focus on assumptions about the inviolability of what a moral citizen is, and what a righteous citizen is. A postcolonial reading of Genesis is a challenge of assumptions about the social and religious worlds, rooted in biblical interpretations, and made by cultural beneficiaries of the legacies of colonialism and imperialism. It is not done for the sake of subversion or deconstruction alone. It seeks to expose a method of reading that is inclusive of human identities and dignities, one that makes space for others to present their own bodies and person outside the categorical limitations of any dominating framework.

The conclusion of this work weaves together the main themes exposed throughout my analysis. It does so not to offer a new strategy, because I think postcolonialism itself should be that strategy. Rather it will be to highlight the fruitful possibilities, the benefits, of continuing to read the biblical texts via postcolonial methods, as well as looking, looking to how we might amend, change, subvert, repair, and expand upon dominant traditions.

The struggle for civil rights, the struggle for the rights of the colonized, the recognition of the colonized is very much the struggle for human rights. In that sense, I am a firm believer that postcolonial method should be part of what I have defined as a larger method of relational dialogue, which seeks recognition of the human nature and potential of others through their differences and their similarities.[40] Such a dialogue must also be capable of navigating the different intersectionalities that resist conforming to an imposed language and meaning structure. Moreover, as Bhabha reminds us, the language of critique is not effective because it preserves the distinction between dichotomies of power relations. It is effective when it opens up space for hybridity and translation.[41] It does that when it challenges the forces holding together the mutantized body of the "other" as the fetishized object trapped in the gaze of those claiming power over it.

A WORD ON THE METHOD
EMPLOYED IN THIS WORK

Postcolonialism, and perhaps we can briefly entertain the term "neo-post-colonialism," as a method with an expanded arsenal, seeks to dismantle the Frankensteinian monster of the marginalized and oppressed "other" cast to the periphery and fabricated by colonial and dominant power centers. It exposes how the colonialist perspective constructs the body of the colonized and imposes upon it an identity defined within the cultural context of the

16   *Chapter 1*

colonial power. In that way, the body of the "other" becomes a fabrication of a dominant power defined based on its own categories and systems of meaning. Erasing (erasure) aspects of an "unacceptable" body that do not conform to the (predetermined) categories upon which the stability of the colonizing culture rest. In that process of "colonization," it becomes unrecognizable to the social world of the precolonized culture and body; it becomes a "monster," or "daemon" even, to itself, as defined within the cultural frameworks of an external power and culture. Its body thus contains, em-*bodies*, not its own but the values of the dominating culture. It becomes the fetishized symbol of the desires and values of the culture that exists outside the boundaries of moral and ethical stability (or the perceived sense of it). In that sense, it is the monster that reminds the culture of the function of categorical boundaries upon which the dominant collective identity rests. "I thought that if I could bestow animation upon lifeless matter, I might in the process of time . . . renew life where death had apparently devoted the body to corruption."[42] The heuristic of "body" functions on several levels: (1) it refers to the author's ideal vision; (2) it refers to the interpreter's imagined ideal; (3) it is the symbol constructed to embody (1) and (2); and, (4) it is the grotesque reduction of the "profane" other, outsider, non-ideal person who is not a member of the community that has claimed the power to define her.

Let me also say a word about a technique I employ in this work. At various points, sentences will be written in italics. Where those are not from a source I am quoting, or where I am not drawing emphasis to the words alone, which should be obvious in the context, the sentences represent a type of chorus in the Greek style. They offer critique and additional commentary, sometimes as alternative perspectives or challenges, in order to emphasize the complexity or multifaceted nature of important ideas. At times, they challenge what I argue. At other times, they challenge what someone else argues. They help explore different angles or perspectives for understanding and dialogue. And sometimes, they are, beyond a simple challenge, my own critique of my own argument. Sometimes I respond to a presented alternative perspective, where a discussion exposes a better understanding. Other times, I leave the alternative voice to speak for itself.

I have also tried to be attentive to three primary audiences: the scholar, the educated layperson, and the inquiring student. For that reason, I frequently use "biblical author" in the singular sense. I do this to be less cumbersome and to avoid the snares of tradition and redaction criticisms. While I accept that those critical traditions have given us a great deal of productive insight, and while I accept Genesis has multiple authors and editors, their identification would only distract from my purpose here. Not dealing with the differences between a "J passage" and an "E passage," in my educated opinion, does not undermine a postcolonial reading of a text whose interpretation a

Introduction   17

dominating tradition has imposed upon colonized bodies. My focus is more on interpretation than on authorial location.

As I mentioned, I draw upon several methods and styles to better emphasize the continuing relevance and need for postcolonial analysis. I adopt social-scientific method, various biblical critical methods, such as postcolonial, liberation, Neo-Marxist, feminist, and others, as well as incorporate an essayist style that allows me to draw upon experiences, of myself and others, to include as part of the discussion. An essayist style, to be clear, also permits inclusion of the conviction of ideals as authorial motivation. I should also note that my application of postcolonial analysis accepts that postcolonialism is similar to affect theory (sometimes called prosthetic theory in Ableist studies). The latter analyzes how interpretations, cultural mores, values, norms, assumptions, and more are rooted in preconceptions of what the individual or community is. Both challenge the assumption that those who are different must be changed to fit an idealized image imposed upon them. Affect theory analyzes how "affects" are impingements upon relations, hierarchies, and the ideological bodies and how those affects are ushered into discrete categories of existence. Sometimes that is done at the expense of a marginalized body who does not fit clearly into presupposed categories. In that sense, postcolonialism and affect theory map out the cultural, ideological assumptions that must be challenged when the colonized or minoritized body is subjected to "prosthetics" to make its "grotesque" image fit within the acceptable mores and aesthetics of the dominant community.

Given that my subject of analysis is the Bible, I must clarify several points at the beginning of this work. There are several points where I mention God and associate the third masculine singular pronoun with God. At those times, I mean to invoke or centralize the dominant interpretive tradition. I do this not to take it for granted but to identify what, among other issues I discuss, must be subject to postcolonial analysis. Where I am not trying to make this point, I have tried to use gender-neutral references to God. At all points, I do not use "God" to refer to an objective reality. Instead, I interpret "God" to be the symbolic embodiment of a community's most cherished values and ideals. Why defining God in that way is important for postcolonialism will be clarified in the following chapters.

My purpose in this work is not to be exhaustive but to be subversive of *dominant* popular readings and interpretations. As I described earlier, postcolonialism challenges the imposed dominant traditions and meanings, subverting them to make space for the voice of the marginalized. Such a reading must challenge the dominant symbols, which in Genesis the literati marshalled toward its function as a national foundation myth. Some stories in Genesis, such as of Dinah and Tamar (chapters 10, 11), inversely reinforce the more patriarchal aims of that myth while not expressly discussing it.

18   *Chapter 1*

These, and others, will need to be "unpacked." Because dominant traditions of interpretation treat the Bible (Jewish and Christian) as a blueprint toward the foundation of a nation (the restored Kingdom of Israel, Heaven, etc.), postcolonialism must begin with the stories and symbols that are central to the articulation of that myth and its history of interpretation.

That raises another important point. Weaving the history of biblical interpretation and how it has been applied to modern social and political issues will inevitably raise the hackles of some readers. This work is not intentionally pro- or anti-Israel, pro- or anti-monotheistic, pro- or anti-Palestine. It is critical of much, but it is so in the spirit of postcolonial critique. As a means to expand dialogue, it must challenge dominant and dominating narratives, and it must do so in ways that do not simply reinforce the status quo, academic or otherwise. In that spirit, for example, when I refer to the modern State of Israel, it is often reference to the dominant nationalist narrative of the political apparatus. It is not a reference to all Israelis, some of whom reject the narrative that has been used to justify conflicts and settlements with and in Palestinian territories (for which Benjamin Netanyahu is becomingly increasingly known, due in part to his impressive tenure as Israeli prime minister). Neither is it a specific reference to Jews, since not all Israelis are Jewish—a point that must be sadly emphasized in US classrooms. Likewise, when I refer to Palestine as analogous to a colonized body, it is in reference to the current relationship between Israel and Palestine as political bodies and how dominant trends in biblical interpretation, and even Western cultures, have reinforced a particular perspective of that tense relationship. There are many Israelis, Palestinians, Jews, Christians, and Muslims who agree on the fundamental need for peace and coexistence. Unfortunately, theirs are not the narratives that are being culturally and internationally imposed through law, international relations, nationalist ideologies, theologies, and more. This work challenges the dominating narratives to create space for dialogues of greater diversity unencumbered by the few in positions of political, cultural, religious, or economic power.

The virtual same can be said about those times where I criticize dominant trends in US Christianity. Postcolonialism should be uncomfortable. It should challenge us. It should inspire us. It should force us to consider where and why narratives that once told the stories of specific communities became imposed upon others. Yet because as a methodological approach it begins by reading against hegemonic power structures, in biblical studies it naturally gravitates toward a binary of power-powerless, colonizer-colonized, victimizer-victim. While those binaries should not be ignored, they should be partly resisted. They are not the sum of what the Bible, Israel, etc., are. Nor are the cultures, peoples, and histories of Israel and Judah from the ancient past the "negative foil" by which we should read the Bible. (*Nor an overly positivist one!*) Doing so has been a tendency in biblical interpretations that have been largely shaped by an "either-or" assumption that has emerged out of cultures shaped by monotheistic sentiments. Whether in popular readings or academic ones, many interpreters from those cultures (or taught at schools in those cultures) approach the biblical texts with the assumption that one must either embrace the Bible as a sacred text or reject it. The former tends toward maximalist readings. The latter tends toward skeptical, if not sometimes negative, readings. One of the difficulties, however, is that our knowledge of the history of Israel and Judah is largely restricted to the Bible, and the Bible is the sacred text for both Judaism and Christianity. Thus, criticisms of theological concepts are often hard to distinguish from historical, social, and political ones. My analysis does not view the historical kingdom of Israel, or Judah (which would also be referred to as "Israel" by some 6th century BCE and later biblical authors), as a colonizer or a colonized body. It focuses on how dominant trends in Jewish and Christian interpretations, especially those given birth to in imperial or colonial cultures, have imposed theological concepts upon the past, infusing them with meanings that reinforce distributions of power and authority, in various ways, for the benefit of a self-defined community. That community is not any ethnicity of the past. The concept of it began as the fruit of literati, who were responsible for writing the biblical texts, and who re-imagined Israel in the wake of the kingdom's imperial defeat. And it flourished among legions of interpreters that have seen themselves as audience and subjects of the Bible as a universal divine revelation. In addition, the projection of biblical Israel, and Judaism as its assumed descendant, as a negative foil ("good Christian/bad Jew") has been a tendency in Christian biblical exegesis.[43] So much so that its presence often goes unnoticed by the exegete trained in Western modes of academic inquiry and discourse. Postcolonial analysis, however, cannot be defined with the problem of anti-Judaism—a view that had a profound impact upon the historical development of Christianity. It must instead challenge meanings, values, categories, and structures of power that have or threaten erasure of others. While those things may be part of a religious tradition, they are not the sum of it, nor is defining itself an antithesis to any specific group.

The inherent risk of any critical analysis of history or culture is describing the subject in categories defined by one's own linguistic system. In such a situation, the community of the past becomes what the speaker, with limited understanding, says it is. Imposing dominant traditions of interpretation becomes an act of ideological colonization. Postcolonialism seeks to expose that. While also recognizing that responding productively is difficult. It demands that readers be vulnerable enough to acknowledge that some conclusions and meanings have been based on assumptions about the past that are

20   *Chapter 1*

the imagined or ideological products of later interpreting cultures. Religions, for example, are guilty of this when they assume objectivity in their sacred texts accessible through interpretation refined by later institutionally organized authorities.

Finally, given the nature of this work, I must say something about my own location and motivation. I have been increasingly convinced that biblical scholars must be more diligent about moving out of their silos. Where in the 20th century CE biblical scholarship was celebrated in Western cultures as part of the lofty pursuit of knowledge for the sake of knowledge, the world of the 21st century demands something else. Defining the fields of esoteric knowledge "for the betterment of mankind" is no longer a suitable aim. Students have voted with their course selections, and patrons have done so with their monies. Biblical Studies and Religious Studies departments in universities and colleges across the Western world are shuttering or being merged with "other humanities" due to lack of interest and funding. The job market for graduate degrees in those areas is atrocious. Some general conservative backlash in the United States against "leftist" and liberal ideologies has only served to justify rejection of (and in some cases make illegal) ideas that challenge the status quo as they aim for informed and complex dialogue about the human condition. This has forced an existential moment upon disciplines like Biblical studies, which despite having the Bible as its main subject, have continuously ignored or failed to translate their own relevances to lived experiences on the ground. The last several protests for equality that ignited across the globe were not shepherded by the religious faithful. That is because the paradigm is shifting. People are no longer easily convinced to conform themselves to a foreign way of thinking. They want instead to know the relevance of the Bible and religion for themselves in who they already are. They demand to know how the knowledge of any given field benefits the lives and experiences of people in their diversity and complexity, rather than in some homogenous concept of an idealized personhood and body. Some of this has to do with people becoming more aware of the existence, struggles, and needs of others. (Choosing to act in response to that knowledge is a different matter.) One can argue that the Internet, for example, is good or bad, but one cannot deny it has changed how we see the world, ourselves, and others in it. Another part of this change has been due to recognition that the "narrative of knowledge" upon which academic disciplines, histories, politics, religions, and economies of Western Europe and the United States have been based have favored a largely Western, white, masculine, heterosexual, and able worldview. That narrative has left many individuals and communities out. A postcolonial approach demands, however, that we ask what it would be like to treat knowledge, narratives, histories, and politics as things that can no longer be controlled by a those who benefit from a particular perspective.

Introduction 21

Part of doing that means we must challenge conventional assumptions, interpretations, ideologies, theologies, meanings, values, and distributions of power in ways that will be uncomfortable, challenging, condemning, and even accusing. Doing this shouldn't merely dismiss the past or the traditions that have preserved specific histories. Constructing negative foils only tends to reinforce the divisions that inspired a response in the first place. Challenge and subversion are meant to expose what otherwise goes unrecognized. And in doing that, those actions create spaces for us to respond in ways that enhance the diversity of a complex world. These changes and needs are what I see when I look out the front door of the metaphorical house that gives shape to my identity.

Why Genesis? There is an unfortunate lack of dedicated postcolonial analyses of Genesis, which leaves dominant traditions of interpretation unchanged in their colonial positions. This is exacerbated by the fact that many popular and academic assumptions about God, revelation, marriage, gender, role distribution, and ethnic hierarchies are rooted in interpretations of Genesis. The stories of Genesis echo in the writings of the New Testament, as well as biblically based assumptions about what the state of the world and God's people should be. They echo in the modern world, such as in rationale for US political and economic for Israel in contrast to Palestine. They echo in the systematic inequalities that continue to influence interpersonal relations in the US and other parts of the Western world. Those echoes must be challenged, and where change is needed, changed. This postcolonial analysis of Genesis is only a small contribution to that challenge. I hope that more biblical scholars will take up the charge in the future.

Given the nature of this work, and that postcolonialism necessitates somewhat of rude methodological and narrative approach, I should also say something about the position from which I understand my own ideological inclinations. Part of that position will shape ways that I interpret the theological influence of Christianity in the world, and especially the United States, where I currently live. In my past, I was a conservative Christian for over 25 years, first as a General Baptist then as a United Methodist, a "pastor's kid," a "missionary kid," a "Navy brat," even taking steps for my own ordination before I began looking elsewhere for a greater understanding about human relationships and cultures, one not constrained by theological assumptions about the human pursuit of God, whose nature always seemed to benefit communities of believers, who were also very concerned about the boundary between them and the "worldly sinner."

In that pursuit, I also became frustrated with biblical scholarship that continued to treat God as an active agent in history. In my opinion, the job of scholars is to sift through the evidence, and there is no scientifically compelling evidence that the—rather, *one* of—version of God described in

22 *Chapter 1*

the Bible is objectively real. The uncritical adoption and application of that assumption is rooted in the imperial and colonial past of religion. As scholars, because one of our primary sources is the Bible, we should be discussing God not as a real historical agent having a singular identity and desire, which believing communities can and do, but an idea or symbol portrayed by the biblical authors and interpreting communities. Failing to be attentive here only preserves the colonial apparatus that framed the foundation of Western knowledge and religion. Not only that, but I think more scholars need to bridge the divide between Academia and popular culture. The issues scholars, especially biblical scholars, discuss have relevance beyond their own shrinking numbers. However, much of the discourse in Biblical Studies has become stale because scholars continue be fascinated by ideas that never make it out of the ivory tower. To be more effective, scholarship must simultaneously advance new ideas and make connections to the lived experiences of people in the world. This work is one of my attempts to find some of the better ways of doing that.

I am not a secularist in the sense that I think human beings will eventually get past the need for religion. Perhaps that is a product of the haunting echoes of my past, but it seems irrefutable that religion continues to remain a cultural reality. That should be said even if the different traditions see changes, both in positive and negative directions, in their membership rosters. In the United States, to note one example, we are witnessing a conservative and fundamentalist push led by those who believe education and politics have been tainted by "leftists" and liberals—terms that are often conflated. (Yes, liberals make similar accusations in return.) The current push is perhaps not unrelated to the Fundamentalist Movement of the 18th and 19th centuries. All this said, I am motivated by the conviction that scholars who practice postcolonialism, feminism, and other ideologically based methodological criticisms should not make as their goal to lay the burial shroud upon religion. They should focus instead on those areas where religion might amend itself to incorporate increasingly diverse concerns, identities, and needs. In that sense, much of my criticism about all religion is directed at finding ways that it can persevere. My goal in this work isn't to debunk religion or the Bible, which is inherently difficult to do. It is, however, to challenge both, especially in areas where they have aided in the marginalization of others.

Finally, unless otherwise noted, I translated all Bible quotations for this work.

OVERVIEW OF CHAPTERS

In this chapter, I introduced postcolonialism. I argued that dominant traditions of biblical interpretation have been so influenced by fields of power and of knowledge defined within colonial frameworks that those heritages often go unrecognized. Genesis is a biblical book frequently cited, as I mentioned, in defense of marriage, gender, family, the right to the land, and more. It is even appealed to for definitions of the attributes of the community of God, including ethnic distinctions that include those that mark a separation between the community and the "descendants of Ham," who were cursed to slavery.

Chapter 2 explores how the story of Adam and Eve might be read from a postcolonial perspective in a manner that challenges traditional assumptions about marriage and gender. Such assumptions continue to perpetuate a dominant framework that benefits the group in power but does not make space for those who are on the margins.

The third chapter discusses the story of Cain and how, in contrast to Abel, Cain embodied a type of Orientalized figure. The chapter argues that colonized peoples do not natively share the same sociopolitical institutions as their colonizers. They are not bound by the same concept of moral citizenship. But in order to be "accepted" within the tolerable limits of the colonizer's culture, they must, in fact, adopt those things. Should they not, they will remain on the margins, seen as an uncivilized potential threat. In that position, they embody chaos and a threat to stability, ideas that have been used to justify violence, physical and ideological, as a means by which to control them and their potential influences.

In the fourth chapter, I focus on the story of Ham and how, in several traditions, and even still today, the story provided a justification for slavery. That interpretation was so pervasive that even some slaves themselves assumed that slavery was what God had deemed to be correct because they were influenced by Christianity, the contours of which had been fashioned by white, European and colonial experiences.

Ham also gives us the concept of, using Wiredu's phrase, "conceptual colonialism," which was rooted in prejudiced notions of divine election, and which continue to shape race relations in the United States. I argue here and throughout that the very notion of divine election is an imperialist or colonialist claim. That God would elect one group of people over another and put that group in a position of power over others is the very expression of empire. To confirm the prevalence of that idea, interpreters might begin with passages from the New Testament, which discuss Christians becoming co-heirs with Christ, and trace that idea out in traditions of biblical interpretation and Church doctrine.

24   *Chapter 1*

To explore the previous idea further, the fifth chapter focuses on the story of Noah and its emphasis upon the value of saving one family over all other peoples of the earth. It explores where the boundaries between insider and outsider were mapped around a certain conceptualization of family, morality, and values which were embodied within a particular family, which symbolizes the cultural ideal of the elect community. Those who did not share those values and moralities were categorized as threats, dehumanized as agents of chaos. Because of that, interpreters of the Bible could rest easy on the knowledge God wiped out "bad" people in order to preserve the stability of his community.

Chapter 6 reads the story of the Tower of Babel in an inverted manner. It interprets the people gathering together to build the tower from a postcolonial position. It looks at how the force of Yahweh, disrupting creating chaos and confusion, might be interpreted as an imperialist, colonialist exercise.

In the seventh chapter, I analyze Abraham and his choosing of Isaac over Ishmael, and how Ishmael became associated with marginalized and minoritized communities even today. The story of the brothers is frequently interpreted through the lens of more modern competition and strife. Jews and Christians view Islam as a chaotic threat, and that actions taken against the Islamic body, wars, killings, imprisonments, and so on, can be justified. Recall some justifications proffered by conservative Israeli Jews and US evangelical Christians modern Israel for taking land from the Palestinians and that their displacement can be justified because of their being outside the favor of God.

In the eighth chapter, I discuss Lot and how concepts of sexuality reinforce the dominant institutions of power. I also discuss how interpretation denigrates Lot's daughters while frees him from any blame. He is not susceptible to any blame. His daughters were and because of that, their children, the ancestors of the Ammonites and the Moabites, suffered. I explain why that story describes the relationship that Israel and Judah had with the Ammonites and Moabites, who were their political and cultural enemies.

Chapter 9 analyzes how the story of Sarah and Hagar builds on the story of Abraham and his two sons. It reaffirms the prejudices inherent within Abraham's story. It analyzes how the story of Hagar and Sarah's rejection of her, along with Abraham's acquiescence to Sarah's demands, reaffirms the prejudice of the cultural superiority of the master over the slave, or colonized. Hagar symbolized a colonized, or enslaved body. And her body is used for the benefit of her master, Abraham, and his wife. When Hagar sees in this a possible liberation from her colonized position, Sarah drives her away, exposing her to the chaos of the wilderness, reinforcing the need for individuals not to challenge the cultural norms and traditions.

Introduction   25

Chapter 10 analyzes the story of Jacob and Esau, and how the story of Jacob is primarily one about the preservation of lineage, society, and communal stability for a particular ethnic body. That idea is reinforced by the location of the story within the so-called Ancestral Narratives of Israel. As part of the national foundation myth, a concept discussed throughout this work, those stories focused on explaining the origin and identity of Israel and of Judah.

That discussion continues with the story of Joseph (chapter 11) and how Joseph's ascension into power could be interpreted as a celebration of Israelite imperialism and colonialism. But even in his ascension, the Hebrews fell out of favor, which made way for their liberation from the cultural institutions of Egypt in order for them to colonize Canaan and build their own nation. The stories of Joshua and Judges, which I do not discuss at length in this book, tell that with their descriptions of God's role in taking over (*like an imperial conquest?*) the land of Canaan to create space for the "people of Yahweh."

The question that drives the discussion in all chapters is this: what must change to liberate the body of the disfigured "other" with whom I share humanity? Explaining what constitutes disfigurement must be part of answering that question.

NOTES

1. See also Hjamil A. Mártinez-Vázquez, *Made in the Margins: Latina/o Constructions of US Religious History* (Waco, TX: Baylor University Press, 2013), 4–5.

2. Cf. Northrop Frye, *Words with Power: Being a Second Study of the Bible and Literature* (New York: Harvest/Harcourt Brace Jovanovich, 1990), 134–35.

3. Gustau Nerín, *Colonialismo e imperialismo: entre el derribo de monumentos y la nostalgia por la grandeza perdida* (Barcelona: Shackleton Books, 2022), 12, translation mine.

4. As, for example, Keith Whitelam has argued in *Invention of Ancient Israel* (New York: Routledge, 1996) and *idem*, "The Poetics of the History of Israel: Shaping Palestinian History," ed. David M. Gunn and Paula M. McNutt (Sheffield: Sheffield Academic Press, 2002), 277–96.

5. Staff, "Most U.S. Evangelical Leaders Expect Persecution in Coming Years," National Association of Evangelicals, November 28, 2016, https://www.nae.org/u-s-evangelical-leaders-expect-persecution-coming-years/.

6. Stephen R. Haynes, *Noah's Curse: The Biblical Justification of American Slavery*, Kindle (Oxford: Oxford University Press, 2002), location 1577.

7. For an in-depth study of this motivation in monotheistic traditions, see Jeremiah W. Cataldo, *Biblical Terror: Why Law and Restoration in the Bible Depend Upon Fear* (London: Bloomsbury / T & T Clark, 2017).

8. MC Gaza, *From Gaza to Aleppo*, Youtube, 2017, https://youtu.be/ah1nzHJjKzc.

9. Cf. Jeremiah W. Cataldo, *Breaking Monotheism: Yehud and the Material Formation of Monotheistic Identity*, LHBOTS 565 (London: Bloomsbury, 2012); Cataldo, *Biblical Terror*.

10. Cf. Fernando F. Segovia, "Introduction," in *Colonialism and the Bible: Contemporary Reflections from the Global South*, ed. Tat-Siong Benny Liew and Fernando F. Segovia (Lanham, MD: Lexington Books, 2018), xi-xxi.

11. Bogdan Ştefănescu, "The Complicated Selves of Transcolonialism: The Triangulation of Identities in the Alternative Peripheries of Global Post/Colonialism," *Metacritic Journal for Comparative Studies and Theory* 8, no. 1 (2022): 64.

12. Ştefănescu, 63.

13. Louis Althusser, "The Object of Capital," in *Reading Capital: The Complete Edition*, trans. Ben Brewster and David Fernbach (London: Verso, 2015), 293.

14. Cf. Althusser, 293.

15. To co-opt somewhat Gilles Deleuze and Félix Guattari, *Anti-Oedipus: Capitalism and Schizophrenia* (Minneapolis: University of Minnesota Press, 2005), 12.

16. Here I am re-appropriating the quote from Deleuze and Guattari, 11.

17. Mary Wollstonecraft Shelley, *Frankenstein; or, the Modern Prometheus* (London: Henry Colburn and Richard Bentley, 1831), Letter IV.

18. Again Ştefănescu, "Complicated Selves."

19. Vijay Mishra and Bob Hodges, "What Was Postcolonialism?" *NLH* 36 (2005): 375–76.

20. Mitri Raheb, *Faith in the Face of Empire: The Bible Through Palestinian Eyes* (New York: Orbis Books, 2014), 55.

21. Deborah Schiffrin, "Narrative as Self-Portrait: Sociolinguistic Constructions of Identity" 25, no. 2 (1996): 167.

22. Elinor Ochs and Lisa Capps, "Narrating the Self," *Annual Review of Anthropology* 25 (1996): 32.

23. Cf. Musa W. Dube and R. S. Wafula, eds., *Postcoloniality, Translation, and the Bible in Africa*, Kindle (Eugene, OR: Pickwick Publications, 2017), 12; Pramod K. Nayar, *Postcolonialism: a guide for the perplexed* (London: Continuum, 2010), 4.

24. Postcolonial theory has moved in this direction, cf. Nayar, *Postcolonialism*, 34.

25. On prosthetic and ableist criticism, see Jennifer Scuro, Devonya N. Havis, and Lydia X. Z. Brown, *Addressing Ableism: Philosophical Questions via Disability Studies* (Lanham, MD: Lexington Books, 2018), xx–xxi.

26. Cf. Michela Baldo, "Queering Translation as Performative and Affective Un-Doing: Translating Butler's *Undoing Gender* into Italian," in *Queering Translation, Translating the Queer: Theory, Practice, Activism*, ed. Brian James Baer and Klaus Kaindl, Routledge Advances in Translation and Interpreting Studies 28 (New York London: Routledge, Taylor & Francis Group, 2020), 200.

27. Cf. Nayar, *Postcolonialism*, 4; Mishra and Hodges, "What Was Postcolonialism?" 376; Mosese Ma'ilo, "Celebrating Hybridity in Island Bibles: Jesus, the Tamaalepō (Child of the Dark) in Matatio 1:18–26," in *Islands, Islanders, and the Bible: RumInations*, Semeia Studies 77 (Atlanta: SBL Press, 2015), 66.

28. Cf. Rasiah S. Sugirtharajah, ed., *Voices from the Margin: Interpreting the Bible in the Third World*, 25th anniv (Maryknoll, NY: Orbis Books, 2016); Rasiah

Introduction 27

S. Sugirtharajah, ed., *Still at the Margins: Biblical Scholarship Fifteen Years After Voices from the Margin* (T & T Clark, 2008).

29. Malcolm X, "The Ballot or the Bullet," cited in Kai Wright, ed., *The African American Experience: Black History and Culture Through Speeches, Letters, Editorials, Poems, Songs and Stories* (New York: Black Dog & Leventhal, 2009), 545.

30. For further definition and discussion of the "monotheistic body" see Cataldo, *Breaking Monotheism*, 13–18.

31. Christian obligation of U.S. support for Israel was a point that Jerry Falwell made frequently, cf. Speech given to the "Strengthening Families" seminar of the Christian Life Commission conference, April, 1982, in FAL 4: Speeches and Sermons (FAL 4:1–3 Box 1).

32. The very point that Raheb, *Faith in the Face of Empire* protests.

33. Cf. Darren Dochuk, *From Bible Belt to Sunbelt: Plain-Folk Religion, Grassroots Politics, and the Rise of Evangelical Conservatism*, Digital (New York: W.W. Norton, 2011), location 2748.

34. Cf. Steven J. Cole, "1. Why God Designed Marriage (Genesis 2:18–25; Ephesians 5:31–32)," Bible.org, 2017, https://bible.org/seriespage/1-why-god-designed -marriage-genesis-218-25-ephesians-531-32.

35. Cf. Jeff Johnston, "Male and Female He Created Them: Genesis and God's Design of Two Sexes," Focus on the Family, September 13, 2015, https://www .focusonthefamily.com/get-help/male-and-female-he-created-them-genesis-and-gods -design-of-two-sexes/.

36. Cf. Lisa Loraine Baker, "What Is God's Purpose for Our Family?" biblestudy-tools.com, September 30, 2022, https://www.biblestudytools.com/bible-study/topical -studies/what-is-gods-purpose-for-our-family.html.

37. Cf. John Hagee, *The Promised Land* (San Antonio: CUFI University Press, 2020), 10, 15; John Hagee, *Why Christians Should Support Israel: The Apple of His Eye* (San Antonio: CUFI University Press, 2016), 5–7, 26, 47, 58.

38. See also the discussion in Jeremiah W. Cataldo, *What the Bible Says about Sex: Why We Read It the Way We Do* (Abingdon, Oxon; New York, NY: Routledge, 2023), 4–5, which highlights some of the concern for controlling the definition of family through marriage and sexuality.

39. Cf. Jeremiah W. Cataldo, *A Social-Political History of Monotheism: From Judah to the Byzantines* (London: Routledge Press, 2018).

40. See Jeremiah Cataldo, "Biblical Strategies for Reinterpreting Crises with 'Outsiders,'" in *Imagined Worlds and Constructed Differences in the Hebrew Bible*, LHBOTS 677 (London: T & T Clark / Bloomsbury, 2019), 143.

41. Homi K. Bhabha, *The Location of Culture* (London; New York: Routledge, 1994), 25.

42. Shelley, *Frankenstein; or, the Modern Prometheus*, chap. IV.

43. Cf. Amy-Jill Levine, "Roundtable Discussion: Anti-Judaism and Postcolonial Biblical Interpretation," *Journal of Feminist Studies in Religion* 20, no. 1 (April 1, 2004): 91–132.

Chapter 2

Adam, Eve, and Steve's Serpent

> Males and females are both the same in essence as fully human beings, but at the same time they are different. . . . Quintessential questions related to gender in church ministry are usually expressed in the following way: What can women do in ministry? Should a woman hold an office such as elder, bishop, or deaconess? Should women be ordained? Should women lead men? What do *submission* and *headship* mean? The answers we give to these questions for community life, marriage, and Christian ministry represent our theological framework for gender.[1]

Traditionally, the answers to those questions posed in the preceding epigraph have reinforced hierarchies that are rooted in the male as the ideal for authority, instruction, and ministry. Do the stories about Adam and Eve provide a framework for marriage in Gen. 1–3? Conservative readers have argued, or rather assumed, that it does. It is a comforting and timeless strategy: God made Adam and Eve and bound them together in marriage as though "one flesh." Such is the desire to see God in control over marriage and sexuality, which benefits the Church's control over the family as a social unit, that Genesis need not even mention marriage. Interpreters find all the proof they need in its oblique reference to a man and woman created and "united." As the National Association of Evangelicals put it on its website, "Indeed, marriage is instituted as a God-given covenant–place for deep relationship, happiness, and for multipurposed sexual expression."[2] No need to undergo the sometimes uncomfortable process of change; the idealized body was defined and its contours etched in the echoes of a universal and absolute revelation.

One can certainly acknowledge there are a few biblical passages that can be interpreted as *suggesting* the joining of a man and a woman to be a divine act. To see those passages as expressing absolute certainty, however, implies that the Bible is more universally relevant than any other text or tradition, the interpretation of which has been regulated by a historically white, heterosexual, and masculine community. For instance, in response to a question about divorce, Matt. 19:6 states that what God has joined human beings should not separate, and that the two people became one flesh (compare Gen. 2:23). This idea is frequently interpreted as a reference to marriage as a divine union rather than a commentary on the social impact of divorce. Rather than interpreting the social context, which takes education in that historical area, many interpreters want instead to see confirmation of their own theological positions. Those positions are frequently developed within the dominant traditions of religion, which are largely the fruit of Western, heterosexual males. But is that a universal mandate for marriage, especially if "flesh" may be better read as a metaphor for the kinship body and not some romanticized blending of a married couple? This latter romanticized idea is quite common among faithful Christians. James Brownson, for example, claimed, "humans are not free to enter marriage without accepting the binding commitments and responsibilities of a kinship bond decreed by God to accompany marriage." And further, "human society . . . rightly holds them accountable to fulfill the commitments they have made. To the extent that church and society do this, they honor the God who has decreed that a husband and wife shall become one flesh."[3] Marriage, as it was defined in Western, patriarchal cultures, became a mode of worship, and it is one that is rooted in a dualistic modeling of the private and public spheres.[4] What the woman represents is linked to the private sphere: the bedroom, subordination to masculine authority, her culturally imposed role as caretaker of domestic affairs. Men represent the public face, the exercise of authority, and the forging of alliances. To deviate from dominant definitions of that model, to assert the uniqueness of one's own body and its relational pairings is deemed "sinful," a profane divergence, which is the quality of body upon which is cast all things the community of members does not want to be true of itself. It highlights an absence that must be obscured through a prosthetic, the image of a heterosexual distribution of authority, before one's body can be (re-)integrated into the community.

The symbolism in the Matthew passage identified above refers to the proposed impossibility of divorce, which numerous interpreters assume to be regulated by divine commandment. But, as I mentioned, the idea of "one flesh" isn't specific to marriage, especially as a divine union or sacrament. It refers to a kinship bond that society legitimates as the basis for collective identity—that the society is grounded on accepted lines of kinship. Nor is it specific to marriage as a sacrament, as held by Catholics, or divine union, as held by Protestants. For both, and for monotheism generally, definitions of "marriage" are attempts to define a building block of the social-political body. Such concerns began with kinship and evolved into communities defined by a common creed, such as nationalism or religious ideology. The attempt to regulate marriage (and sexuality) is an attempt at defining the cornerstone of the community, or social-political body.[5] Marriages were moments of definition, as Maurice Godelier states, that categorized and valued social relations and groups, such as the village where a couple lived and built a home, and the lineage that would be perpetuated.[6] Perhaps it should be clear where control over marriage might lend itself to real and ideological colonialism. Not only can that be seen in the Bible's rejection of intermarriages but also in circumstances where marriages between races are either explicitly outlawed or socially condemned, such as marriages between black and white individuals in the historical United States.[7]

When we understand the implication of what I am describing about historical interpretations and traditions, it should be obvious that the notion of "becoming one flesh" emphasizes the development of a new kinship body or lineage. Within patriarchy, lineage was traced through fathers. The patriarchal name was passed on from one generation to the next, typically through the firstborn son, who in the general historical contexts of the biblical texts usually received the birthright and blessing. When the son left his father and mother, he built his own family and "branch" in the lineage. He didn't become an independent family, unless he was cursed by his father, in which case the familial ancestry was cut off (as, for example, was the case of Noah's son, Ham, which I will discuss in chapters 4 and 5).

"One flesh" doesn't mean an autonomous or independent family unit, which would keep things completely constricted at a nuclear level. Such is the inevitable assumption in interpretations of "one flesh" as a reference to a spiritualized act of marriage. In historical reality, the husband becomes the patriarch of his own social unit, or kinship body, while preserving continuity in the ancestral line. As Adam said of Eve in Gen. 2:23, "She is bone of my bone, flesh of my flesh." Such, however, is only a claim men can make, according to dominant traditions of interpretation. Women, the whole of monotheistic traditions must confess, became the first colonized bodies.

I recall hearing marriage vows that included proclamations by men to be "loving leaders" (when stripped of the florid vocabulary, it was often "don't cheat and provide economically") and women to be "obedient." The sense of it was frequently gleaned from Eph. 5:22 and 1 Peter 3:1, the former which instructs wives to subordinate (ιδιος) and the latter to subject (υποτασσω) themselves to their husbands. The passage in Ephesians denotes making oneself the exclusive property of someone in authority. The one in 1 Peter denotes subjecting oneself to the authority of another. Passages such as these have encouraged modern marriage vows that might instruct the husband to love and honor his wife but the wife to love, honor, and *obey* her husband.[8] Some marital vows couch that expectation in biblical narrative, along the lines Ruth's full-throated commitment to Naomi (cf. Ruth 1:16–17). As Ruth gave up of herself to a greater authority, the bride gives herself to her

32 *Chapter 2*

husband and his direction. A similar hierarchy of relationship can be seen in Eph. 6:5–8, which instructs slaves to obey their masters. In these cases, those of women, wives, and slaves, obedience entails adopting the expectations of an authoritative "Other" imposing its will upon them. It should not be surprising that many colonial conquests sought to "feminize" "lesser" peoples in order to "civilize" them according to colonial or imperial culture. Conformity to the practices and ideals of the colonizer's concept of marriage was one way of doing that. *How frequently, after all, were polygamous marriages broken up by missionary colonizers?* I recall one of my undergraduate professors from Nigeria telling my class how European missionaries came into his family's village and "explained" why polygamy was against God's will. As a result, many women were divorced (and abandoned) so that marriages comported to Christian expectations. Marriage is the basis of power rooted in the structure of the family (for comparison with later portions of this work, ancient Near Eastern societies often considered slaves to be property of a patriarchal household). That is why it is regulated with such ideological fervor that conflicts and kicking members out of communities may result from challenges to prevailing assumptions about marriage.

Within Christian tradition, which has had a dominant influence over Western attitudes, ideological convictions about marriage and family find their links to divine creation.[9] Such views are rooted in assumptions that God made Adam and Eve as human beings, and therefore as the prototype of a married couple, that gender roles were clearly established in Gen. 3:14–19, and that the family's expectations included bearing (obedient) children. Adam and Eve, assumed to be husband and wife, became the foundation for the more modern theological concept of *heterosexual* marriage. But the institution of marriage is never mentioned in the story of Adam and Eve. Instead, its elevation as an objective institution is a theological strategy, celebrated by theologians and other biblical interpreters, for defining the social world in terms of their own ideals symbolized in their chosen concepts of God. This strategy is rooted in the assumption that Gen. 1–3 tells the universal and objective story of creation, including the mapping out of gender roles and obligations and the contours of "family" as the foundation of God's elect community, but which become redefined from strict biology to a metaphor—a transitional pattern that can be seen in interpretations of texts such as the Song of Songs, which are full of sexual imagery but are interpreted as a metaphor of the relationship between God and people, and the one's unrequited desire for the other.[10] Consequently, in the hands of those who defined the traditions and histories—as the stories of ourselves we present–that are dominant, the story offers universal confirmation of what men and women, husbands and wives, should *be* as gendered and sexual sociopolitical agents.[11] Because that is the foundation of the family, and the family is the foundation of society, as such assumptions go, it is not amenable to any deviation or difference from that basic, fundamental binary between *heterosexual* males and females. *Marriage, after all, was instituted by God! So too the State! God save the king!* When these ideas are imposed upon others as the basis for a moral society, it demands that others conform to a standard by which they must live in order to be accepted as a member, citizen, or insider. This amounts, in short, to a type of moral and ideological colonialism.

But what if the text is acknowledged as something more mythic, and that the intent wasn't to explain marriage? No marriage ceremony exists in the story, nor is there any clear sign that the man and the woman were married. The Bible's references to children born to the two don't assume marriage. In fact, several children that played pivotal roles in the Bible were born outside of marriage! And in the ancient world, marriage did not have the same value that it does for modern lesbians, as a physical and emotional union devoid of masculine bodies, in the more modern context. In other words, biblical marriage was not always based only on love. It was a legal contract between men. Neither was it in the biblical text considered the property of the church or cult denoting some spiritual, sacred, or otherwise, union. And it typically occurred on a local level, apart from any church, synagogue, or temple. The idea that marriage was something only the church could grant developed later on.

Allow me to briefly provide a historical example and reference. The 4th Lateran Council (1215 CE) presented marriage as a sacrament and the Council of Trent (ca. 1545–1563 CE) solidified that idea. Even before its official codification under the Holy Roman Empire, marriage became a tool for controlling the populace and those who had access to political authority.[12] These expectations for what marriage entails were not part of the narrative in Genesis. They became codified in dominant traditions of biblical interpretation as religious leaders sought to define the identity of the Christian community, casting it into the mold of the universal "body of Christ." The masculine authorities of that body worked toward refining the citizen of an "invisible empire" under the banner of Christ in parallel to existing political institutions.

In Genesis, the Hebrew term *ishah*, which refers to Eve in relation to Adam, can be translated as "woman" or "wife" depending on the context. That nuance has been a boon to theological interpretations presenting the story as a basis for marriage. But *ishah* does not refer to a woman or wife as part of a sacred bond in the way that modern Christian traditions assume. That assumption imposes a category of meaning upon an ancient context, stripping it of the multi-peripheries and poly-centers that define its distributed relations. It casts a dichotomized lens of an insider-outsider perspective defined within a later monotheistic framework upon a historical context to which the biblical author belonged. In that situation, diverse bodies are not appreciated

34   *Chapter 2*

for their diversity but are fragmented and foisted into a mold defined by the community controlling the histories and traditions preserved as those that form the skeletons of the body of the "idiot," the senseless body that must be civilized according to dominant cultural ideals celebrated by the community, now self-delusional, as objective. Defining the past through modern categories subordinates it to modern cultural ideals and values, an act that postcolonialism protests and calls for its condemnation. References to "wife" refer to a woman who was obligated to a man not her father or brother, but one with whom she, and her father through her, has entered a covenantal agreement.

Let me restate the point. Use of the term *ishah* in the narrative from Gen. 1–3 is *not* a clear sign that the reference is to a wife rather than a woman. There was an exchange between men, namely God and Adam, which would demand that we also challenge the typical view of God and conclude that God is not the universal deity but one who is interested in establishing a relationship with a particular lineage symbolized in Adam. If that is true, Adam is a universal man only where he establishes the lineage that can be refined for the sake of Israel because Genesis is a text rooted in the cultural and sociolinguistic systems of Israel, or more realistically, Judah. Let's consider the possibility—and I would say "likelihood" with strong confidence—Genesis followed the pattern of other creation myths: two types of beings were created, had sex, and bore children. If read as a myth, the story in Genesis presents an ideological rather than an objective historical position. The authors imagined the origins of creation in a way that was fairly consistent with other types of stories throughout the ancient Near East. Nevertheless, it was that cultural vantage point, the singular interpretation of their own community, that would later get adopted into the position of a universally sacred text. Rather than Yahweh being an auto-fellating male or having sex with a goddess, as other cultures describe of deities in their own origin myths, the biblical author cast the messiness of sexuality upon humans. The national god of Israel formed human beings to have sex and procreate in order to build a nation, an emphasis I will discuss particularly in chapter 7, regarding Abraham's story as part of Genesis as an Israelite national foundation myth.

Another point must be acknowledged. Gen. 1–3 refers to Adam and Eve, but the references may not be as proper names. *Adam* could simply denote "man," as well as "land," "soil," or "ground." In Hebrew, *chavvah* (which is translated as "Eve") denotes the mother of living things. The names of the characters identify their function and their positions in the story. Ancestral links to land and society (through procreation) were blended in the literary characters. It would be their children from whom the initial division of humanity into "good" and "bad," which would later become the ideological foundation for *herem* (cf. Deut. 7), other wars, and rejection of foreigners, that would provide the narrative stream for the biblical author.

None of this should be read without acknowledging that the Bible was written in a patriarchal culture, codified in historical sociolinguistic systems, and by authors targeting an Israelite/Judean cultural context, and with a particular audience of land-owning males in mind. When they discussed the world around them, they explained things based on the normative values, ideas, and meanings with which they were familiar. And nowhere does the Bible (including texts of Jesus and the prophets) try to upset that norm. In fact, Jesus, who Christians see as God and the universal model for a godly life, addresses women in the framework of his patriarchal context.[13] In almost all cases, to and about them, he speaks as a masculine authority. The uncritical, unquestioned adoption of that hierarchy bolstered later theologies about Jesus as being so pure that he did not marry is rooted in patriarchal assumptions about women as inferior and sources of profanity.[14] Can one not but conclude that this tendency to universalize the historical particular in theological glorification breaks with the historiographic and cultural framework in which the text and its claims about women were written?

Kwasi Wiredu may help answer that question. Wiredu argued from a postcolonial perspective that universals are not fixed but are influenced by cultural particularities.[15] I would argue that that position, that the universal is not unassailable by cultural and historical translation and interpretation, offers an accessible starting point for any postcolonial analysis of Gen. 1–3. That said, there is a sense in which one has to acknowledge that position is also fairly postmodern. As part of its *modus operandi* it expects the decline or de-emphasis upon the notion of objective meaning in the sense that the modernist position held. Postcolonialism is, by nature, a challenge to the very assumption that there can be any objectivity. Such an ideological starting point, against which postcolonialism reacts, benefits a particular majority and clearly does so while also being inaccessible to minoritized or colonized peoples. It problematically maintains that the only way that they could reach or access the "objective" truths, values, meanings, or that the only way they could benefit from them would be to encounter them and to engage them through the cultural and meaning system of a dominant majority.

Perhaps that can be better said in terms of an analogy. Take, for instance, the old missionary model (still practiced by some conservative evangelical denominations) rooted as it was in Orientalist histories and definitions of the world.[16] Missionaries coming out of colonial and imperial cultures would encounter tribal-based societies and operate under the assumption that where cultures did not reflect the missionary's own levels of civilization, they were ignorant, less intelligent, less culturally sophisticated, and unaware of fundamental issues such as private property, legal systems, the institution of marriage, and so on. Such ideological assumptions, which were also at the heart of Orientalism generally, assumed that they did not, prior to the missionary's

36   *Chapter 2*

arrival, have access to the truth or its authorized interpreter.[17] Because of
their uncivilized and savage minds, uninformed by Western cultural ideals
and values, if they ever encountered it without an interpreter, the missionary
and his cultural value system who symbolized the ideal body, they weren't
intellectually aware enough to understand the nature of that encounter. And
so missionaries would teach them the "truth." But in that teaching, they also
taught them the linguistic systems, the meaning systems, the value systems,
the ethical systems, and the moral systems that defined the cultures of the
missionaries, which were foreign to the new context. In that, I am reminded
of the movie, *The Mission*, which as a fictionalized story portrayed Jesuit
missionaries going to the Paraguayan jungle to convert Guarani communities, was nevertheless based on a historical event. While they presented
themselves as "saving" the Guarani from slavery under the Portuguese, and
indirectly the Spanish through the Treaty of Madrid (1750), their salvation
could only come through their conversion to a different foreign authority, the
Catholic Church and the pope as its head. Slavery and salvation both came
through colonization. Either result required the colonized people to leave
their own cultural traditions, narratives, identities, values, ethics, morals,
and politics behind. What if imposing the idea of heterosexual marriage as a
universal absolute, and a sacrament, upon Gen. 1–3 was itself also an act of
ideological colonization?

While Wiredu argues that scholarly assumptions about universals should
be more culturally specific, the author doesn't reject the possibility of shared
fundamental values across cultures. Cultures can share values. Sometimes
they develop independently, other times they are a consequence of cultural
borrowing. Wiredu argues that our understanding of what makes up a "universal" value must be understood more in culturally specific terms. And in
that, Wiredu refers to the subjectively objective nature of a culture's values
and ideals that are, as Peter Berger describes, internalized as objectively real
without awareness of their strictly cultural origin. Individuals live as though
these *were* objective because they *perceive* them as such.[18] Even when a value
appears to be shared across cultures, how it is translated and subsequently
internalized remains culturally specific. What that means, then, is that imperialism and colonialism are willfully dismissive of how limited the imperial
or colonial culture's own definitions are. What better response, then, rather
than colonized cultures accepting without challenge the traditions determined
by Western cultures, which has also become foundational to norms in biblical
comprehension, that cultural groups be given the freedom to interpret texts
and values from their own perspectives? Regarding the Bible, that might look
like resisting the urge to assume that there is a real universal and absolute
essence in its meaning and interpretation. In that, one would also resist the

urge to rest in the arms of such comforting (to a particular perspective) statements as "everything about man points to God."[19]

If that is a valid basis for interpreting Genesis, and I think it is, and one can accept that real universals were not fixed in the story itself, and that modern assumptions about marriage were not "revealed" in the ancient text and are unassailable to change, then one can accept that even *if* Adam and Eve were the first two human objects of creation, they were presented as such simply for the function of procreation. It was not to establish a more modern concept, one *assumed* to be objective, of marriage as divinely ordained. It described an interpretation of how human beings propagate. Not only that, but the biblical authors wrote such interpretations presupposing Israel and Judah as social and political realities. That is why Genesis begins in its first chapter with general humanity and ends in chapter 50 with the Hebrews on the cusp of becoming a nation in the land "promised" to Abraham by Yahweh, Israel's and Judah's national god (a point I will discuss further in chapter 7).

This tension between textual interpretation, as though of a codified law, as a restriction upon bodies as an expression of self reminds me of books now that are in vogue that target younger children to explain sexual body parts, hormones, and attraction, including procreation. Genesis is kind of like that, only dressed up in adult fashion. I am not making the naïve and antiquated modernist claim that mythic narratives *are* on the level of children's stories. Such narratives *were*, however, written in ways to make them memorable and repeatable. They were done so in ways that made sense and allowed for people to interpret them within their own contexts. Put differently, the reason the stories are so simplistic and fantastical is to make them memorable vehicles of cultural values that could be interpreted in them. They were not devoid of a culturally contingent sociolinguistic and meaning framework. As Northrop Frye wrote,

> The reason for presenting the past, real or legendary, in such a form is already given in the word presenting. Early societies at least may not have any very clear idea of their own actual history, but they do know that their lives will end in death, that there have been many disasters and setbacks in those lives, with the prospect of further ones, and that their world is full of cruelty and injustice. Myth exerts a counterbalancing force to such history as they know, with its suggestion that the events they encounter are repeating their ancestral myths or working out their decreed meanings. Such myths are not really 'tales of the fathers,' in Thomas Mann's phrase, but confrontations with a present significance, drawing out the reserves of courage and energy needed either to maintain routine or meet a crisis.[20]

But what does it mean then if we are not seeking universals as things that are true at all times and for all people? Rather, that we interpret the story of

38   *Chapter 2*

creation as a *counterpoint* to traditional readings that have reinforced imperial and colonial norms? It interrogates practices and traditions that have
facilitated appropriation, exploitation, and oppression of minoritized and
native cultures by a dominating power and culture.[21] How does one do that?
I have already alluded to certain strategies, such as challenging Adam and
Eve as objective realities. But what do the figures of Adam and Eve represent, as well as the serpent in the garden, from a postcolonial perspective?
To answer that, their portrayals must cease to be equated with the "truth" of
gender, sexuality, and family. Assuming such equivalence is part of the project of building a "commonwealth" among peoples of the world—a colonial
enterprise. It takes part in the activity of constructing a narrative by which the
minoritized and colonized body is portrayed as, "primitive, depraved, pagan,
criminal, immoral, vulnerable, and effeminate."[22] In other words, "sinner" as
the concept has been aggressively reinforced in Western Christian cultures
and theologies. To read in such a fashion, to take part in the restrictive defining of others' bodies and identities, entails, as Dube put it, the willful suppression of others. "To establish any form of 'commonwealth'—be it Christian,
economic, political, social, ideological, environmental, military—always
involves the suppression of cultural differences and the imposition of a few
universal standards."[23] Marriage is the vanguard of that commonwealth. For
those who make marriage a divine institution, ideological commitments and
conversions reinforce the unity of the body as long as marriage, and sex and
gender, which are its necessary components, is regulated. As one Catholic
priest put it, conflating marriage and family, "We have to rebuild marriage.
And the reason why it is under full-blown attack is because the demons know
that marriage, that is the family, is the building block of society—not the
individual."[24]

How often have we heard from religious communities that God made the
particular the model and basis for the universal? That Adam and Eve were the
first attempt at creating a stable world? Their failure to comport themselves to
imposed but fairly obfuscating rules became the later basis for the Christian
doctrine of "original sin." Such an impact did that doctrine have that what
was given voice to by early authors, such as St. Augustine, remains in force
even in the present age. Christians assume "original sin" to be objectively real
and described in Genesis. Yet the real narrative explanation for why man and
woman were kicked out of the garden, in contrast to theologies built around
the idea of an original sin, was so that they wouldn't eat from the Tree of
Life and become gods (cf. Gen. 3:22–23). This was a protection of hierarchy, which the divine's punishments of the man and the woman reinforce
(cf. 3:14–19). But the contingencies of those are quickly overlooked when
the interpreter's values and agenda are inserted. For a modern example of

that ideological colonization, in a response to what they identify as "LGBT affirmations," the Christian Missionary Alliance Church writes, "People naturally embrace a lie and rejects [sic] God's truth (Rom. 1–2; Eph. 2:1–3; 4:17–18). Christian doctrine calls this condition *original sin*. We are born sinful (not simply committing sins), our very nature is *fallen*."[25] Their position is that anyone who doesn't match up to their interpretation of *imago Dei*, which does not include "practicing members" of LGBTQIA communities, are those who have not moved past a sinful state into a sanctified state of divine grace. From where does that grace come? In a "fallen world"—the concept of which justifies the judgment and condemnation of cultures and ideologies not shared by most Christians—this occurs *only* through the Crucifixion, the meaning of which Christians privatize and protect with their very essence. One must become a member of the community, of the Body of Christ, by redefining oneself based on the dominant cultural expectations of the dominant community, sacrificing oneself to the demand of others, to receive the "universal gift." The gift of Christ's body is conditional upon losing oneself to an imposed ideal defined as the will and expectation of God. That, of course, runs contrary to the Unitarian Universalist belief, which represents a minority within the Christian tradition. I mention them here because they are a group trying to separate the fundamental idea of Christianity from the evil of its imperial, colonial, and theological past. Postcolonialism demands that we challenge any idea grounded in the traditions of colonial and imperial cultures that assume a single center and a concomitant periphery into which anyone who does not support the ideals of the center will be cast.[26] Universalists share that pursuit.

Controlling the dominant narrative of biblical interpretation has been aided by the editorial formation of Genesis. The work is a *political* document in that it is a Judean national history. We cannot say "Israelite" without qualification in contrast to the tendency of most Jewish and Christian interpreters: during the 6th century BCE and later, Judean authors and editors co-opted the ethnic identification for a re-imagined kingdom that unified the territories of the northern kingdom of Israel and the southern kingdom of Judah (cf. 1 Kgs. 4:21–28 ET; 5:1–8 HB; 9:26).[27] That vision lives on not only in theology but also political strategy from legal regulations of family to the embodiment of nations. It is, for many Jews and Christians, the basis by which the modern State of Israel should define its borders and its policies on expansion. As Johannes Gerloff, for example, writes, "the borders of a country depend on the relationship of the respective people with the living God. Their course, therefore, indicates something about this relationship."[28] It's hard to take Gerloff seriously. The belief that God gets God's hands dirty sustaining the current state of human politics is one only found in cultures where significant power resides. In contrast, was it God's will that Ukraine define its own

40 *Chapter 2*

borders? Or that Russia restrict them? That Native Americans be defeated? That the Acholi, Lango, and Rohingya peoples be the targets of genocide? That numerous interpreters can claim that the movement of history is guided by God only testifies to the space and position of relative comfort in which their theologies were developed, codified, and broadly enforced.

It's easy to obfuscate under theological aspirations of universalism the intent of the redacted form of Gen. 1–11. It sets the mythical stage for Gen. 12–50. From creation to exile, from the garden to the flood, from one conflict to another between early patriarchs, to Yahweh's promise to Abraham that the land of Syria-Palestine will be the property of his descendants, to Joseph's ascension into power over Egypt, all tell the story of the formation of a *specific* group of people, a collective body, the Israelites. Universalizing that story lends to beliefs in God forming *his* community into a holy community. It is the type of determinism that drives the ethical justification of empires and colonizers, who see themselves as the embodiment or constituency of God's elect community, and therefore descendants of "biblical Israel," which is itself a fictional idea that never existed in history.[29] The more extreme variations of this belief are British and American Israelisms, which I will discuss later. Given birth within that framework, traditional readings of Gen. 1–3 reinforce an ideal image of gender and family that reflects the self of those who control the dominant traditions of interpretation and who do so to advance a particular idea of community. But those readings have emphasized the idea and the nature of a definably single and elect community. In doing that, it has shut the door on different communities that could access or approach the text as applying to themselves. *One can say, then, that restricting discourses around or to one center and one periphery is a means of controlling the narrative.*

Under colonialism, meaning and interpretation of the Bible become the property of the dominant heritage and tradition. This history of the Bible as God's revelation is expressed through the framework of the culturally dominant vocabulary. The particular becomes the model of the universal, which is why monotheistic traditions have become inextricably wrapped up in imperialist ideologies.[30] Access to restoration, or salvation, entailed adopting values, morals, and ethics that were already known in the imperial culture. Not unlike the female body enculturated first as a daughter to a patriarchal male then exchanged under the guise of masculine reciprocity to another male, who becomes her husband, lord, and master, according to the Bible.

EVE AS A POSTCOLONIAL HEROINE? EVEN IF NOT, LET'S TRY TO HEAR HER VOICE.

The more one wants to be an atomist, the more some figure of the big Other is needed to regulate one's distance from others.[31]

The ideological power of colonialism is its ability to reduce, homogenize, and overwrite, as though a palimpsest, the identities and cultures of others. It turns diversity into a single controllable and definable body—mutantized to fit into the existing categorical framework for a dominating culture.

To counter the oppressive weight of colonialism, postcolonialism must be subversive.[32] It must challenge the dominant traditions of interpretation and open space for marginalized and minoritized communities.

In that pursuit, one strategy for reading Gen. 1–3 is to see Eve as the hero of the story. If God represents colonial or imperial power, and Adam represents the extension of the appointee, and so the designated of that power, Eve, in *her* choice to pursue knowledge, represents resistance to any imposed idea and expectation. When she chooses the Tree of Knowledge, when she *chooses knowledge*, she puts herself in front of any imposed patriarchal framework selfishly expected by God and Adam (cf. Gen. 3). She claims her body as her own, but we also know her autonomy is not celebrated by either the author or dominant traditions of interpretation.

Ingrid Faro writes, "the humans move from the state of stewards of God's creation . . . to independent masters outside the garden."[33] But that interpretation, which is common, assumes an ordered hierarchy in which the woman is categorized by the needs and expectations of the man. Take, for instance, the punishment given to the woman in contrast to that given to the man. The woman receives increased labor pains, which are associated with her assumed gendered role of producing heirs for the man. She will perform her function through pain. She will desire her man. She will want the authority and control of her man, and he will dominate her. In all this, Eve symbolizes a colonized body. The man, because he obeyed his wife (Gen. 3:17), was condemned to struggle against the earth to produce food. There is clearly a prioritization here, in that the judgment of the woman necessitates the existence of the man. The judgment of the man, however, does not necessitate the woman. This type of categorization and hierarchy is at the root of ideologies justifying claims over the bodies of others. For example, if we read the man and the woman as a metaphor for cultures, the idea that a subordinate culture will be dominated and would be reliant upon the superior culture is one that is consistently found in the ideologies of colonizing cultures. This explains resistance by minoritized bodies against power centers that seek to restrict them on a subordinated periphery. For example, the trend of women cutting their hair in

42   *Chapter 2*

2022, an Iranian protest which became global, as a protest against masculine, or patriarchal, oppression of women calls people to listen and understand the perspectives of women, and how they are subordinated bodies.[34]

Eve models a revolt against imposed gendered expectations that reinforce the authority of a "big Other," whether God or a masculine, patriarchal ideal. That she is not entirely free from her ideological shackles, however, is clear from her punishment and from her lack of voice in the account, save to blame the serpent, and her early attempts at resisting the serpent's encouragement to pursue knowledge. *We want our minorities quiet and complacent!* Compare the act of controlling knowledge to shape the contours of community by the South Carolina assembly which prohibited slaves, whose bodies were ideologically feminized by their "lords and masters": "and whereas, the having of slaves taught to write, or suffering them to be employed in writing, may be attended with great inconveniences; Be it therefore enacted . . . that all and every person and persons whatsoever, who shall hereafter teach, or cause any slaves or slaves to be taught, to write, or shall use or employ any slave as a scribe in any manner of writing whatsoever, hereafter taught to write, every such person and persons, shall, for every such offence, forfeit the sum of 100 pounds current money."[35] Like enslaved persons in South Carolina, Eve's rejection represents an attempt to control the distribution of knowledge and who benefits from it—acts that also define the dominant contours of community.

Regarding Genesis, Gerhard von Rad notes that the distinction between the man's punishment and the woman's strikes "at the deepest root of her being as a wife and a mother"; whereas, the man's strikes "at the innermost nerve of his life: his work, his activity, and provision sustenance. It does not, however, strike at the man himself."[36] Even in that assessment, von Rad assumes that the identity of the woman is wrapped up in (masculine assumptions about) what she is, not what she does, as a wife and a mother. Those attributes are defined by necessity in relation to the man, who, in contrast, is defined by what he does and what he can accomplish.[37] The same thing can be said for colonized bodies.

The traces of that "other" are there, despite attempts to obfuscate it under the banners of universalism and divine plan. *Let us never forget that God is portrayed in masculine terms!* As Northrop Frye put it, "God is male because that rationalizes the ethos of a patriarchal male-dominated society."[38] Adam is made in the image of God. Eve, however, is made from a *small piece* of Adam relinquished to create a subordinate helper. We can do all the theological gymnastics we want, but we cannot get around the implication that Eve is a watered-down version of the image of God from a theological perspective With her status and identity linked to divine revelation through the man, she is the perfect colonized body: subordinate, dependent, quiet, and defined entirely by her connection to the man. That diminished view, together with her "errant" pursuit of knowledge, would also be part of why interpreters flocked to her as justification for views on the evil and seductive tendencies of women. Take, for instance, Martin Luther's claim made in a sermon: "for the devil holds the female sex organ . . . And who can enumerate all the ludicrous, ridiculous, false, vain, and superstitious ideas of this seducible sex? From the first woman, Eve, it originated that they should be deceived and considered a laughingstock" (*Ten Comm.*, p. 407).

That Genesis was concerned about theological premises such as *imago Dei* is not true. As I discussed already, Genesis fits more in the genre of a political document than a theological or devotional one. Emphasis upon Adam and Eve as universal models of human relationship to God, to each other, and of sex, gender, and family is a theological imposition from a later time. Nevertheless, dominant traditions of interpretation have conflated the story with their own theological impositions so that a co-opted meaning has become the norm and is frequently cited as the basis for views such as complentarianism. For example, "The man is created first in the Old Testament, and possesses what the New Testament will call *headship* over his wife," as Owen Strachan, the former president of the Council on Biblical Manhood and Womanhood, claimed.[39] If Gen. 3 articulates the foundational roles of society, then the suppression of the minoritized body, of the difference it symbolized, is given legitimation through connection to divine revelation as the objective blueprint for the world. For those in authority, deviance is threatening. There is a reason that Eve was described as creating problems when pursuing knowledge of her own accord. While Genesis expressed a patriarchal model of relationship—without ever mentioning marriage—it was entirely historically particular to the biblical author's social location. Biblical interpretations, however, which have long been controlled by the enjoyment of men, have enthusiastically embraced the idea that man was closer to presenting that ideal body, as defined as the model to be emulated, and which would be associated with Christ's body (cf. 1 Cor. 15:45–49 where Christ is referred to as the "last Adam," who is the life-giving counterpoint to the living body; see also 1 Cor. 15:21–22; Rom. 5:12–19). Woman, in contrast, was subordinate to the man (based on Gen. 2:21–24; 3:16). And legions of masculine, biblical interpreters remind us with an unbridled passion that it was Eve who ate from the Tree of Knowledge and rejected that imposed hierarchy, which held that women were intellectually inferior and were driven by emotion and sensual desire. *A reflection of masculine ignorance that perseveres even in the modern world!*

When Eve took the "fruit," which is a symbolic object of consumption by bodies, from the Tree of Knowledge, she sought to move past her limitations as a sexual being. But the subordinated body, because of its position,

44   *Chapter 2*

is restricted by what it may consume, lest it create chaos by overturning the conventional assumptions and institutions. Recall, for comparison, laws in early US states that made it illegal to teach slaves how to read and write, which I referred to earlier. Eve moves past imposed, suppressing patriarchal expectations. She presents herself as someone of intellect, subverting patriarchal ideals embodied in God and man (although God is typically portrayed in idealized masculine terms). That is a problem for the biblical author, and the legions of biblical interpreters through the millennia. There are countless examples of biblical commentaries, treatises, sermons, and more, for instance, who cast Eve as diabolical and even as a tool of Satan.[40] I already mentioned Luther. In addition, the revered St. Augustine, for example, makes the following statement in his discussion of marriage and semen, which I will discuss in more detail below (cf. *Good Marr.*). He also strips the intellectual accomplishment of Eve from the female body, "Woman is of small intelligence and . . . lives more in accordance with the promptings of the inferior flesh than by the superior reason" (*Gen.* 9.5.9). In addition, Thomas Aquinas wrote, "As regards the individual nature, woman is defective and misbegotten" (*Summa* I.92.1 Reply to Objection 1).

Augustine believed that sin was passed through the man's semen into the consuming body of the woman (cf. *City* 13:14), which, one might assume, only perpetuates her status as a profane, consuming creature. Her body consumes what is given her by the man, who symbolizes the community or culture in power, stripping her of autonomy. *The subordinated body is restricted through what it is allowed to consume.* That might suggest that Augustine was willing to overlook Eve's choice to eat from the tree as the delusional nature of women generally. That is, it could have been treated as a one-off event, until she condemned all women by corrupting the man. Put more directly, Eve's choice didn't condemn all of humanity until she seduced Adam into making the same choice (Gen. 3:6). When Adam made the same choice, it was then that sin, like a belligerent gene, ecstatically took residence in the testicles of every man. Presumably, then, if Adam refused to make the same choice that Eve had made in terms of the Tree of Knowledge, Eve could have been removed from the story without problem and replaced (similar to the Jewish tradition of Lilith, Adam's first "wife"). But Eve, as a minority, acts in a way that makes sense to her. She applies her intellect unencumbered by any imposed framework and acts in a way that does not obligate her to an imposed set of expectations and ideals. She represents the choice that colonized cultures might make for themselves. Her body also symbolizes that which is punished for rejecting the imposed hierarchy and authority by the colonial power. (Recall that I identified women as the first colonized bodies.)

Modern readers frequently interpret the serpent who spoke to Eve and convinced her to eat from the Tree of Knowledge as Satan, although that connection is not clear within Gen. 1–3. Satan, as theologically understood as the embodiment of absolute evil, is a much later development.[41] Rather, in Gen. 1–3 the Hebrew term in question is *hanachash*. With a definite article, the term is not a name but a a category or type including a description of function.[42] Toward that purpose, the serpent is not an antagonist of right versus wrong. It represents antagonism toward imposed imperial power. So again, we return to the idea that names indicate functions and relations to the material world. In Hebrew, *adam* can be translated as "mankind" or "land" (as *adamah*), because part of Adam's curse, for instance, is to work the land and return to it when he dies (cf. Gen. 3:19). Eve, which is *chavvah*, can be translated as "life." She is described as the "mother of all living" (cf. Gen. 3:20) because her body is the fertile ground from which the bodies of men are raised. Regarding the *dramatis personae* of the serpent, Adam, Eve, and even God, interpreting names as functions offers greater credence to understanding the story as a metaphor for bodies distributed within a hierarchy of power.

Many readers see death as punishment for disobedience, but the couple were kicked out of the garden so they would not eat from the Tree of Life and *become like gods* (Gen. 3:22–24).[43] The couple are kicked out of the garden *not* as a direct punishment for eating from the Tree of Knowledge. We can only conclude then that even in the garden, they existed on a linear path toward death. In great colonial imagery, God claimed the land upon which the couple lived and forces a new mode of production upon them while demanding a new set of cultural norms. *You must now live **this** way.* So the story of the expulsion isn't one of divine punishment as much as it expresses a function of divine control, preventing human beings from becoming like gods, which includes displacing people to protect the dominant institution of power. What does that say about communities who see God as a model to aspire toward? Are we then also surprised by the fact that Western empires saw justification for their conquests in divine will? *You savages must now live **this** way!*

EVE AS A SYMBOL OF SUBVERSION?

If postcolonialism demands subversion. If it challenges dominant traditions of interpretation, those that have restricted and in some cases obscured the cultural narratives and meanings and values of colonized or minoritized or marginalized peoples, then we might interpret Eve as representing the potential and need for challenge. She reminds us not to accept meekly unwarranted subordination but to resist, to speak, even if we are met with greater "judgment." Because one day we might be free. Groaning under the dominating symbol of a cultural context that did not appreciate her individuality, she reached up and exposed the frailty of God and man. We might remember

46   *Chapter 2*

that what God declared to be the consequence of eating from the Tree of Knowledge ("you will die") was incorrect. In fact, it revealed an insecurity in the character. *They might become like us . . .*

In the narrative, the actions of God reflect the biblical author's view of man and his connection to the bodies related to him. That interpretation fits the image of Eve less as a historical character and more as a function. In the same way, Adam and God can be interpreted less as historical characters and more as functions. Reading that way opens the door for postcolonial strategies of challenging imposed ideals, roles, and other cultural behaviors. It makes space for subverting traditional interpretations that get caught up in the idea of defending God, man, and the actions of God and man in Gen. 1–3, as well as seeking confirmation of the ideologies that govern the modern context, especially those that control marriage, gender and family. It demands recognition that such traditional and dominant interpretations are obsessed with finding confirmation of their own masculine (and Western, as I'll explain in later chapters) ideals as universal mandates.

In biblical interpretation, the potential for and the problems of life, relationship, even love begin in the garden and the tyrannical thumb of a chauvinist god. So reading Gen. 1–3 as a paradigm for divinely ordained marriage, family, and gender is to miss the point. As Elaine Pagels observes of Augustine's interpretation, for instance, "As woman's fertility brings involuntary suffering, so also does sexual desire: the blight of male domination has fallen upon the whole structure of sexual relationships."[44] In other words, according to Pagels, women are subordinate to sexual males because they fucked up through Eve. Their punishment is to have their bodies fucked and to produce heirs, "new bodies," for the social affirmation of the patriarchal male. The assumptions that the biblical author, or that historical misogynist interpreters, who ascended into the role of "church father," such as Augustine, had are not, or should not, be those that define the contexts of modern readers. To hold to the archaic view of the world means we have to cut out some human potential. And in doing that, we perpetuate forms of ideological colonialism. And that is where some problems are occurring with pursuits of equality. If we accept Gen. 1–3 as interpreted by the dominant traditions of Christianity, then we accept women are subordinate to men, and that they should be subordinate to men in *all* cases. Not only that, but that men are closer to God.

But that is not the culture in which those who have been marginalized want to live. A postcolonial reading of Gen. 1–3 demands that we celebrate the attempt at independence and autonomy by Eve, whose body God and the man colonized. It demands that we challenge conventional assumptions about marriage, family, gender, and role. We should challenge them in ways that remind us that one community's definition may not be shared by another's. More than that, we can adopt a humanitarian concern with such a challenge, especially if it reminds us of how much sexual aggression and offense against women continue to be perpetrated in monotheistic cultures.

When a dominant culture imposes itself upon minority communities or marginalized communities and peoples, it must be addressed. Where the Bible and biblical interpretation is used to oppress women, it should to be addressed. Where it's used to oppress LGBTQIA communities, it should be addressed. Where the Bible is used to justify slavery, it should be addressed. We should challenge any assumption that the marginalized, as Bhabha put it, "articulate the 'death-in-life' of the 'imagined community' of the nation."[45] We should challenge assumptions that they represent that which threatens the possibility of the national community, and that their differences must be merged into a singular body and category, as though representing a function and metaphor of the fate that awaits the national community, if power were stripped from its insecure hands.

Eve's story encourages us to seek knowledge. It encourages us to seek knowledge that makes sense to us within our communities. It also reminds us of how easy it is to justify and enculturate oppression, thereby subordinating the bodies of others under the oppressive weight of our own in real and symbolic missionary positions.

NOTES

1. Octavio Esqueda, "Much Ado About Gender Roles," ChristianityToday.com, August 22, 2018, https://www.christianitytoday.com/ct/2018/august-web-only/complementarian-egalitarian-debate-gender-roles-explainer.html.

2. National Association of Evangelicals, "Theology of Sex" (National Association of Evangelicals, 2012), 3.

3. James V. Brownson, *Bible, Gender, Sexuality: Reframing the Church's Debate on Same-Sex Relationships* (Grand Rapids: W.B. Eerdmans, 2013), 94.

4. Cf. Carol Meyers, *Discovering Eve: Ancient Israelite Women in Context* (New York: Oxford University Press, 1988), 32.

5. Cf. Cataldo, *What the Bible Says about Sex*, 59–68.

6. Maurice Godelier, *The Metamorphoses of Kinship*, trans. Nora Scott (London; New York: Verso Books, 2011), 60.

7. A number of states had laws against miscegenation. The US Supreme Court ruled those laws to be unconstitutional with *Loving v. Virginia, 388 U.S. 1* (1967).

8. Cf. Andre S. Bustanoby, "Love, Honor, and Obey," *CT* 13, no. 18 (June 6, 1969): 3–4.

9. Cf. Carol Heffernan, "God's Design for Marriage," *Focus on the Family* (blog), January 1, 2002, https://www.focusonthefamily.com/marriage/gods-design-for-marriage/; Christopher Ash, "A Biblical View of Marriage," The Gospel Coalition, January 14, 2020, https://www.thegospelcoalition.org/essay/biblical-view-marriage/.

48   *Chapter 2*

10. Cf. Cataldo, *What the Bible Says about Sex*, 179–200.

11. Cf. Heffernan, "Marriage"; Focus on the Family, "Oral and Anal Sex: Biblical Guidelines for Intimacy in Marriage," Focus on the Family, nd, https://www.focusonthefamily.com/family-qa/oral-and-anal-sex-biblical-guidelines-for-intimacy-in-marriage/.

12. See again Cataldo, *What the Bible Says about Sex*, 59–67.

13. Compare Cataldo, 77–91.

14. Cf. the assumptions in Candice Lucey, "Was Jesus Ever Married with a Wife and Children?" Christianity.com, July 27, 2020, https://www.christianity.com/wiki/jesus-christ/why-is-there-a-theory-that-jesus-had-children.html.

15. Cf. Kwasi Wiredu, *Cultural Universals and Particulars: An African Perspective*, African Systems of Thought (Bloomington: Indiana University Press, 1996), 1–10.

16. For more on the pervasiveness of this type of thinking and ideological orientation, see Edward W. Said, *Orientalism* (New York: Vintage Books, 1994).

17. Again, cf. Said.

18. Cf. Peter L. Berger, *The Sacred Canopy: Elements of a Sociological Theory of Religion* (New York: Anchor Books, 1990), 4–11.

19. Gerhard von Rad, *Genesis, Revised Edition: A Commentary*, OTL (Louisville: Westminster John Knox Press, 1973), 60.

20. Frye, *Words with Power*, 26.

21. Cf. Nayar, *Postcolonialism*, 1.

22. Nayar, 2.

23. Dube and Wafula, *Postcoloniality*, 12.

24. Michael W. Chapman, "Catholic Exorcist: 'Transgenderism Is a Full-Blown Attack Against Motherhood,'" CNSNews.com, 01/09/2023, https://cnsnews.com/article/national/michael-w-chapman/catholic-exorcist-transgenderism-full-blown-attack-against.

25. The Christian Missionary Alliance, "Staying on Mission: A Guideline for How Alliance Churches Respond to Obergefell v. Hodges" (The Christian Missionary Alliance, November 2019), 30.

26. Cf. Nayar, *Postcolonialism*, 1, 4.

27. Compare the maximalist portrayal in William Schlegel, *Satellite Bible Atlas: Historical Geography of the Bible*, Second Edition (Jerusalem: The Bible Society in Israel, 2016), 75, map 5–6.

28. Johannes Gerloff, "Biblical Borders of Israel (Part 1)," *Christians for Israel International* (blog), July 3, 2020, https://www.c4israel.org/_teachings/biblical-borders-of-israel/.

29. Cf. Thomas L. Thompson, *The Mythic Past: Biblical Archaeology and the Myth of Israel* (New York: Basic Books, 1999); Mario Liverani, *Israel's History and the History of Israel*, trans. Chiara Peri and Philip R. Davies (London; Oakville, CT: Equinox, 2005).

30. See also the study in Cataldo, *Breaking Monotheism*.

31. Slavoj Žižek, *In Defense of Lost Causes*, Kindle (London; New York: Verso, 2008), location 770.

Adam, Eve, and Steve's Serpent   49

32. See also Mártinez-Vázquez, *Made in the Margins*, 4.

33. Ingrid Faro, *Evil in Genesis: A Contextual Analysis of Hebrew Lexemes for Evil in the Book of Genesis*, Studies in Scripture & Biblical Theology (Bellingham, WA: Lexham Press, 2021), 117.

34. David Mouriquand, "Iran Protests: Why Is Cutting Hair an Act of Rebellion?" Euronews, October 6, 2022, https://www.euronews.com/culture/2022/10/06/iran-protests-why-is-cutting-hair-an-act-of-rebellion.

35. Stephen C. Wright and Micah E. Lubensky, "The Struggle for Social Equality: Collective Action Versus Prejudice Reduction," in *Intergroup Misunderstandings: Impact of Divergent Social Realities*, ed. Stéphanie Demoulin, Jacques-Philippe Leyens, and John F. Dovidio (New York: Psychology Press, 2009), 54.

36. Von Rad, *Genesis*, 93–94

37. Von Rad, *Genesis*, 93–94.

38. Northrop Frye, *The Great Code* (New York: Harcourt Brace Jovanovich, 1983), 107.

39. Cited in Eliza Griswold, "The Unmaking of Biblical Womanhood," *The New Yorker*, July 25, 2021, https://www.newyorker.com/news/on-religion/the-unmaking-of-biblical-womanhood.

40. Cf. the discussion throughout Cataldo, *What the Bible Says about Sex*.

41. Cf. T. J. Wray and Gregory Mobley, *The Birth of Satan: Tracing the Devil's Biblical Roots* (New York: Palgrave Macmillan, 2005), 51–73, esp. 72–73.

42. See also Wray and Mobley, 58–64.

43. Faro's assertion that this story refers to a spiritual death and a delayed physical death is unconvincing (*Evil in Genesis*, 48–49). The biblical author did not share the same definition of spirit that modern Christians do, indebted as the latter are to Greek philosophies.

44. Elaine H. Pagels, *Adam, Eve, and the Serpent*, 1st ed (New York: Random House, 1988), 133.

45. Bhabha, *The Location of Culture*, 164.

Chapter 3

Colonizing Cain

About to drop you like Cain / like Cain dropped Abel.[1]

The biblical story of Cain echoes condemningly through history. Yet its antagonist, while guilty of murder, at least according to the biblical author, bears the possibility of being interpreted in different, perhaps even more compelling, ways. *After all, how many biblical heroes are also guilty of killing but are celebrated for their positive contributions to the development of Israel, or as moral examples?* In contrast to his symbolic confinement in biblical reception history, what if Cain could be read as symbolic of a colonized body? In addition, that his actions against Abel's body symbolized his rejection of an imposed cultural body (or conformity to it), which Yahweh embodied? I am aware of what my hypothetical protestor will say, that I am making the text say something it doesn't. I do not accept that. There is no evidence that Cain and Abel, or Adam and Eve, or Noah, or Abraham, and so on, were actual historical personages. Rather, Genesis was written within the literary framework of a mythic genre, which a basic knowledge of mythic studies reveals that myths convey some historical values and meanings through symbolism but are not intended to convey modern expectations for historiography. Reading Cain as a symbol is hardly a step away from the original intent of the literary genre. That type of reading is also what interpreters have been doing in their Bible readings for millennia. Of course, *what* gets read symbolically versus as historical fact has less to do with the genre of any writing or the authorial intent, and more to do with the interpreter's own agenda. For example, and I must return to this example because it betrays interpretation's attempts to define and control bodies, how often have we heard that the Song of Songs is a metaphor for Christ's relationship to the Church or Yahweh's relationship to Israel? The Song is erotica *par excellence*![2] But it is frequently interpreted as a metaphor to match the aims of the dominant interpreting tradition, which does *not* celebrate sexuality and desire, rather quite the opposite.

52   Chapter 3

That tradition maintains sex is a utility for producing more members, who
must be raised in Christian households and, according to former Secretary of
Education Betsy DeVos, for the US example, taught with *Christian* curricu-
lum to be good moral Christian citizens.[3]

The example of the Song of Songs also betrays how the interpreter's fear
over female sexuality is not far from Cain's story, as I will argue in later chapters of this work. The man, Adam, had sex with the woman, Eve, and she gave
birth to Cain (Gen. 4:1). It's easy to gloss over the statement that the biblical
author attributes the woman, "I have created a man just like Yahweh did." But
it feeds the traditional interpretation of the woman as a necessary evil. The
woman who took from the Tree of Knowledge, who claimed to create like
Yahweh, was also in her overt sexuality the symbol of masculine weakness.
To confirm that, we need only ask, how many interpretive accounts describe
Eve as a positive force? Very few. Instead, she presents the foil against which
masculine concerns are cast. The author, in his commitment and affiliation to
Israel, makes those concerns a primary emphasis. And one can know this for
several reasons. Genesis 4 is part of the larger ethnic-political mythology of
Israel, where Gen. 1–11 lays the groundwork for the so-called ancestral legends of Gen. 12–50, the latter which itself lays the groundwork for the exodus narrative in which Yahweh leads the Hebrews out of Egypt into Canaan
to establish them as a nation. Laden with authorial assumption, the Hebrew
phrase attributed to Eve is *qaniti*, "I created," and it seems to be a clear play
on the name Cain, *qayin*. On this issue note Tammi Schneider, who embraces
a traditional monotheistic position that keeps Western assumptions about God
as a causal agent in the story: "The creation verb Eve uses is one of the verbs
used to refer to the divine's role in creation ([Gen.] 14:19, 22; Deut. 32:6),
and of the Deity redeeming the people (Exod. 15:16; Isa. 11:11)."[4] While
she draws similar connections to the larger story of a "people," she treats
the narrative as an objective theological account of divine revelation rather
than a historically contingent myth. Such interpretive tendency runs rampant
in biblical scholarship and reinforces, as postcolonialism wants desperately
to remind us, colonial vocabularies and meanings. In dominant Western and
colonial traditions, the "people" who are the subject of God's plan are associated with the "righteous" community, which in Christian tradition is defined
as the Body of Christ. The bulk of all commentaries, doctrines, translations,
decrees, etc., associated with the Christian Bible emerge in the cultures of
Western Europe, and later the United States. Their inroads into non-Western
cultures were facilitated by historical imperialism and colonialism fashioning
those cultures into a "civilized" image. *I created! But through the power of
the word of the gospel message. So I am not like Eve, am I?*

Let me propose again that the names of the characters in Genesis reflect
the function of their bodies. Cain is the result of a human creation. Rather,

his birth results from the *woman* taking initiative. *I created!* Consequently, like his mother—*"Please! You won't really die" (Gen. 3:4)!*—he resists the imposed moral order that is given to him. The result? Like Eve's actions resulted in a denial of immortality, insuring an endpoint for all human life, he takes the life of his brother (Gen. 4:8). And so it would seem that for the author, female initiative, which has been the heart of a colonizing ideology (and justification)—the foreign, uncivilized body is so very close to the uncontrolled female body in the patriarchal mind—which Cain may now embody, destroys a stable moral order and threatens life. The proximity between the female body and the colonized body is not one of factor but degree to which both are recognized as bodies that must be relegated to a periphery.

Cain's actions do not appear premeditated in the modern sense. Rather, they may be better understood as driven by a type of passion. Not a lover's passion, of course, but the passion of anger. In fact, Yahweh asks Cain, *"Why* are you burning with passion?" and *"Why* did your face fall?" (Gen. 4:6; emphasis mine). The latter question likely means the loss of any expressed willingness to engage in cultural exchange. While some scholars will translate the phrase as "downcast," that term does not fit well with "burn with anger" (*charah*). It may be better translated as the fuming body posture that someone gets when they are livid and a breath away from being violent. But that connection to unrestrained passion ending in murder is also behind why the "mark of Cain" is associated with blackness in some predominantly white traditions of interpretation. Historical white cultures and their dominant biblical interpretative traditions were influenced by Orientalist assumptions about Africa, the Middle East, and Asia as home to uncivilized, exotic, barbarian, pagan bodies driven by fragile control over sensual pleasures and emotions rather than rational and intellectual sophistication. I will discuss this issue in more detail later.

Faro claims, based on Gen. 4:7, Yahweh gave Cain an opportunity "to do good."[5] But it is more a hypothetical than an instruction. "Is it not true that if you do good, you will be dignified." (Gen. 4:7). For that reason, in part, I am not convinced by Shubert Spero's interpretation of *Bereishit Rabbah* that Cain "regretted his deed and sought to do penance."[6] That interpretation presupposes the author's moral "law," which is also attributed to divine revelation in monotheistic traditions, as the basis by which Cain assessed his own person. Rather, Yahweh already set the wheels in motion for what Cain will do by rejecting Cain's sacrifice without reason. *Nope, not good enough. You're insufficient. Wait a second, don't get mad about it! You need a "can do" attitude!* Thus, what Faro claims was Cain's choice was not a choice at all. Rather, we should read 4:7 like a judge patronizing a condemned

54   *Chapter 3*

criminal: "isn't it true that if you do good that you will be exalted, but if you don't, sin waits to rule over you"? But note an alternative reading. The term *robets*, frequently translated as to "lie down," may be better translated in apposition to "sin." In Akkadian, *robets*, and if the author was in Babylonia, this history may have been accessible in scribal circles, referred to a demon.[7] Instead of sin laying at the door, one can translate the phrase as, "the demon, Sin, is at the door."

The tenacity of that connection led Joel Kemp, for example, to dedicate an entire study to the connection between the mark of Cain in Gen. 4:5 and modern prejudiced assumptions about "black" as "dangerous, deviant, and depraved."[8] Why that connection? From a sociological view, there is an easy explanation. Groups seek clear rules for preserving the distinction between insider and outsider. All that threatens the homeostasis, or stability, of the group, is categorized as an outsider and chaotic. It is that fundamental need that resides at the historical emergence of the figure as Satan in monotheistic traditions as the antithesis to the "people of God." In the history of the United States, the black body was first defined as property, then as a corrupted outsider, then as a tolerated minority. Even in the 21st century, one would be naïve to maintain that the black body is fully accepted within the value systems of a white dominant society. As Kemp put it, "the villainy associated with Cain throughout biblical, early Jewish, and Christian traditions becomes racialized in America to help construct these 3Ds of Blackness [dangerousness, deviance, and depravity] and ultimately to demonize Black people. . . . Biblical interpretation provides an ideological foundation for America's racial systems, and the law gives these racial ideas their structure and force."[9]

I don't want to focus on the role that US law plays in giving racism structure and force; my focus is on biblical interpretation. Even Kemp's study focuses on the institution and praxis of law enforcement and not on the body of codified law. The point that he highlights, however, is that cultural interpretations of law manifest the qualities and values of the idealized body. It is that faceless body that is the basis by which concepts of citizen, insider, member, even human are imagined. Difference from that generates collective anxiety that must be eased through at least one of several ways: a structural reorganization of how "body" is defined, such as what the 15th and 19th Amendments of the US Constitution have partially done; creation of categories of tolerance but not expressed acceptance (*"black bodies are acceptable in black spaces, but we're a little uncomfortable with them in white spaces"*),[10] with imposed ideologies of how the tolerated minority must conform to dominant cultural norms; or, outright rejection.

There is an important inverse to what I just described that highlights the depth of an institutional enculturation of prejudice, which has historically influenced biblical interpretation. As a high school student, I gained a better

Colonizing Cain 55

appreciation of distinguished "spaces," though without the intellectual apparatus to frame it in the form of a sociological theory, when I was one of the only white youths at a gathering of inner-city young black people. On the bus to our destination a young black male asked me who my favorite rapper was. During this cultural time, rap was a form of associated identity. Naively, however, I said, "Beastie Boys," and I couldn't understand at first why everyone around me laughed. (Today, with greater intellectual sophistication and cultural awareness, my friend Dwayne Tunstall and I laugh about my response.) As I write this, I can't remember why the intended audience for this gathering was black youth, but I have a suspicion. This was also around the time N.W.A., Public Enemy, Tupac, Dr. Dre, and Rodney King were highlighting the violent outcomes of inequality, and the majority culture was trying to figure out appropriate responses. It's possible the organizers were motivated by the cultural focus on the "black minority"/"white majority" dichotomy that defined US culture in the early to mid-20th century CE—a dichotomy that also became the foundation for later affirmative action strategies. The overall aim of this gathering, as I remember, was to show inner city youth that violence wasn't the only way out of their circumstances. (The ideological problem behind that motivation or assumption should be apparent when recalling who comprised the majority of attendants.) My encounter on the bus was innocent if not socially embarrassing, but it was not the only situation I had to navigate. One night, a group of young black boys cornered me as I was going to bed. One individual who seemed particularly angry got in my face, "Don't go to sleep, white boy. I'm going to kill you!" At the time, I didn't know how to react because we had never spoken before, nor did I understand how this was a "proving ritual" reinforcing a social hierarchy, one in which I was being defined on the lower end.

I'm writing this book because neither he nor his friends touched me, nor did they approach me again. I later heard that an older black male, who reputation said was a member of the Bloods, issued a dictum, "nobody touches the white boy." In a cultural environment in which I was the "tolerated" minority, my savior wasn't the white Jesus found in nearly every church in the United States. Nor was it the dominant majority. My savior was a black man whose intent was likely not to save me personally but to protect his community, guarding them against being vilified any more than they had already been by the dominant culture in the United States, and who had himself sought meaning in a gang because society had turned a blind eye to the suffering and oppression he and his community experienced on a daily basis.

Even in a space dominated "black bodies" there remained some tension in relation to my identity as a member of the dominant culture. With a wisdom gained from experience, the "OG Blood" knew that if something happened to me, some repercussion might be felt by his community. In the cultural milieu of the United States during that time, violence against a representative of majority culture in a space where they were not a threat would only reinforce the dominant society's prejudice of black people as villains. Inversely, it can also be said that those majority culture representatives who dismiss or denigrate movements in the modern context, such as BLM, continue to see black bodies as those upon whom violence can be acceptably exercised without accusations of villainy.

Just as the threat of becoming villains likely motivated the OG Blood to warn against harming me, villainy itself serves the aims of the status quo by dissociating bodies that would otherwise challenge it. According to Gen. 4:5, it was Yahweh who planted those seeds in Cain, making Cain's inevitable rejection part of the divine plan. Cain could either complacently accept his inferior status to Abel or respond. Either way, his position in the relational hierarchy (a subordinated body) was established. As Elihu Coleman described in his description of a common defense of slavery, "a Mark set upon Cain, and they do believe that these Negroes are the Posterity of Cain, because of their hair, and their being so black."[11] In reassurance of both the permanence of categories *and* how the distribution of those categories reinforces hierarchies that benefit their subject in contrast to the other, physical attributes are categorized according to interpretations rooted in perceptions of the self and one's own community as the ideal, or the image closest to it. Difference is a threat.

The biblical portrayal and definition of Cain, as I will explain in the following discussion, is obsessed with his response. His is the scapegoated body. Contrast his murder, for but one example, with that of David's (2 Sam. 11:14–17), the glorified king of Israel (*frequently portrayed as being white in artistic representations*) from whose line Jesus would descend (cf. Matt. 1:1). David's act does not result in his rejection like Cain's does. In fact, David ultimately gets what he wants: the woman, Bathsheba, and an "eternal" dynasty. Where David is forgiven and his unborn child as the scapegoated body bears the weight of his sin (2 Sam. 12:13), Cain and his descendants are forever symbolically the emotional beast that threatened the lineage of the patriarchal father. What is the basis for the difference in response if not that one body represents the outsider while another represents the insider? Driven to the margins, Cain is like the precolonized body who must be controlled and removed from the social community, lest his "chaos" break the stability of the community. He is also like the colonized body in that his labor benefited the dominating society, which is represented by Adam and Eve. Cain cultivated the ground (recall the nature of his offering). And we recall the punishment in Gen. 3 that the man, Adam, receives is that by the sweat of his brow will he work the land. One could also assume that Cain worked the land *for* the man, or at least along with him.

Colonizing Cain   57

Of course, not all scholars interpret it that way. For example, Westermann suggests Cain's curse connects him to the serpent, who is also cursed (cf. Gen. 3:14), both representing the diabolical body of the "other."[12] The land is also cursed because of Adam's transgression (cf. Gen. 3:17). In each case, being cursed implies continued existence as a cursed body, but one established as a foil against which dominant attributes of the author's community are established. *Like the body of the savage standing before "civilized" society?* Cain's story does not end with his being a condemned murderer but a subordinated body marked by Yahweh for labor and as a body marked in remembrance for the benefit of the members of the community.[13] That theme would be further embellished by New Testament writers. The author of 1 John 3:11–12, for example, associates Cain with evil as a contrast to the gospel message. Hebrews (11:4) celebrates Abel's sacrifice as "greater" than that of Cain's, through which Abel was commended righteousness, leaving Cain only to represent the unrighteous in his body contrasted with that of Abel. *Even Jesus, while casting out indictments against the pharisees, weighed in on the tradition of Abel's righteousness (Matt. 23:35)!* But what did Abel do in the story except offer a sacrifice and die? He becomes the foil against which Cain's profanity is cast. Consequently, his actions were memorialized as acts of faith so that Can would forever be cursed.[14] The New Testament authors clearly establish the moral dilemma for their audiences, composed of Christians trying to make sense of their crucified savior. Faith brings understanding, while a lack of faith turns one into Cain (Heb. 11:1–4; see also 12:1–3). *Don't be like Cain (see 1 John 3:12)!*

Remember, the author implies how Cain's anger erupted after he offers Yahweh the first fruits of his own labor. Yahweh was more pleased with Abel's offering. The Bible offers us no real reason for the favoritism. Faith? That is a New Testament interpretation of an Old Testament passage. But Genesis doesn't discuss faith as a theological concept devised by early Christian apologists such as the author of Hebrews. Genesis states Yahweh gazed with favor upon Abel's offering, which was the firstborn of his flock (Gen. 4:3–5). But so rooted is the Christian view in numerous interpretations that the justification for divine whimsy moves away from exegesis: Cain's judgment becomes a matter of the heart, of faith, and of commitment to religious practice.[15] But the Christian concept of those ideas would have been unknown to the author, much less to Cain if we entertain the fanciful idea he was a historical personage, the son of the world's first two people who were themselves only recent beneficiaries of the Tree of Knowledge which God was trying to keep from them. Or, at least, claimed it was inaccessible to them while also teasing them with its presence.

My grandfather did something similar when my brother and I were living with him. He put two new toys and magazines on the kitchen table and left

58   *Chapter 3*

them there before my brother and I returned from school. My brother, like Eve, opened one toy and began playing with it, cajoling me with how fun it was, eventually convincing me to open the other one. When my grandfather returned home from work, like God in Genesis, he cast judgment upon us for opening the toys without being told we could (even though they were intended for us).

Perhaps the Genesis story was nothing more than priestly commentary making a preferential case for meat sacrifices over agricultural ones. *Steaks before salads, boys!* After all, priests were fed, in part, by the sacrifices of the people, which may also be an argument to consider the sacrifices as being of equal value; a more modern practice is tithes and the past collection of indulgences.[16] It may also have had something to do with birthright and blessing in the culture, coupled with the woman's claim to have created a man just as Yahweh did (Gen. 4:1). *Perhaps the taint of the woman was the corruption of her son?* That may be closer to the point. After all, Cain worked the land in subservience to Yahweh's punishment of the man (Gen. 3:19). Was there some suggestion that Cain, like Esau (see chapter 10), would lose his birthright and blessing to his younger sibling, especially when he bared challenge to the authority of the patriarch (cf. Gen. 25:31–34; 27:18–29)? Perhaps even more condemning, where was the man, *ha'adam*, while Cain was working the field with the sweat of his own brow producing the crops he would eventually offer as a rejected sacrifice? *Lying around drunk like Noah and Lot?*

In most traditions, Cain is portrayed as the ancestor to cultures east of Eden, which, if we locate Eden in Babylonia (perhaps inspired by Nebuchadnezzar's Hanging Gardens), would associate him with the Babylonians or the Persians, or people beyond the known world at the time. None of those were Israelites or Judeans, and *all* were considered foreign threats by different authors of the biblical texts. The Assyrian and Babylonian Empires defeated and displaced peoples from the kingdoms of Israel and Judah. Genesis tells us that Cain cultivated the ground by farming and building a city (cf. Gen. 4:17). One could interpret those actions as symbolically carving order out of chaos.[17] One might even be tempted to go so far as Spero to claim that the cities reflect Cain's new appreciation for society, making room for the "other" after he struck down Abel, showing remorse and embracing "cooperative living."[18] Still, it is a weak proposal. Presumably, if the city was a symbol of Cain's remorse then Cain cannot become the villain he became in the view of New Testament writers and later traditions of biblical interpretation. After Cain's death, the city would be a constant reminder of his "return" to the author's moral code, something the New Testament authors could appeal to as *proof* of God's power. And what an appeal that would be even if we are not sure where the city was, though von Rad suggests that Kenite cities can be identified in 1 Sam. 30:29, possibly also Isa. 66:19 and Ezek. 27:13, with the last two referring to people groups. The geographic layout of these would provide a possible geographic reference point for the first city.[19] These would locate Cain's city, which he named after his son, Enoch (cf. Gen. 4:17), in the land of the Tigris and Euphrates Rivers in Babylonia. To bring this full circle, Babylonia is the author of Revelation's favorite metaphor for the worldly threat to the Body of Christ. It is not, contra Spero, a possible testament to Yahweh's power.

Ted Smith's argument that the passage should be read as evidence of a "divine negation of the spiral of fratricidal violence" is not convincing.[20] That imposes as a lens the later monotheistic view of God as an active agent in the natural world *and* it belligerently ignores the world of violence, divine and human, that the Bible's covers struggle unsuccessfully to contain. Even Ambrose's interpretation (*Cain*, 434) that God let Cain wander the earth to highlight God's kindness (God let Cain live) appeals not to an exegetical analysis of the story but to theological sentiment about a Christian view of God, God's sovereignty, and divine forgiveness. But such interpretive tendencies, I have been arguing, and will develop in the rest of this work, reinforce a dominant narrative or language, even dialectic, that gives legitimacy to colonialist thinking about the "other" and the "other's" moral responsibility to God's sovereignty, reflected in the body of the dominant community.

That need to mark out a distinction between insider and outsider may be implied in the lineages of Cain and Seth, as well as Yahweh's putting a mark on Cain in order to define him as a body of *difference* that lives *only* by the permission of Yahweh (cf. Gen. 4:15). Von Rad's suggestion that the author refers to a tattoo is not convincing.[21] It overlooks the function of Cain as the danger of a willful antagonist and as one defined by restlessness (von Rad does, however, connect Cain, through the land of Nod, with restlessness).

Following Abel's death and Cain's expulsion, Seth was born to Adam and Eve. This time, the woman claimed that God *gave* her a child, not that she created one. She subordinates herself to the expected hierarchy, and the result is a living son to carry on the man's lineage. The man, "Seth," is etymologically linked to the term for "foundation." It is his body, not Cain's, produced through the acknowledgment of a "proper" hierarchy and distribution of roles, that represents the future of God's "chosen people." The inverse of that image, however, can be seen in interpretations of Cain. In addition to what I've discussed already, Josephus interpreted Cain as *the* progenitor of the threat to that lofted body (*Ant.* 1.53–66). John Byron also noted that *1 Clement* 4:7 describes Cain as the prototype of hatred and envy; that *Hero* 5, an epistle attributed to Ignatius, refers to Cain as the successor to the devil; and, that the *Apocryphon of John* (II, 24, 16–25, 118–19) labels Cain the epitome of unrighteousness.[22] In contrast, Seth (*like Abel?*) symbolizes the inverted image of Cain, who is the monstrous "other."

60 *Chapter 3*

Both Cain and Seth have descendants named Lamech (Gen. 4:17–18; 5:25–28). In fact, there are several unexplained, generalized similarities.[23] Within Cain's lineage, Lamech is born to *Metushael* (Gen. 4:18). While within Seth's lineage, Lamech is born to *Metushelach* (Gen. 5:25). The author portrays Cain's descendant as an even greater threat, when he pens the well-known adage, "if Cain is avenged seven times, then Lamech will be seventy-seven times" (Gen. 4:24). In contrast, Lamech in the line of Seth is the father of Noah (Gen. 5:28). The author of Luke connects the lineage of Jesus to God through Lamech and Seth (Luke 3:23–28). And with the enthusiasm found only among members of the elect community, the author prioritizes that lineage, and its patriarchal implications, by referring to Adam as the son of God, therefore the recipient of the divine birthright and blessing, which includes the land that would be promised through Abraham, and which would be the location of the kingdoms of Israel and Judah. The ingredients for an imperial ideology, which will be coopted by later monotheistic traditions, are there. In contrast to the celebration of Seth's lineage, Cain's Lamech represents the inverse of Seth's descendant. Here, Lamech only survives because of the permission of Yahweh, the national god of Israel. *What a colonial sentiment!* That a foreign culture, recall that Cain may have lived in the land of the Tigris and Euphrates Rivers, survives because of the grace and fortitude of another claiming superiority over it can be nothing else. Cain's function symbolizes the need for a superior culture to embody a civilized counterpoint. *Was that not also a justification of slavery by Western imperial cultures?* Note, for instance,

> But even Cain's death did not bring an end to the story. His children, beginning with Lamech and his sons, continued to perpetuate the evil of their ancestor. They were held responsible for introducing idolatry, sexual immorality and the demise of the Sethites and sometimes even the angels of heaven. The result of this interpretive activity is that the legacy of Cain continues on and becomes an explanation for the continuing presence of evil in the world. . . . Cain was conceived in evil, committed evil, and evil continued through his progeny.[24]

Driven by enthusiasm for the superiority of the self in the Bible's reception history, and "mythoracial" ideas developed in Western cultures to legitimate categorical distinctions between insider and outsider, Cain became symbolic of evil. He embodied that which was uncivilized, immoral and unaware of sociopolitical frameworks or consequences.[25] That, for instance, is the sole reason titles such as, *The Curse of Cain: The Violent Legacy of Monotheism*, work in their appeals to Western audiences.[26] Cain forever is associated with violence and chaos, even though he becomes a builder of cities, which is an act of civilization. Doing so carves order out of chaos, creating the

Colonizing Cain 61

socially foundational boundaries between insider and outsider. But only from a particular perspective. After all, rarely did political colonizers of the past acknowledge that the cities of those colonized did not need an imposed moral framework. Moreover, Cain's act of murder reflects his need to be civilized and his embodiment of chaos. What does that tell us about biblical interpretation when readers from the 19th and 20th centuries CE interpreted the "mark" of Cain as blackness?[27] Might it be that the foreigner, or outsider, is both a threat and useful? Such was the ideological definition of slaves in the US territories and British imperial territories. Even Phillis Wheatley (ca. 1753–1784 CE), an African American poet—I should note that the reference "African American" didn't gain traction until after Jesse Jackson, Sr., convincingly argued in the late 1980s for the use of the term to refer to the descendants of enslaved Africans and free black peoples in the United States—seemed convinced that her traditional heritage was something she must be liberated from and that there was some form of distinction between "Christians" and "negroes":

> 'Twas mercey brought me from my *Pagan* land, Taught my benighted soul to understand That there's a God, that there's a *Saviour* too: Once I redemption neither sought nor knew. Some view our sable race with a scornful eye, 'Their colour is a diabolic die.' Remember, Christians, Negroes, black as Cain, May be refin'd, and join th' angelic train.[28]

In both the text of the Bible and later adoption of it by biblical interpretation, "Cain" as a symbolic body denotes an outside and subordinate identity. His story begins that way. Regardless of Cain's success in building cities, his status, and that of his people, is portrayed in the Genesis story as dependent upon the kingdom of Israel/Judah through the symbol of Yahweh. In resisting the tendency of dominant interpretive traditions to totalize the sin and curse of Cain, a postcolonial reading subverts the claim made by Western colonial powers to divine right over the desired territories of land. It challenges the ideological position that because colonized peoples did not share the same sociopolitical institutions, they were not bound by the same concept of moral citizenship and they must be civilized. Compare, for instance, the papal bull *Dum Diversas*. "In it, Pope Nicholas V endorses [the Portuguese] king's invasion of West Africa and subjugation of all 'pagans' and 'enemies of Christ' therein."[29] And in the *Romanus Pontifex* two years later "the pope directs King Alfonso V to 'restrain the savage excesses' that occupy the lands south of Africa's Cape Bojador, destroy their kingdoms, and enslave them in the name of God and for the salvation of the world."[30] The bull assumes they may build cities (establish order) but they have done so outside the control of God's "chosen community." It is of necessity. Their salvation—the true control of their chaotic and violent tendencies—will come through their enslavement to a dominating power as their bodies reflect their subordinate, and dependent, position. That is the true colonial position, that the colonizer is "saving" the colonized from themselves.[31] These examples are but a few that expose the oppressive underbelly of biblical interpretation. And I am not alone in drawing attention to that. Africana scholars have breathlessly sought to make that point. As Hugh Page put it in the preface to the *Africana Bible*, the "Christian Bible has been a source of disruption and instability in the lives of Africana people."[32] That history has made the Bible a "weapon to create, support, and legitimate colonial enterprises that dehumanize and oppress individuals."[33]

Even though Cain built cities, which could be the basis for arguing that he was civilized, he remains an outsider defined by his separation from Yahweh. Not only that, but with the burden of "divine inspiration," holding that the Bible is *the* revelation of God in the monotheistic sense, and therefore objective, means Cain's story, because it is a *biblical* one, denotes he will *always* be deemed an outsider. Consequently, the ideological category of the "mark of Cain" provides a legitimatized way for those who hold the Bible as a central, sacred object to exercise prejudice. More directly, it provides the space for legitimated prejudices.[34] The ease with which that could happen in the dominant traditions of biblical interpretation and their associated cultures was, again, a reason Cain became associated as a symbol of black bodies among predominantly white Christian cultures. Some, as I alluded to earlier, even correlated the mark with the origin of peoples from the African continent.[35] Many of those interpretive leaps link the curse of Ham to the curse of Cain. John Fletcher, for example, sees Ham's marrying into the line of Cain as Ham's transformation of his descendants into black bodies. Moreover, "The history of man since the flood is accompanied with a sufficiency of facts by which we are enabled to determine that the descendants of Ham were black, and that the black man of Africa is of that descent" (*Studies*, 251). Cain's "deviance" and his subsequent "mark" burden him as aberrant to normative attributes that define "personhood" in the biblical context. Failing to challenge that association in interpretive traditions has, for some in Western Christian cultures, linked blackness to notions of savagery, heathenism, barbarism, and demonic natures.[36]

This notion of a divine protector and the inferior status of outsiders or non-members is one that permeates the colonial mind, both as a theoretical construct and as an ideologically driven historical practice. Colonizing cultures view themselves as superior, frequently with divinely legitimated obligations either to civilize "tribal cultures," typically through slavery, or to wipe out their self-autonomy. Ideological justification for those ideas runs a range of things but includes the belief that a superior culture is saving an

Colonizing Cain 63

inferior one. Read from that perspective, it's hard to miss the assumed power relationship. Yahweh, the god of Israel and Judah, becomes Cain's "protector." In that, Cain, who represents in part a colonized culture, survives only with the protection of a greater power, Yahweh, who represents the political authority and ideals of Israel and its cultural superiority. In response, Cain's body will always only be known by its difference *and its dependence*.

Let me return to the function of Cain's lineage. Gen. 4:17–24 marks the beginning of Cain's lineage, which is typically passed on through the first-born son. But, of course, contrast that with Isaac, who was Abraham's second son and who received the birthright and blessing of the patriarchal lineage, which I will discuss further in chapter 7. Cain built a city, naming it after his son Enoch. Enoch bore a son, Irad, who was the father of Mehujael. Mehujael was the father of Methushael. Methushael was the father of Lamech. Lamech took two women for himself. The first was Adah, and the second was Zillah. Adah gave birth to Jabal. According to 4:20, he was the first of those who lived in tents and kept livestock. The reference seems to be to semi-nomadic peoples, perhaps along the lines of the Kenites.[37] If so, this seems to invert the process of civilization, showing a collective body moving from urban to semi-nomadic modes of production, which may emphasize the restlessness of Cain that must be controlled. *Like the historical slave owner's assumption about black persons seeking freedom from the physical and institutional oppressions of their white "masters"?*

Jabal's brother was Jubal, who was the first of all people to play music (Gen. 4:21). Zillah, Lamech's other wife, or possibly just his "woman," also gave birth to a second son named Tubal-Cain, whose name may identify an ethnicity in east Asia Minor (*tubal* may denote Cappadocia). He shaped metal and tools made of bronze and iron. Josephus links Jubal and Tubal to the pleasures of the body, which may emphasize their connection to Cain and his emotional temperament (cf. *Ant.* 1.60–66). His sister was Naamah. After Naamah is named, Lamech, in verse 23, proclaims to his wife, "I killed a man for wounding me, a young man for bruising me! If Cain must be avenged seven times, then Lamech must be 77 times revenged!"

It is an interesting proclamation. And it is one that makes sense from the perspective of the Israelite author, but not from the perspective of Lamech. The Israelite author imposes an awareness of Yahweh upon Lamech. If Lamech and his family were historical figures, it is unlikely they would have known anything about Yahweh, who was the deity of Israel and Judah, not Enoch, or wherever Lamech was staying. They would have had their own local deities. In the ancient world before the prevalence of empires, gods were restricted to geo-political boundaries, which were the boundaries of the spaces in which communities dwelled and moved as agents. Their more "objective" attributes, a type we assume for modern nation-states, were a

64 *Chapter 3*

direct influence of imperialism—an influence that would later continue to be found in Christian missionary activities. Doctrines on the universalism of deities were not an assumption of pre-imperial societies. Instead, the biblical author seems to imply that Cain and Lamech, and their descendants, can only know themselves based on the perspective of the Israelite and Judean culture. Similar are the assumptions made by colonial cultures about those colonized: without exposure to a "civilized" culture, they do not understand or know who they are. After all, Lamech must appeal to the tradition of Cain and his interaction with Yahweh as the basis by which he justifies or reinforces his own sense of identity and morality.

While Cain's lineage is described in subordinate and divergent terms, Seth's establishes the kingdoms of Israel and Judah. In Gen. 4:25–26, Adam impregnates Eve, who gives birth to Seth. This time, however, Eve isn't named. We can assume that it was Eve, but she is not explicitly named. Where the named woman as an active agent might be a threat, the nameless woman's body is a function of patriarchal procreation. And in 4:25, in contrast to when Cain was born and Eve proclaimed, "I have created like Yahweh" (Gen. 4:1), the woman claims that Yahweh has *given* her a son. Note further her diminishing narrative presence highlighted by the fact that her speaking role is stripped in 5:3. There it says that the man produced a son in his likeness and image, and named him Seth, which may be a play on *shiyt*, "to place," or *shat*, "foundation." He is named that by the man who sees in him the perpetuation of his own lineage.

Seth fathered a son named Enosh (a name that can also be translated as "humanity"). According to the biblical author, people worshipped Yahweh. So it can be claimed that Seth, born in response to Cain's transgression, establishes—as his name may imply—the worship of Yahweh. Cain, in contrast, represents a deviation from the idealized cultural identity and political body that Yahweh represents. One body is defined by its rejection of what Yahweh represents, the other by its ritualistic internalization of what Yahweh represents. In contrast to common theological assumptions, Yahweh does not represent the more modern, universal sense of a monotheistic god. He is the god of a particular ethnic kingdom. Cain represents a cultural identity that acts apart from the moral, ethical, and social framework symbolized by Yahweh. And because of that, he acts in uncivilized and immoral ways, according to the biblical author.

And yet, Cain was marked by Yahweh so to protect him. As I have already discussed, the nature of that mark has been the fascinating fodder of generations of biblical interpreters. One of the more blatant traditions that I identified has been to identify the mark as physical blackness, which justified prejudices and even legitimated slavery. It is well acknowledged that this was motivated by a desire to preserve a theory of monogenesis, meaning that all peoples came from Adam and Eve, who were white in European-American renderings. One need only consult the numerous paintings of biblical texts, many of which were commissioned by the church to educate illiterate people on God's will and revelation through Bible stories easy to remember (recall my earlier discussion about the function of myths). One of those commissions was called for by the Council of Trent as a counter-Reformation movement.[38] Fueled by a blatant lack of scientific understanding but a passion for the God of Western Christianity, biblical interpreters were eager to see blackness as the mark of Cain, particularly black-skinned peoples from the continent of Africa.[39] They were different, exotic, and their possibly uncontrolled influence was deemed as a threat to white civilized society and the mode of production from which white aristocracy benefitted. That idea only helped fuel views that cursed Ham was also black. Francis John Harrison Rankin, for example, wrote after traveling to West Africa in 1834, "We are taught to picture the Evil one as black." But he also recognized the alternative perspective, "[t]he African is certain that Satan is white."[40] And African American scholar James Baldwin wrote, "In the same way that we, for white people, were the descendants of Ham, and were cursed forever, white people were, for us, the descendants of Cain."[41]

It is also worth noting that Marcus Garvey, one of the "fathers" of the American Black Nationalist Movement, which emerged in response to prevailing racial inequalities in 20th century United States (ca. 1919–1926) describes the theory that Cain, who was originally black, turned white after killing Abel.[42] There is a clear play on "turning white with fear" here, but it is also a direct challenge to the dominant view that Cain was marked with black skin. The "white race" ended up in Europe, Garvey argues, because the black descendants of Adam and Eve drove Cain's white descendants out of Africa.[43] And further, note Vastey,

> Others affirm that our colour and our reprobation can be traced back to Cain, for killing his brother Abel. I have strong reasons for believing that it is actually the whites who are of the race of Cain, for I find in them that primitive hatred, that spirit of envy and arrogance, and that passion for riches of which scripture speaks, and which led him to sacrifice his brother.[44]

Garvey saw a symbolic function in Cain's act: "yes, it was on the principle of injustice that Cain killed Abel, it is on the same principle of injustice that England exploits Africa, that France exploits Africa, that Italy exploits Africa, that Belgium exploits Africa, that the stronger nations of the world exploit the weak."[45] It is easy to miss Garvey's subversion. Dominant traditions of interpretation already accept that Cain is the progenitor of murder, if not the embodiment of evil. But like Nathan standing before King David to accuse

66   *Chapter 3*

him (2 Sam. 12:7), Garvey condemns those cultures who profited from slavery and colonization, who justified that profit under the auspices of divine curses and blessings. *They*, not the humbled body of the black individual, are like Cain.

In subversive interpretations such as Garvey's, and in those cultivated as the dominant traditions in white, Western cultures, whiteness and blackness are physical markers of function. In both perspectives, Cain has become symbolic of the "other" and a representative of assumptions about hierarchies of power and distinction. But it was within white interpretive traditions that the mark of Cain became associated in the 19th and 20th centuries CE with violence and uncontrolled, impulsive behaviors.[46] They found support in the New Testament and other related literature. In dominant western cultures, Cain came to embody the antithesis of civilization and morality that could be scapegoated with New Testament passages such as Hebrews 11:4, which says that Abel, by faith, offered a greater sacrifice than Cain. That idea is mirrored by Philo (*Confusion* 124), who accuses Cain of keeping the best of his harvest for himself, and the Midrash (*Ber. Rab.* 22:5), which suggests a link between Yahweh's favorable gaze and the ideal of deliverance, highlighting Genesis's possible etymological play on *yasha'* ("deliverance") and *sha'ah* ("favorable gaze") in what could be a foreshadow of the Babylonian experience of the Judeans in the 6th century.

Faith, to which the New Testament book Hebrews refers, replicates the commitment and loyalty one would have to a kingdom or empire and offers for Hebrews a counterpoint to the Roman Empire. I will discuss that idea in more detail later. For now, I must point out that, according to dominant interpretive traditions, where by faith Abel offered a "greater" sacrifice than Cain, giving himself to a "greater ideal," that is, the dominant collective one, and through his faith he was commended as righteous, Cain and his sacrifice were rejected. First John 3:11–12 contributes to the rigid separation between insider and outsider when it instructs that believers should love one another and not be like evil Cain who murdered his brother. Cain was the embodiment of Satan, who in various Western cultures is frequently portrayed as being red or black, while Abel, who did nothing in the story but offer a sacrifice and die (*the ultimate sacrifice?*), highlights the righteous, faithful individual.

In European and American traditions of biblical interpretation, Cain becomes the symbolic figure of justified colonization. Postcolonialism challenges that, demanding that we see the agendas, values, and ideologies that lay behind such interpretations. Regardless of the communities to which they belong, it demands that we acknowledge how our own readings of Cain and Abel reinforce *our* assumptions about *our own* civilizations and their systems and traditions of interpretation. In recognizing that, we may better see how we use them to reinforce subordinate statuses upon those who are not members of our own communities.

There is more to this interpretive angle, but it expects us to look ahead in Genesis and to the figure of Ham. The tendency to conflate the stories of Cain and Ham betrays a cultural tendency to prioritize a particular tradition as universally authoritative, one which has provided historical justification for atrocities like slavery. Note, for example, "During the heyday of slavery in America, a racial understanding of Genesis 9–11 was so much a part of cultural common sense that defensive arguments were no longer required. The significance of Noah's curse in American slavery debates cannot be appreciated until we grasp the way Genesis 9 provided the implied racial context that other biblical arguments lacked."[47] The racial context behind that curse? Western Christians assumed Ham, the son that Noah cursed, was black. Such was the pervasiveness of the assumption that it made ready justification for slavery *and* the colonization of countries on the African continent. Sexuality was linked to the curse, especially within the influence of the more aesthetic traditions of European Christianity. Richard Jobson, viewed it flaccidly when he wrote that "the enormous Size of the virile Member among the Negroes [was] an infallible Proof, that they are sprung from Canaan, who, for uncovering his Father's Nakedness, had (according to the Schoolmen) a Curse laid upon that Part."[48] Nowhere in the Bible does it say that God cursed Ham's penis. Neither does it say explicitly that Ham's curse was because of a sexual transgression. However, to acknowledge an interpretative connection, there is some linguistic possibility to link his transgression to a sexual nature, though the specifics will forever elude us. To "uncover" another man's nakedness (cf. Gen. 9:22) *can* mean sleeping with his wife. It can denote sexual advancement upon the man himself. It can also mean exposing his buttocks or penis. It can also mean shaming him so to make him lose honor.

The ease with which culture made that assumption *and accepted it as veritable fact* is emphasized in modern cultural portrayals of black male sexuality. From immature high school jokes to erotica and pornography in the United States, black men are often stereotyped as having large penises and enjoying unrestrained, near bestial sexuality. But we shouldn't assume that association is merely one of jealously. Obsession with black male sexuality by white culture in the United States began *at least* during Segregation. When black men could no longer be lynched, the justification for which was often that a black male had sexually imposed himself upon a white woman, black men were stereotyped based on imposed ideas about their sexuality. Though lynching was outlawed, they continued to be portrayed as sexual predators and beasts in white culture.[49] Even in the 21st century, assumptions about black families and unwed mothers perpetuate modern translations of the age-old fear and

68 *Chapter 3*

prejudice. Cain, also Ham, didn't have to be black in the Bible for readers to use him as a symbol of ideological colonialism. Finding in his cursed body justification for their own ideological agendas, he is, however, frequently interpreted as black in dominant interpretive traditions of white Christianity. His disfigured body is symbolically burdened with the consequences of deviance from the ideals of an imposed moral and cultural code.

NOTES

1. Puscifer, *The Rapture (Fear Is a Mind Killa Mix)*, Conditions of My Parole (Puscifer Entertainment, 2011).

2. Cf. the larger discussion in Cataldo, *What the Bible Says about Sex*, 179–200.

3. Cf. Benjamin Wermund, "Trump's Education Pick Says Reform Can 'Advance God's Kingdom,'" *Politico*, December 2, 2016, http://www.politico.com/story/2016/12/betsy-devos-education-trump-religion-232150.

4. Tammi J. Schneider, *Mothers of Promise: Women in the Book of Genesis* (Baker Academic, 2008), 171–72.

5. Faro, *Evil in Genesis*, 157.

6. Shubert Spero, "Was Cain the Father of Civilization?" *JBQ* 48, no. 2 (April 2020): 111.

7. See also Joseph Blenkinsopp, *Creation Un-Creation Re-Creation: A Discursive Commentary on Genesis 1–11* (New York: Bloomsbury / T & T Clark, 2011), 94; Cataldo, *What the Bible Says about Sex*, 184–85.

8. Joel B Kemp, "Racializing Cain, Demonizing Blackness, & Legalizing Discrimination: Proposal for Reception of Cain and America's Racial Caste System," *Perspectives in Religious Studies* 48, no. 4 (2021): 377–99.

9. Kemp, 379.

10. Cf. Elijah Anderson, *Black in White Space: The Enduring Impact of Color in Everyday Life* (University of Chicago Press, 2022).

11. Cited in Kemp, "Racializing Cain," 388.

12. Claus Westermann, *Genesis 1–11: a Commentary*, trans. John J. Scullion (Minneapolis: Augsburg, 1974), 311.

13. See also von Rad, *Genesis*, 107.

14. Compare Thomas Schreiner, *Commentary on Hebrews* (Nashville: Broadman & Holman, 2015), 490–91.

15. See also von Rad, *Genesis*, 104.

16. Cf. Walter Brueggemann, *Genesis*, IBC (Louisville: Westminster John Knox, 2010), 56.

17. An idea Eliade articulated in his *The Myth of the Eternal Return: Cosmos and History* (Princeton: Princeton University Press, 2005).

18. Spero, "Was Cain?" 112.

19. Cf. von Rad, *Genesis*, 110–11.

20. Ted A. Smith, "The Mark of Cain: Sovereign Negation and the Politics of God," *MT* 36, no. 1 (January 2020): 57.

21. Von Rad, *Genesis*, 107.

22. Discussed in John Byron, *Cain and Abel in Text and Tradition: Jewish and Christian Interpretations of the First Sibling Rivalry* (Leiden, Brill, 2011), 208–9.

23. Cf. von Rad, *Genesis*, 109–13.

24. Byron, *Cain and Abel*, 164–65.

25. I am borrowing the term "mythoracial" from Kemp, "Racializing Cain," 380.

26. Regina M. Schwartz, *The Curse of Cain: The Violent Legacy of Monotheism* (Chicago: University of Chicago Press, 1997).

27. Cf. Haynes, *Noah's Curse*, location 326.

28. Phillis Wheatley, "On Being Brought from Africa to America," Poetry Foundation (February 7, 2023), https://www.poetryfoundation.org/poems/45465/on-being -brought-from-africa-to-america.

29. Jessica Wai-Fong Wong, *Disordered: The Holy Icon and Racial Myths* (Waco, TX: Baylor University Press, 2021), 51.

30. Wong, 51.

31. Compare Rashid Khalidi, *The Hundred Years' War on Palestine: A History of Settler Colonialism and Resistance, 1917–2017*, First Metropolitan paperback edition (New York: Metropolitan Books, Henry Holt and Company, 2022), 6–7.

32. Hugh R. Page Jr et al., eds., *The Africana Bible: Reading Israel's Scriptures from Africa and the African Diaspora* (Fortress Press, 2009), xxvi.

33. Kemp, "Racializing Cain," 382.

34. For further discussion on legitimated prejudice as distinct from genuine prejudice, see Christian S. Crandall and Amy Eshleman, "A Justification-Suppression Model of the Expression and Experience of Prejudice," *Psychological Bulletin* 129, no. 3 (2003): 414–46.

35. Cf. David M. Goldenberg, *Black and Slave: The Origins and History of the Curse of Ham* (Berlin: Walter de Gruyter GmbH & Co KG, 2017), 40–42, 153–55, 238–49; David M. Goldenberg, *The Curse of Ham: Race and Slavery in Early Judaism, Christianity, and Islam* (Princeton University Press, 2003), 178–82; Ruth W. Mellinkoff, *The Mark of Cain* (Eugene, OR: Wipf and Stock Publishers, 2003), 76–80.

36. Cf. the description and works cited in Kemp, "Racializing Cain," 380.

37. Von Rad, *Genesis*, 110–14.

38. Cf. Cataldo, *What the Bible Says about Sex*, 65.

39. Cf. Nyasha Junior, "The Mark of Cain and White Violence," *JBL* 139, no. 4 (2020): 662–63.

40. Cited in Junior, 663.

41. Cited in Junior, 673.

42. Cf. Junior, 666–68.

43. See Junior, 670.

44. Cited in Junior, 671.

45. Marcus Garvey, *Selected Writings and Speeches of Marcus Garvey* (Mineola, NY: Dover, 2004), 87.

70   *Chapter 3*

46. Cf. Junior, "Mark of Cain," 661–62.

47. Haynes, *Noah's Curse*, location 267.

48. Cited in Haynes, location 591.

49. Cf. Patricia Hill Collins, *Black Sexual Politics: African Americans, Gender, and the New Racism* (London: Routledge Press, 2004), 64, 161.

Chapter 4

Highbrow Hamitic Hypothesis

You can take my body. You can take my bones. You can take my blood but not my soul.[1]

According to Genesis, Ham shamed his father, Noah, following the family's survival of the flood through which God killed every living thing *except* Noah's family. Such is the precedent set for what will become a foundational assumption in theologies about Ham in contrast to the righteousness of Noah, and the pervasiveness and danger of profanity and sin. It is also the background of the so-called Hamitic Hypothesis, which maintains that Ham's descendants were perpetually cursed because of Ham's actions.

While the Hamitic Hypothesis was found in historical British and American cultures providing legitimation for slavery, and while most Bible readers would not openly espouse the the idea, there remain scribal echoes of it in modern race relations. Marcel Kabanda, for example, wrote about its ideological impact on the Rwandan genocide.[2] His opening line, clearly a rhetorical question, could well be the banner for postcolonialism (translating the quote): "Should one be concerned that so many people have remained indifferent to the tragedies of Africa's Great Lakes [region]?" The answer, of course, *should only* be "yes." We *should* be concerned when the voice of any community is lost in beneath the oppressive weight of a dominating community and narrative. The oppressing of others is what should make us angry about things like the Hamitic Hypothesis, which link justifications of oppression to physical appearance and perceived differences of bodies. Correlating Ham with blackness *because* he was cursed by Noah, who in contrast is assumed to be white, or that Cain, which I discussed in the last chapter, was black because he was cast out and associated with evil, legitimates prejudice, fabricated superiority, inequality, and more. More condemning, it justifies those human oppressions, and everything entailed in the exercise of them, with the will of the divine. It is also worth noting, as Haynes emphasizes,

72   *Chapter 4*

that it wasn't until the age of exploration and colonialism that medieval European sentiment assigned Ham to the continent of Africa. That exploration, and the concomitant rise of European imperialism and colonialism, laid the groundwork for the colonialist assumptions about black bodies, which not only destined them to the yoke of slavery but sought to erase the cultures and histories with which they identified.[3]

The association of black skin as punishment for gazing upon those naked can even be found even earlier. Ibn Mas'ud, who died on 653 and was the companion of Mohammed the prophet, is quoted by Ibn Hakim (d. 1014/1015 CE), who wrote, "Noah was bathing and saw his son [Ham] looking at him and said to him, 'are you watching me bathe? May God change your color!' And he is the ancestor of the *sudan* [i.e., blacks]."[4] That connection between blackness and curse continues to animate more modern portrayals of the story. For instance,

> IN MAY 1999, the National Broadcasting Corporation telecast its widely anticipated TV version of Noah's Ark. Commentators claimed that the production had taken liberties with the biblical text; they were silent, however, about aspects of the Bible's history of interpretation that were retained in the television miniseries. For instance, the movie linked Noah's son Ham with Africa (by casting a woman of African descent as his wife), with unrestrained desire (by including scenes in which Ham makes sexual overtures toward his fiancée), and with rebellion (by depicting Ham as the instigator of mutiny on the ark).[5]

Those qualities are present in traditions of biblical interpretation but not in the biblical text itself. The notion of the Hamitic Hypothesis, therefore, should be understood within the framework of ideological colonialism. While it provided a seeming justification for physical or political colonization, it has consistently been used to create ideological boundaries around sometimes physical and political borders: those boundaries categorizing identity and personhood. This is the type of colonialism that refers to the overwriting and erasing of a minority community's self-narrative, including its history, cultural values, and mores. While with the more modern international recognition of geopolitical borders physical colonization does not occur on the level of what it used to, the consequences of the frameworks built upon it are still felt, though at the time I write this Russia has been waging a war to expand its borders and forcibly (re)patriate Ukrainians for a little over a year (Feb. 24, 2022, marks the official beginning of that war). For that reason, it's clear that we need to understand that ideological colonialism speaks to the continuing overwriting of minority cultures and the oppression and objectification of their bodies. It refers to the colonizing of culture and identity to the extent that even in the absence of wars or territorial claim, even apart from laws rooted in prejudice, the ways we define the identities of others performs a similar function. Like Dr. Frankenstein, we define others according to our own cultural views and values. We manipulate their bodies into "acceptable" images based on our own ideals and aims. In such circumstances, to be accepted, the outsider must prove him or herself to be *like* us, to place themselves within the tolerable limits of our own cultural expectations and identity. Proving, in that, that they will not threaten the stability of our social worlds.

The impact of ideological colonialism carrying on the work of its ancestor, physical colonization, was something that motivated scholars like James Cone, who helped to elevate Black liberation theology into academic discourse, though many scholars continue to seem content to keep it on the margins of dominant academic discourse.[6] Cone explained an important aspect of his motivation: "My initial challenge was to develop a liberation theology that could be both black and Christian—at the same time and in one voice. That was not easy because even in the black community the public meaning of Christianity was white."[7] *How deeply rooted is the colonial mind in religious education!* Most academic bibliographies in published works within Biblical studies—a core discipline in which change could and *should* happen—for example, do not include the works of James Cone or other Black liberation theologians. Why is this a problem? The ways we discuss the past, knowledge, and how we *gain* and develop knowledge reinforce, if they are not changed to accommodate diversity, an already defined understanding of the past. *Knowledge is rooted in the histories we tell.*[8] The history of the West, including biblical interpretation as its handmaiden, has been primarily that which was developed within the cultures of Western empires: white, heterosexual, Christian, patriarchal, and able. To ignore the voices of those who do not fit those categories is to be complicit in their oppression or erasure from the real archives of history.

The issues that concern Black liberation theologians such as Cone, the importance of Black culture and identity, are not a part of the larger public conversation, or even among the dominant topics in academic discourse. Even most university classrooms, for instance, which might tend toward Left-leaning or liberal perspectives, while they might reference racism, segregation, movements such as Black Lives Matter, or even critical race theory do not include bibliographies leaning heavily on the works of those that would challenge the fundamental structures of knowledge upon which even liberal academics depend. The best that is seen is typically a letter from Martin Luther King, Jr., or a paragraph or two from Kimberlé Crenshaw, Angela Davis, or Ta-Nehisi Coates. Such writings have been selected, filtered, and suitably tamed so that they don't threaten the foundation of the status quo. Academia, like religion and politics, has its own conservative and self-delusional demons that it must learn to acknowledge.

74 *Chapter 4*

For an additional perspective, note the ideological angle from which Wong approaches this issue, "[t]he oppressive structures of Western society against which we battle are predicated upon our established acts of worship."[9] Religion justified the world defined under imperialism and colonialism. And while it's easy to protest that reality and to voice support for equality, it's something else to remap the infrastructure of one's meaning and knowledge systems. Cone challenges not only academics of theological and biblical studies but also a dominant religious culture that pays lip service to equality without investing itself in required structural changes.

No one knows if Ham was black, though there is a long history of associating Ham with blackness.[10] And because one cannot verify whether Ham was a historical person, one should also not assume he is anything more than a metaphor or function of prejudice. He is assumed to be black by interpreters who see "black" as the antithesis of themselves. Some even maintained that the curse changed Ham's semen and its consequences were passed on generationally through sex.[11] That tendency found support in the supposed link between Ham's descendants and various peoples of the African continent. Thus, his function is as the outsider, the antithesis, the uncivilized body who will wreak havoc upon the community by challenging its mores, values, and ethics. He represents the black body that must be subordinated until it learns to be a moral, rational being. As even Charlie Aaron, an ex-slave, claimed, buying into the historical narrative fed to him, "According to what was issued out in the Bible, there was a time for slavery. People had to be punished for their sins."[12]

And then we must also consider the statement by Reverend E. W. Warren, the depth of whose cultural whiteness is overwhelming in his literary passion, who wrote,

> "Hear, O Heavens, give ear, O Earth, for it is the Lord that speaketh." This quotation was made by Mr. T. with solemn emphasis, then turning to Genesis ix:25, he read, "Cursed be Canaan [i.e. Ham]; a servant of servants shall he be unto his brethren, and he said Blessed be the Lord God of Shem, and Canaan shall be his servant. God shall enlarge Japhet and he shall dwell in the tents: of Shem and Canaan shall be his servant." Here, Nellie, is the origin of slavery, it comes directly from God through His servant Noah.[13]

As is often the way of things, ideas accepted culturally without evidence but which reflect dominant shared values often over time become assumed as facts. That tendency and influence of values that reflect white, European (and later, American) cultures, which became the primary linguistic framework for dominant traditions, bolsters modern biblical discourse and interpretation of Ham who is often assumed to be black and identified as being in league with Satan (*like Eve?*). As Bede, representing Anglo-Saxon literature, writes, "the old enemy is always born as though anew from a black nation of infidels through the wicked execution of teaching or deed."[14] This connection of wickedness to blackness found perhaps its greatest support in the 18th and 19th centuries CE in western Europe and the United States through a theologically justified racialized curse claiming divine legitimation of slavery.[15] As a testament to this general cultural mind in the Americas (ca. 1700), Massachusetts judge Samuel Sewall rejected the common assumption that "these blackamoors are of the Posterity of Cham, and therefore are under the Curse of Slavery."[16] But while he rejected the idea, that it was common enough that it needed to be addressed is a testament to its prevalence. The institution of slavery was frequently justified with the belief that God cursed Ham in perpetuity to be a slave of Shem, the latter being the ancestor to the Israelites. And with both Jews and Christians claiming ancestry through that lineage, the descendants of Ham became subordinate to "God's chosen people." Thus, European and American white Christians could justify being slave owners because they believed it ordained by God.

Justification for this sense of divine election was based on the belief that God chose a particular group of people to represent his will on earth. The ideal, abstracted and universalized as it became in traditions of biblical interpretation, was only the reflection of the community's image itself. "God" is always already the sum of the community's highest, most cherished values. The universalizing of the particular would set a dangerous precedent for the justification of prejudices. In that context, any curses and statements of differentiation within the biblical text had universal and diachronic qualities; they became canonized as the revelation of God. As such, they were transformed into the objective bases upon which was built an understanding of a world that reflected the perspective of a dominant group, culture, or tradition. In short, because of Ham's curse, all of his descendants were destined to be slaves to Shem and his descendants.

With its link to the powers of Western Europe, a predominantly white Christianity and its cultures became the dominant image of God's elect community. We see manifestations of that even in the modern context, as well as reactions to it, such as in the form of the Black Jesus movement. In both Europe and the United States, most artistic portrayals of Jesus and God are of white men. I've had conversations about this in and out of the classroom and a popular retort is that Jesus wasn't white, he was Mediterranean, and so likely olive in complexion. While those who give the response may see it as a correction of an incorrect view, it is more a dismissal than a correction. It ignores the long history in which Jesus was portrayed *and assumed to be* white and European-esque. *Can it be said that God is the sum of the*

76   *Chapter 4*

dominant community's most cherished values and ideals? This type of designation or portrayal, which compares to the marginalization of others based on Hamitic ancestry, wasn't restricted to physical attribute. It conveyed and symbolized an imposed value on personhood and body, such that those associated with Ham had no legitimate claim over land and authority in it. As Goldenberg writes,

> Hamitic genealogy was a common French view and was expressed as early as 1553 by Guillermo Posatel, as Gliozzi noted. Writers representing the other colonial powers were not long behind, with evidence for the Portuguese and Spanish before the end of the century, and for the English a few years later. It is argued that this is also the case for the Dutch who colonized Cape Colony in South Africa. Hamitic/Canaanite ancestry was at times used to explain what was seen (and/or desired) as the natives' servile character. The Spanish colonial jurist Juan de Solórzano y Pereyra (d. 1655) believed that the Indians of the New World descended from Ham and were servile because of the Curse. At a later period, the Jesuit explorer and missionary José Gumilla (d. 1750) claimed that the Hamites left their original land and came to South America. There they were joined by the Jews who had been exiled from Israel, and the two nations thus formed the natives of South America. As proof of his contention, Gumilla states that the Indians voluntarily accept the state of servitude, that they are often drunk, and that they do not wear clothes. As Perbal noted, the drunkenness, nakedness and the state of slavery are based on the story of Noah.[17]

Ham's body symbolized rejection of others from lands a Christian colonizing community wanted. *Slaves are not land-owning citizens!* This could be justified as an act of returning land and bodies back into relationship with God, whether through conversion or destruction. And it served the purpose of advancing the power and authority of the (self-designated) "elect" community. That view can be confirmed by early Spanish colonizing views, such as expressed by Juan de Torquemada, Juan de Lucena, Jeróme Osório, and Salinas y Códova, among many others.[18] Torquemada, for instance, writes, "[T]he black color is not from natural causes, but . . . these Indians [of Cuba] and all who in other religions are colored brown are descendants of those children of Ham."[19] His assumption is that the natural world is a creation of God. *Sin,* that theological heart of darkness, is the unnatural expression of unrequited human desire manifest, like rotten fruit, in the discoloration of the skin. Only those in a state of compatibility with the natural world can exercise dominion over it as God intended.

Some of the more extreme manifestations of that idea can also be found in the United States. Numerous extremist groups, such as the Klu Klux Klan, various manifestations of the Proud Boys, and even aspects of QAnon are in line with a number of assumptions and theologies blending Christianity and white superiority. Such groups often find that Ham offers a ready justification for separating white culture from black culture.

Under the oppressive history of slavery, black bodies were disfigured, stripped of their familial and cultural heritages, and re-animated with the breath of "life" by an oppressive "Other." While there are immigrants to the United States, a predominant majority of African Americans in the United States can only trace their ancestry back to the time of slavery. When people were shipped to the colonies and sold as slaves, they were given anglicized names, their families were torn apart, and their traditions prohibited. There was no record written of their lineage. They were dehumanized. The impact upon their cultural identity, which was being written over, happened on not only physical but also political levels. Put differently, it was physical and ideological colonialism. The institution of slavery was built on the idea that slaves were "domesticated," stripped of any cultural and blood links, and taught to depend upon the grace and beneficence of a master from which they could never earn their freedom. Perhaps not too unlike the Christian concept of God as master and sinful man burdened by an infinite debt to God for God's grace.[20] *Slaves obey your masters with anxiety and trembling liberally with your heart as you would Christ (Eph. 6:5).*

It was in this process that ideological colonialism strode ahead as a primary means of re-enculturating the "other." With Ham, this occurred on the fundamental level of a dichotomy between good and evil, insider and outsider, and black and white. Blackness became a negative symbol cross-culturally, a point that should be acknowledged. Not only that, but the abstracted nature of blackness as evil was given bodily form through Christian exegesis. "[A]bstract color symbolism assumed a human face, and by means of writings, sermons, and iconography, this image of the black continued throughout Late Antiquity into the Middle Ages and the Early Modern period in Christian Europe."[21] Within a cultural environment shaped by that ideology, to become a part of the dominant society, the "other" must be stripped of the history, traditions, and values unique to the individual and her community. They may try to hold on to those things, but separated from her culture the individual can longer express them in a way that makes sense within the culture in which they now live. To learn the vocabulary necessary to articulate who they are, to develop a sense of self within their new cultural context, they must adopt the dominant cultural framework. Ideological colonialism begins there in the assumption that the minority body must adopt the value frameworks, vocabulary frameworks, meaning frameworks, and the general cultural framework of the culture in which they now live. Who they are, their sense of self and collective identity, ceases to be defined by themselves in their own native culture. Instead, they are forced into a foreign cultural system that defines them according to its own frameworks. The institution of slavery sought to

78   Chapter 4

erase the slave's past sense of self, assuming with colonial rationalism that the "uncivilized" person who would become a slave did not *have* a sense of self and human dignity. That was why Episcopal bishop George Washington Freeman could claim that evidence of the curse of Ham "of which [the black slaves'] present degraded condition is a manifest fulfillment."[22]

The bishop could be content in his interpretation because the Bible condones and never condemns slavery. It assumes slavery to be just part of the normal way of things, which is an assumption that some of the so-called Pauline Epistles of the New Testament share (cf. Col. 4:1; Eph. 6:5). Some scholars and interpreters have argued that slavery reflected in the biblical context and by the biblical text differed from US and British slavery. It is not convincing because the underlying intent is to defend the Bible in its literal form, even in societies that no longer condone slavery. That tradition of doing so has been long-standing, as Verkerk observes of one example, the Ashburnham Pentateuch, an illustrated version of the Bible's first five books, not only adopted a Roman convention in portraying black bodies but reflects a growing ideological conviction that the physical appearance of blackness was a sign of a sinful nature.[23] With that history, incidentally, the adoption of black in monastic habits and cassocks may reflect an association of an earthly sinful body in need of salvation. The development of that technological interpretation can be seen as early as Origin (d. ca. 253 CE), who systematically applied blackness in contrast to whiteness as a metaphor for sin.[24]

Moreover, arguments that masters in the Bible treated their slaves more fairly than modern forms of slavery are not convincing, which is one I have heard on multiple occasions. Such apologetic positions attempt to liberate the Bible and its associated cultures from modern distaste for slavery as practiced by Britain and the United States. (Incidentally, most people in the West seem to be unaware of slavery practices in other parts of even the modern world.) Take, for example, Exodus's (cf. 21:26–27) discussion of the "ethical" treatment of slaves. According to that passage, it was okay to beat one's slaves, or to treat them like animals. The legal-ethical limit was that one could not knock out, or off, body parts, such as eyes and teeth, which would suggest an overly aggressive beating. But beatings that stopped short were okay to keep slaves in line with the order of the patriarchal household. I agree that the more modern forms of slavery were atrocious. I think to separate them from slavery in the biblical context is a poor attempt at excusing "God" from the atrocity of oppression and disfiguring the bodies and identities of others of difference.

One main difference between the historical and the more modern forms slavery was the depth to which technology facilitated the institution and its Capitalist satisfaction. While black individuals were not the only enslaved peoples throughout history, the theological association of sin as chaos with black, coupled with the emerging emphasis upon profit as confirmation of divine favor, facilitated technological and ideological innovation in slavery within Christian cultures as a market and a business.

The biblical authors lived in cultural contexts in which slavery was the norm. The only time that a slave could be granted freedom was when it was a fellow citizen, usually one who was a subject of debt slavery (cf. Ex. 21:2–11). Conquered peoples were fine to keep as slaves until they died or were sold. And one could treat one's slaves physically and sexually however one desired. That, for example, is why Sarah "gave" Hagar to Abraham (Gen. 16:3), Rachel "gave" Bilhah to Jacob (Gen. 30:4), and not to be out-done, Leah "gave" Zilpah to Jacob (Gen. 30:9).

Not that we should diminish modern slavery to the mild-mannered per-ception interpreters maintain of its practice in the Bible. Rather, we should expose and challenge the dominant perceptions of biblical slavery with the appalling nature of modern slavery. When we do not challenge the nature of the Bible, when we don't challenge the institutions that it promotes or does not condemn, and when we cannot recognize them in the modern context as being problematic and ethically wrong, we justify and perpetuate oppressive structures, traditions, and behavioral patterns that perpetuate inequality.[25] It was the benefit of profit and authority that eased the ideological justification that James W. C. Pennington, an abolitionist, former slave, and Presbyterian minister bemoaned in 1841, "A class of men have gained the high reputation of attempting gravely to theorize themselves into the right to oppress, and to hate and abuse their follow man! . . . Noah cursed his grand son Canaan, and this *dooms* the black man to slavery, and *constitutes* the white man the slaveholder! Astounding!"[26] Cultural discomfort with those ideas continues to remind us of the need for change. In the United States, for instance, in the 21st century, we have seen the rise of movements such as Black Lives Matter. That we have to remind ourselves of that, that individuals who are black matter *as individuals*, is a testament to the fact that white Western cultures have not learned how to get past the issues of segregation. Nor have they challenged the dominant interpretive traditions of the Bible that have directly or indirectly made space for supersessionist ideologies that reinforce the dominance of a single community. Even in 1966, Thomas Holdcroft wrote in a biblical commentary, for example, "The descendants of Canaan become the black races who for long centuries furnished the world's supply of slaves."[27] Several years earlier, Baptist minister Carey Daniel claimed, "The Bible clearly implies that the Negroes' black skin is the result of Ham's immorality at the time of his father Noah's drunkenness."[28]

In what might be a rare moment of lucidity, Žižek wrote, "When [blacks] are treated by whites as inferior, this does indeed make them inferior at the level of their socio-symbolic identity. In other words, the white racist ideol-ogy exerts a performative efficiency. It is not merely an interpretation of what

80   *Chapter 4*

blacks are, but an interpretation that determines the very being and social existence of the interpreted subjects."[29] It doesn't matter if one is overtly, or actively, racist, one may still perpetuate racism and inequality by meekly taking part in a system that defines the "other" based on the values and identity of the majority. The statement, "You are [x]" is the first step into colonial inequality, which imposes restrictions through performative efficiency and contours of identity upon the disfigured body of the other. I do not need to be actively prejudiced against the individual, but if I do not challenge the vocabularies, symbols, and meanings that comprise the dominant discourse, where they reinforce inequalities, I contribute to the perpetuation and performance of inequality and prejudice. And in that, I participate in disfiguring the body of the "other" whose identity is increasingly contingent upon the categorical framework through which the dominating community defines its social world. Inequalities reinforce the idea that the body of the "other" becomes what the dominating culture says it is.

The traditional ways in which Ham's story has been interpreted, as James Cone, Theophus Smith, and others have argued, continue to shape the way the dominant white culture views black culture and individuals in the United States.[30] That dominant perception continues to determine the "social existence of interpreted subjects." That the act of interpretation is one way oppression occurs should clearly show how much inequality has permeated the vocabulary by which culture expresses social reality. It is white, colonial meaning that determines *how* culture interprets others through the ideologically dominant language, and even how the interpreted subjects interpret themselves as part of the culture.

Some will point to the Bible and Christ's command to love one another as evidence that the Bible supports equality. But that is not enough. It is not enough of a challenge from a postcolonial perspective. The reason that we have not seen substantive changes, not only within the religious sphere but also in the broader US cultural sphere, is because we have not challenged the traditions of interpretation that have themselves allowed for communities to justify inequality and slavery. Many in the US appeal to the biblical text to justify extremist ideologies, whether it be regarding slavery of the past, restrictions on LGBTQIA in the present, or the advancement of women in the past. And while US culture no longer practices slavery, while it no longer prevents women from voting, those changes happened on a political level. Religion had to adapt itself in light of those changes; *it did not lead those changes*. While same-sex relations and same-sex marriage have also recently been attended to on a political level, they have not enjoyed the same adaptation by mainstream religious traditions.[31]

What is needed is an interpretative strategy that challenges the dominant traditions that continue perpetuating inequalities. This is what postcolonialism can do in the modern context. And it can do so to open doors for newer types of interpretive traditions and conversations. The intent is not simply to debunk. If that is the case then we do not need postcolonialism, we only need contrarians and nihilists. The intent is to change the nature of the conversation in a way that allows for additional voices to be heard and to take part. But because of the heritage of the past, the way to do that is no longer to see Shem as the favorite one of God, nor to see Ham as the one cursed to be Shem's slave.

Postcolonialism's agenda seeks not only to liberate colonized identities, to dismantle structures of power that reinforce oppression and inequality, to challenge the inequalities and traditions of interpretation that have been built upon them. Those who benefit from the status quo and the dominant traditions of biblical interpretation must acknowledge what postcolonialism has been claiming all along: the body of the "other" is the disfigured product of a dominating language and meaning system, which imposes categories upon diverse individuals in a way that homogenizes differences outside the dominant community, while inversely celebrating regulated and knowable differences within the community. Such belligerence couches itself in statements as "I don't see color," and, "all lives matter." Our responses must be: (1) "you should"; and (2) "yes, *all* lives *do* matter," impregnating our words with the future of marginalized bodies everywhere.

NOTES

1. Rhiannon Giddens, *At the Purchaser's Option*, vol. Freedom highway (Nonesuch, 2017).

2. Marcel Kabanda and Jean-pierre Chrétien, *Rwanda. Racisme et génocide: L'idéologie hamitique* (Paris: Belin, 2016), 1, translation mine.

3. Haynes, *Noah's Curse*, locations 155–61.

4. Goldenberg, *Black and Slave*, 68.

5. Haynes, *Noah's Curse*, locations 119–22.

6. Cf. James H. Cone, *A Black Theology of Liberation*, 40th anniv (New York: Orbis Books, 2010); James H. Cone, *The Cross and the Lynching Tree*, Kindle (Maryknoll, NY: Orbis Books, 2011).

7. Cone, *Lynching Tree*, location 224.

8. This is fundamental, for instance, to Foucault's argument. Cf. Michel Foucault, *The Archaeology of Knowledge and the Discourse on Language*, trans. A M Sheridan Smith (New York: Pantheon Books, 1972), 1–17.

9. Wong, *Disordered*, 8.

10. Cf. Goldenberg, *Black and Slave*.

11. Goldenberg, 69.

82 *Chapter 4*

12. Federal Writers' Project and Library of Congress, *Alabama Slave Narratives: A Folk History of Slavery in Alabama from Interviews with Former Slaves: Typewritten Records* (Bedford, MA; Washington, DC: Applewood Books; Library of Congress, 2006), 5.

13. E. W. Warren, *Nellie Norton, or, Southern Slavery and the Bible: A Scriptural Refutation of the Principal Arguments Upon Which the Abolitionists Rely: A Vindication of Southern Slavery from the Old and New Testaments* (Macon, GA: Burke, Boykin & Co., 1864), 8–9.

14. Cited in Tristan Major, *Undoing Babel: The Tower of Babel in Anglo-Saxon Literature*, Toronto Anglo-Saxon Series 25 (Toronto: University of Toronto Press, 2018), 21.

15. Cf. Haynes, *Noah's Curse*, location 194.

16. Cited in Goldenberg, *Black and Slave*, 146.

17. Goldenberg, 175–79.

18. Cf. Goldenberg, 179–80.

19. Cited in Goldenberg, 180.

20. See also the philosophical description of this in Slavoj Žižek, *Violence: Six Sideways Reflections*, 1st Picado (New York: Picador, 2008), location 2492.

21. Goldenberg, *Black and Slave*, 189–90.

22. Cited in Goldenberg, 223.

23. Dorothy Hoogland Verkerk, "Black Servant, Black Demon: Color Ideology in the Ashburnham Pentateuch," *92372* 31, no. 1 (Winter 2001): 60.

24. Cf. Goldenberg, *Black and Slave*, 190 n. 7; Stephen D. Moore, *God's Beauty Parlor and Other Queer Spaces in and Around the Bible* (Stanford University Press, 2001), 65.

25. Wiredu's "conceptual colonialism" addresses the same idea as ideological colonialism (cf. *Cultural Universals and Particulars*). Conceptual colonialism is rooted in prejudiced sentiments about divine election, and those sentiments continue to shape race relations in the United States. We still have protests. We still have public debates about whether a policeman shooting a black man is a legitimate use of force. We still have to have these conversations because the prejudices that have defined our notion of different interpersonal relationships and race relations are those that have been rooted in a predominantly white culture.

26. Cited in Goldenberg, *Black and Slave*, 224.

27. Cited in Goldenberg, 237.

28. Cited in Goldenberg, 236.

29. Žižek, *Violence: Six Sideways Reflections*, location 984.

30. Cf. Theophus H. Smith, *Conjuring Culture: Biblical Formations of Black America* (Oxford: Oxford University Press, 1995).

31. Cf. Clarence Thomas's opinion in 19–1392 Dobbs v. Jackson Women's Health Organization (Supreme Court of the United States June 24, 2022).

Chapter 5

Flooding the World and Saving a Few

How Wise also was Noah, who built the whole of the ark! [Genesis 6:14] How just again! For he alone, preserved of all to be the father of the human race, which made us a survivor of past generations, and the author of one to come; he was born, too, rather for the world and the universe than for himself. How brave he was to overcome the flood! How temperate to endure it! When he had entered the ark, with what moderation he passed at the time! When he sent forth the raven and the dove, when he received them on the return, when he took the opportunity of leaving the ark, with what moderation did he make use of these occasions! (*Duties* 25:121).

Many read Noah's flood story celebrating Noah as an exemplar of faith and a model for the righteous community.[1] In addition to the previous epigraph from Ambrose, observe the unhesitating confidence of Gregg Hunter, pastor of Fort Howard Community Church, "Compared to the people around him, its [*sic*] easy for one to say that Noah alone walked with God. Noah communed with God. Noah listened to God. And God used Noah to do an incredible thing. . . . My prayer is that the church would be filled with Noah's [*sic*]– people who find favor in the eyes of the Lord not through our own righteous deeds, but through faith in Jesus Christ."[2] But what was the incredible thing that God did? Was it annihilation of the world, or saving a specific lineage of people? And what does Noah symbolize in that sentiment? A lucky but drunken patriarch? A paradigm of faith? Hunter maintains Noah's faith in Jesus is an example to model. I've read and reread Noah's story. I don't see Jesus mentioned once. In contrast, I see references to Elohim and Yahweh. The former was an Israelite and Judean god that emerged from Canaanite traditions and assimilated Babylonian divine aspects. The latter, as I have mentioned already, was the frequent national god of two kingdoms: Israel and Judah. Foisting the Christian image of Jesus into a translation of the

84   *Chapter 5*

narrative repackages the meaning of the text, translating it into the property of a particular community which limits it within the performative efficiency of its own linguistic system. Consequently, what was once the product of a remote historical context becomes co-opted as a metaphor for the agenda of a later community. Thus, Noah becomes an archetypical Christian with faith in Jesus. If translation is a type of "transcreation," as James St. André offers, emphasizing the agency of the translator, then the story of Noah, as well as various others in Genesis, is the vehicle through which the translator expresses his own agenda and meaning.[3] That means, the Christian translates Christian meanings as part of that process. Because of the privatization of monotheistic text and revelation by dominant traditions, when the Bible as defined by a particular community is elevated as an assumed objectively real revelation of God, it is, in fact, the subjectively determined meanings that are themselves the goals and foci of translation that are so elevated, not the essence of anything supernatural. *The desires and values of my community become externalized as objective which you must accept as such to benefit from this community.*

The dominant interpreting community interprets divine favor for Noah and motivation for the flood as consistent with its own body as the righteous community. That idea is imposed upon future members, or converts, such as those colonized bodies who must face a dilemma: adopt a new externally imposed persona or suffer social and political destruction, an idea that has been perhaps most succinctly stated in the historical Christian colonial sentiment, "baptize or die." While there is benefit in having models to follow, this perspective overlooks the possibility of alternative readings. Here again postcolonial criticism challenges us to subvert those traditional readings. As I've mentioned before, the purpose of this project is not solely to debunk or refute such traditional readings. Rather, it's to expand and to challenge them in a way that forces us to reconsider how we have been interpreting texts. It asks us to reassess the meanings we associate with those texts, especially with the Bible, including the values and assumptions about truth that we elevate as objective because of their association with the Bible. Was the flood story simply a story about faith? That's how it's taught in Sunday schools. That's how it's frequently taught in the pulpit, which I can attest to having heard on multiple occasions. That's what most Christians and Jews will say, if you ask them standing in a line at McDonald's. Even LaSor et al. hold, "Nature is, nonetheless, of a personal order, throbbing with the mysterious, powerful presence of the Lord. Viewed against this background, the awesome terror of the cataclysmic destruction of the Flood is raised to almost unutterable proportions as the expression of God's judgment on human sin. Here was *the appropriate judgment of God that came on humanity when 'every inclination of the thoughts of their hearts was only evil continually'"* (6:5).[4] In that description, annihilation is justified as judgment, with those who perished deemed to be bodies irredeemably disfigured by immorality. Where, however, do we ever hear the stories of those who were judged by an outside community and its god? In my lifetime, there have been several catastrophes throughout the world. In many cases, there have been those who ignorantly proclaimed them to be God's judgment upon immorality; but never were the deaths in those catastrophes discriminated. Good died alongside bad. It is too easy to justify the deaths of others as God's judgment when we do not have to listen to the voices of those crying out for mercy.

For those willing to excuse a monotheistic god of atrocities—ones that any human would be deemed wholly evil for committing—such was the cultural importance of Noah to the preservation of humanity that the flood story can be interpreted, as did the patristics and later Christians, as symbolic of Christ and the Church, where Christ saved in his sacrificial body the seed of those who may walk and talk with God.[5] As Gen. 6:9 put it, Noah was (translating the quote) "a wholly righteous man [distinguished as such] among his generation." Because of that, he "walked with God," symbolizing the covenant that God established with Israel but later claimed by Christians for the so-called "body of Christ." Thus, the community that receives the "birth right" and blessing of God to be "co-heirs with Christ" is defined based on the dominant contours of the community itself. *Members, who are beneficiaries, look like us.*

But where is any attention paid to its much darker overtones? Where is the careful attention given to the atrociousness of the story that gets white-washed in metaphorical readings of Jesus or celebrations of Noah's faith? The horrendous actions? The immoral genocide? *God wiped out men, women, children, infants, and animals!* And why is it not read from the perspective of minority communities, who had no clue that there were certain expectations and obligations imposed upon them by an external source? That their non-membership in a "dominant" (elect) community was their downfall? That failure to adhere to the expectations of the dominant community, symbolized by Yahweh, resulted in their annihilation? How many interpreters have dismissed real analysis by claiming that God's actions cannot be judged by human standards? *The step to justifying political actions of colonizers and empires is not far at all!* Terence Fretheim, for instance, can't hide his assumptions about god as an active agent when he writes, "Notably, God does not need to introduce judgment into the situation; the destructive effects of violence were already springing forth from the human deed. The judgment then is not some punishment that is arbitrarily chosen by God but is understood in terms of natural consequence, intrinsically related to the sinful deed. God is mediator of the order of creation, but God does not act specifically to trigger the destructive flood."[6]

Ingrid Faro makes a similar homogenizing claim, "In God's own words, he accepts the current reality that evil intentions have become an integral part of the heart of humanity."[7] How do we know? Because a single scribe claimed it to be that way? Why are we not suspicious that the scribe claimed his own national "lineage" as righteous and all foreigners as "evil"? Or, that dominant traditions celebrate Noah as *not* like the "other," who must be wiped out because evil has become integral to the human experience? How is that not near to what many White Nationalists and Christian Nationalists in the United States say today, for whom the Founding Fathers of the United States seem to hold a Noahic type of status? Recall, for example, Emanuel Leutze's portrayal of George Washington crossing the Delaware while standing in a boat during foul weather to defeat the Hessian army at Trenton. Behind him, of course, was the symbol of what he represented: a "national" flag that was not created until at least six months after the event portrayed. But lest my hypothetical protestor bristle at any assumed correlation between the biblical author, biblical interpreter, Christian Nationalists, and White Nationalists, let me emphasize the rhetorical strategy I am using: I am comparing different subjects on the ground of a similarity. I am *not* saying that one equals the other, nor that all are identical. But I am asking, based on the similarity, what are the degrees of separation that does not make one equivalent to the other? I am also protesting assumptions about narrative all too frequently made by biblical scholars that the biblical narrative was normative.

To say that the *entire* world was evil and therefore deserving of punishment is to impose a certain definition of evil upon and all peoples, one developed within a specific cultural milieu. It is a fundamental statement of power common to monotheistic traditions. *What aspirations for power by men haven't been justified using religious ideals?! Colonial conquest? Yes. Imperial rule? Yes. Slavery? Yes.* It speaks to the dichotomy at the base of the monotheistic claim: power belongs to those who are not slaves to "sin." Ham, the son of Noah, who I would argue to be a poor fatherly role model, was found guilty of some vague transgression and his descendants were cursed to be powerless and slaves! In that situation, Noah can only represent a particular cultural perspective in which obedience to God (Elohim or Yahweh, depending upon the Genesis section) was prioritized. He does not represent the descendants of Ham, the Babylonians, the Egyptians, or other. He represents Israel in both the physical sense and the symbolic one, the latter which was co-opted by Christianity as the "new" people of God. *Such a supersessionist claim!* Because who will rule in that new Israel? God through Christ and his co-heirs, Christians. Not only that, but salvation required committing oneself to the cultural identity and moral system represented by Noah and his family. That spirit can be found in Judaism before Christianity. For instance, the *Legends of the Jews* claims that Noah was the very beacon of civilization:

Flooding the World and Saving a Few   87

Noah had scarcely come into the world when a marked change was noticeable. Since the curse brought upon the earth by the sin of Adam, it happened that wheat being sown, yet oats would sprout and grow. This ceased with the appearance of Noah: the earth bore the products planted in it. And it was Noah who, when he was grown to manhood, invented the plough, the scythe, the hoe, and other implements for cultivating the ground. Before him men had worked the land with their bare hands. . . . When God created Adam, He gave him dominion over all things: the cow obeyed the ploughman, and the furrow was willing to be drawn. But after the fall of Adam all things rebelled against him: the cow refused obedience to the ploughman, and also the furrow was refractory. Noah was born, and all returned to its state preceding the fall of man. Before the birth of Noah, the sea was in the habit of transgressing its bounds twice daily, morning and evening, and flooding the land up to the graves. After his birth it kept within its confines. And the famine that afflicted the world in the time of Lamech, the second of the ten great famines appointed to come upon it, ceased its ravages with the birth of Noah.[8]

What this legend describes of Noah's importance is shared by Christians, the assumption of which would bolster interpretations of the curse of Ham, some of which were discussed in the previous chapter. Both Jews and Christians maintain God saved Noah and his family because of Noah's righteousness. 2 Peter 2:5, for Christian example, describes Noah as the "herald of righteousness." Incidentally, nothing is ever said about the righteousness of his family. Even 2 Peter refers to "seven others" who were saved because of *Noah's* righteousness. Noah's family, like the colonized community, is defined by its authoritative head, the patriarch. How now the statement by Ingrid Faro echoes monotheistic truth! "An assault against the image bearer [cf. Gen. 9:24] is an assault against God, and he takes it personally."[9] What is the "image bearer" if not Noah and the "righteous community"? This is the very expectation of colonialism, of which monotheism is perhaps its greatest cheerleader. *Conquer and convert in the name of God! We bring the truth that all must acknowledge! The truth of God is seen in us!* While "the effects of colonialism and colonization in local contexts are highly variable" colonizers expect that the inhabitants of a colony behave in ways consistent with the morals, values, ethics, and politics characteristic of the dominant, colonizing culture.[10] To find tolerance, colonized peoples must take on prefabricated identities that have been defined within the categories and the frameworks of the colonizer's culture. "Durin' de war us wasn't bothered much, but after de surrender . . ."[11]

So why should we expect the peoples in Noah's story that are deemed evil be anything other than what they were? The otherness of others, deemed sinful by followers of Yahweh or the monotheistic "God," is a yoke cast upon the shoulders of those who are othered. "Humanity," as Faro writes,

88 *Chapter 5*

"is responsible for their choices as God appointed representatives."[12] What God created as good, Faro adds, was distorted by a wide range of "evil" in human autonomy. How to end that world-destroying autonomy? Establish the foundation (can we say "Seth"?) for a dependent relationship that requires the adoption of a new cultural identity. Or, in the words of Matthew, "Make disciples of *all* men." (28:19). Or in Mark, "Go into all the world and preach the gospel to every creature" (16:15). Why should they comport themselves to the value and moral system represented by Noah? At what point in the story was there ever a convincing logical argument made: "my god exists and will wipe you out if you don't become like me"? Isn't that the claim of *every* monotheistic religion? That violent death looms for everyone who does not commit themselves to the cultural expectations of the "righteous" community? *"And if anyone's name is not found written in the book of life, they will be forced into the lake of fire" (Rev. 20:15).* Why do we not protest such readings that do not challenge the dominant interpretation? Why do we accept genocide was legitimate? If the story really is frighteningly historical, why do not more people share Anton LaVey's opinion, "I found God . . . and he's a total asshole"?[13]

Philosophers and theologians among us might say human morality is not divine morality, and God's ways are justifiable based on divine morality. And while they may claim no theological commitment, the claim itself is the child of monotheistic expression and desire in the world. God and the righteous community hold themselves to a different standard than the rest of the "world," such as what was wiped out in the flood, or reflected in the near annihilation of the Canaanites under Joshua (see Josh. 1:24–33). Is it the old Christian adage, "We are in the world, not of it"? Defining identity as justifiable because of what God is and not because of human morality? If that is the case, why is the entirety of biblical interpretation conducted within the framework of human language, vocabulary, morals, ethics, and meanings? It doesn't step outside of that, nor of human translation, which is an act of imparting memes with meanings relevant to the *translator's* cultural context. Why are certain interpretations acceptable when they challenge what is said in the text (such as the unethical nature of *lex talionis*, as modern discussions on the death penalty maintain), but others are not (such as the acceptance of same-sex relations)? When, and especially so, they force us to acknowledge on some level that perhaps the image of God that we have projected (like Warner Sallman's *Jesus* [1940] found in many Protestant churches) is the product of a dominating culture? Why is it acceptable that some passages can be dismissed as passé because they are no longer practiced in the dominant interpreting culture and do not challenge its values? Should women sleep outside the house during menstruation (cf. Num. 5:1–4; Lev. 15:19–27)? *I dare any partner try arguing that!*

Dominant interpretations of the story focus on Noah's righteousness. Joseph Smith's, though he be ostracized by mainstream Christianity and ignored by Judaism, extolment of Noah summarizes much of Christian and even Jewish thought on this: "Noah . . . stands next in authority to Adam in the Priesthood; he was called of God to this office, and was the father of all living in his day, and to him was given the dominion. These men held keys first on earth, and then in heaven" (*Hist. Church* 3:386). Such interpretations are avoidance strategies because they avoid acknowledging that women, children, animals, along with men, were wiped out. And let us go even further. We can assume that disabled individuals did not make it to the ark. Toddlers and babies without concepts of morality or any notion of righteousness were wiped out. And what about pregnant women? How does one reconcile that God killed unborn babies? *That seems like a type of forced abortion! Where was the woman's choice here?* I must reemphasize that a postcolonial reading as a subversive strategy challenges the dominant traditions of interpretation that have imposed an image of body that must be internalized by all people. It asks about how texts impact the "other," such as ethnic and racial identities, children of non-Israelites, and more. It challenges the idea that if we accept what the dominant interpretive tradition has been, then children, women, unborn babies, non-Israelites, and other communities outside of the accepted norm could be justifiably killed because they did not uphold the same values that the author's community did. Dominion and sovereignty are the themes of Noah's story—those of an Israelite god later universalized as a monotheistic one.

This sets the tone for what von Rad claimed,

> God himself liberated the earth for the survivors. After the judgment of the flood, man on his own could not say as a matter of course but the earth was man's domain. It was, therefore, an important matter for the faith of those who came later, a matter about which they had to be sure, but the entrance into the new time, Unto the new earth, did not arise from human initiative but from God's express will. . . . The story of the flood, less familiar to present-day theological thought than other facts of the primeval history, testifies first of all simply to God's power and freedom, which allowed his created world to be engulfed by chaos. It shows God is the one who judges sin, and it stands at the beginning of the Bible as the eternally valid word about God's deadly anger over sin. Thus it protects every succeeding word of grace from any kind of innocuousness (*Verharmlosung*); it undergirds the understanding of God's will for salvation as a pure miracle.[14]

There's a parallel example. In modern American Indian fiction, many main characters have diminished or nonexistent relationships with their absent fathers. According to Robyn Johnson, "the absence of American Indian

90   *Chapter 5*

fathers came about because of predatory colonialism, in which American Indian tribes and families were forcefully uprooted and relocated onto reservations that were alien to them and their millennia-old sociocultures or were merely fractions of the land they used to occupy. Hence, their metaphysical lives, their religious ritual practices, which are profoundly attached to specific geographical places, were irreparably disturbed and damaged."[15] Even though the colonization American Indian communities has already happened, the identities of those communities continue to be shaped by the dominant culture in the US. In other words, the ways in which cultural stories are preserved, told, or even rewritten confirm the ideological convictions of the community in power. As Bhambra warns, "The silencing of colonial encounters is only one aspect of a wider narrative of global domination."[16] A narrative, I would argue, that has become the silent manifesto of monotheism.

But let me add this element as well, deities of the ancient Near East were often simple. They were symbolic and conveyed national symbolism. I offer that a more modern parallel of this symbolism is national flags. Deities represented the higher ideal of their kingdoms in a similar sense that flag represents not only the country but also the ideals of that country.

In the story of Noah to expect that non-Israelites would worship the god of Israel, who is the dominant subject of the Bible, rejects space for different bodies and identities. Perhaps this speaks to a principle of scarcity at work in monotheism, which sets individuals into rivalry for God's favor.[17] Such rivalry would reinforce the monotheistic obsession with the boundaries separating insider and outsider, so well symbolically portrayed in Cain and Abel, Shem and Ham. The excuse, again, that everyone apart from Noah's family was evil in all of their behaviors is not only reductive, it is the type of statement that promotes prejudice and discrimination. Not only that, but if Wilson is correct, the reference to the image of God in Gen. 9:6, the likeness of God, *tselem 'elohim*, which he translates more loftily as the Christian concept of *imago Dei*, denotes that whoever sheds the blood of a human by human should that person's blood be shed, thus following the God established archetype for killing outsiders who have "profaned" the divine image. The narrative of Gen. 6–9 would define the procedure for retributive violence by appealing to humanity's creation in the image of God. Such violent actions and an emphasis upon blood reinforce the boundaries between insider and outsider. They reinforce the categorical distinctions that support such boundaries, and those which give way to things such as prejudice, racism, exclusion, and even colonization by several degrees of connection.[18] Such strategies reinforce the contours of the interpreting community as the ideal community, marking out the distinction that separates it from those who have been identified as sinful or profane. After all, if sin was enough for God to wipe out the disabled, infants, and pregnant women, then we must see this story as nothing but one intended for a very specific community of insiders. *Jesus loves **me** / this **I** know / for the Bible tells **me** so . . .*

Wilson writes further, "if examining the way that God wields royal power in the creation story helps clarify the matter in which humans are to employ their power to 'have dominion' and 'subdue' the earth (Gen. 1:28), then likewise, observing how God uses power in the flood narrative provides a template for further clarifying the human imitation of God."[19] If that is the case then how is it not that genocide, infanticide, and ethnocide are not justifiable because of the actions of God, so long as they can be theologically explained and justified as being consistent with divine will?

So I must return to the question, why was Noah's family saved and everyone else worthy of destruction? That justification can only come through translation, through imposing one's own perspective, through making reductive communities that are not part of the dominant majority, through assembling the body of the monstrous "other" against which one's own fears and bad experiences may be cast. In that, it facilitates a colonialist assumption that people outside of one's own community do not have the right to the land, that their bodies must be transformed into the divine image, and that their occupation of the land does not have to be respected by the colonizing community because the colonizing culture has physical and ideological power. As Jules Ferry declared in a speech to the French Chamber of Deputies (translating the quote), "Gentlemen, we must speak more loudly and true. It must be said openly that superior races have a right vis-à-vis the inferior races. . . . I repeat that the superior races have a right, because they have a duty. They have the duty to civilize the inferior races."[20]

So why was Noah's family saved? Because from Noah's lineage through Shem, according to the biblical text, come archetypical figures for both Judaism and Christianity. Carol Kaminski sees the primeval blessing repeated to Noah's sons (compare Gen. 1:28 and 9:1, 7). In that, she states, the author confirms that despite judgment, God's plan for creation will not be "thwarted."[21] William LaSor et al. share that view, "The Flood story, although the supreme example of God's judgment on human sin, also subtly reflects his preserving grace. At the end there is a word from the Lord that is not found in other ancient traditions (Gen. 8:21f). This word offers a glimpse into God's own heart. The Flood is seen as a measure of the grace of the living God as well as of his judgment."[22] That is a nice sentiment, but if one holds it to be a historical account, then it excuses the slaughter of an innocent many. How often, I must return to my original question, do we imagine the flood story and see the eyes of the women, children, and disabled bodies gasping for air in the floodwaters as they lose strength? How often do we care about the unborn children who perished only because their pregnant mothers were drowned? How often do we challenge the idea that we justify the deaths of others, the genocide of others, because they are different, that their cultures were not as "civilized" as ours? Fretheim concludes that God shared power initially with human beings. When sin entered the world, it was pervasive and consuming, those humans failed earning destruction by using that power inappropriately.[23] That position is supported by the general theological assumption that the community must stand against the human tendency to be corrupted by sin, and that sin can justify divine genocide, like Ham's curse did for slavery. But such a position is little more than motivated by the desire to disqualify individuals and communities from positions of authority, or even justifying the misuse and destruction of their bodies. *Sin is a function of rejection!*

The spread of monotheistic traditions, such as Christianity, were driven by the very idea that salvation is wrapped up in a dominant cultural identity. One way to facilitate that was not only canonization but also a standardization of interpretation. Canonization was a long process, in part because there were such disagreements, which were driven by diversity. Power and established authority were necessary for one tradition to emerge as victorious. The struggle to create uniformity, to impose a dominant interpretive framework, coincided with the development and spread of Christianity. In the emergence of Christianity as something that was part of the dominant, and dominating, culture, it found its way into the political tool set of emperors. But such interpretations again, as I noted in chapter 4, don't focus on the struggle of minorities. They ignore the suffering of peoples stripped from their homes and sold into slavery. Or a more modern example, they do not pay attention to the experience of Hispanic populations who immigrate into the United States, for instance, and who find a culture capable of using biblical interpretation to support building walls to prevent them from entering the country.[24] The flood story reminds us we can easily justify genocide, prejudice, even evil if it benefits our own community. And, we do. For further example,

> In today's world, a clear distinction would have to be made between moral-order events, such as 9/11, and cosmic-order events, such as the tsunamis, but not an absolute distinction. The question needs to be asked: Given the interrelated spiderweb of a world in which we live, has not human sin had an adverse effect on at least some natural events? Think of Hurricane Katrina, for example, both from the perspective of inadequate human preparations and responses and of the possible effects of global warming on the storm's severity. If at least some such natural events can be so understood where moral order and natural order are linked, it is difficult to deny an interpretation of such events at least partially in terms of God's judgment, not least if one understands judgment as the effects of sin. Again, issues of discernment are immediately at hand, and divine judgment needs closer definition.[25]

Sin serves as the justification *only* for the insider who sees himself as having access to authority through the figure of a God who belongs to the community itself.

Atrocities linked to God are rendered as tension between divine judgment and human corruption, an idea that believing communities holding divine revelation within their own frameworks of meaning maintain. As the creator, God is removed from blame because the creator can do whatever God wants with God's created. *"I found God,"* LaVey said. Human beings, as the argument goes, can't hope to understand the fullness of divine intent or plan. They can only know their obligation to obey. That is why Fretheim can write, "While the flood is understood to be the judgment of God, that reality is not presented as arbitrary or capricious. Genesis 6:11–13 states clearly that violence, the violence of 'all flesh,' is the reason for the disaster. . . . The divine motivation for judgment is made very clear indeed. Notably, socio-moral evil is the focus of the divine motivation, not idolatry or other matters of worship. Violence is inhumanity to others, illustrated in the prior stories of Cain and Lamech."[26] But God reflects the dominant majority, and nothing is known of God beyond what ideologically motivated human beings have written. It is easy to postulate divine reason that supersedes human understanding, but one can never truly know that it exists. Any telling of it is always bound to a particular cultural language. *It must be translated!* Like the lofty philosophers of classical ages, this is precisely what postcolonialism demands that we recognize: that religious traditions and philosophies are not universal languages; to claim they are makes a claim to power. It calls us to recognize that biblical interpretations do not capture the true meaning and essence of human obligation to divine revelation. That is precisely why we have stories of broken families, such as among the American Indians who wrestle with absent fathers, mentioned above. Fretheim tries to preserve the concept of a universal and absolute moral order against accusations of divine misbehavior that human sins of violence demanded consequences. That itself, he maintains, is a testimony of a functioning moral order preserved through the judgment of God.[27] I humbly offer that it's easy to say that when one is not a victim. It's easy to uphold one's own perspective on God, morality, and human responsibility because it is already consistent with who one is. For others outside of one's community to accept the same thing demands that they understand it based on external meaning and cultural frameworks. That expectation tells us that while physical colonization is no longer a moral imperative, ideological, or conceptual, colonialism still is. "History is our judgment and God enables history—carrying the world along, not in mechanistic ways but with a personal attentiveness in view of a relationship of consequence."[28] Yet what are the contours of that relationship?

94   *Chapter 5*

Reading the flood story without recognizing the atrocity or pain it entails is to fall into the trap of justification of the self and the dominant ideals by which one benefits. A subversive strategy should demand that we see it as highlighting the willful blindness of the dominant tradition. It should remind us that if we ignore or forget the plight of others outside of our communities, we justify their ideological oppression solely for what benefits us.

Too often the flood story, particularly Gen. 9:1–17, is read for the conclusion that God saved humanity, represented by Noah and his sons, namely Shem and Japheth, but not Ham. *Or, was he saved to be a slave?* With the story's end, God established a covenant (Gen. 9:12–16) never to destroy the earth again. *Although oppression, slavery, ethnocide, and genocide were still very real possibilities!* The symbolism there should be noted: the earth represents the image of the interpreting community. The flood story is a cold reminder of what colonizers have been doing for centuries: wiping out the histories and traditions of others, and then promising never to do it again, sometimes even by incorporating romanticized accounts of colonized histories in a show of tolerance. In that sense, I would argue, postcolonialism demands that we see that the flood story is not about salvation but condemnation of the authentic and non-assimilated body of the "other," who is only "other" within the meaning and linguistic frameworks of and beneath the authority of a dominating community.

NOTES

1. A point also made by William S. LaSor, David A. Hubbard, and Frederic W. Bush, *Old Testament Survey: The Message, Form, and Background of the Old Testament*, 2nd ed. (Grand Rapids: William B. Eerdmans Publishing Company, 1996), 29.

2. Gregg Hunter, "Righteous Noah (Genesis 6:5–13)," *Fort Howard Community Church: Fort Howard, MD* (blog), July 19, 2021, https://www.forthowardcc.com/blog/post/righteous-noah--genesis-65-13-.

3. James St. André, "In All His Finery: Frederick Marryat's *The Pacha of Many Tales* as Drag," in *Queering Translation, Translating the Queer: Theory, Practice, Activism*, ed. Klaus Kaindl and Brian James Baer, Routledge Advances in Translation and Interpreting Studies 28 (New York London: Routledge, Taylor & Francis Group, 2020), 86.

4. LaSor, Hubbard, and Bush, *Old Testament Survey*, 29–30, emphasis mine.

5. Cf. Marvin R. Wilson, *Our Father Abraham: Jewish Roots of the Christian Faith*, 2nd ed (Grand Rapids: William B. Eerdmans, 2021), 99.

6. Terence E. Fretheim, "The God of the Flood Story and Natural Disasters," *Calvin Theological Journal* 43, no. 1 (April 2008): 31.

7. Faro, *Evil in Genesis*, 39–40.

8. Louis Ginzberg, Henrietta Szold, and Paul Radin, *Legends of the Jews*, 2nd ed., JPS Classic Reissues (Philadelphia: Jewish Publication Society, 2003), 134.

9. Faro, *Evil in Genesis*, 40.

10. Christine D. Beaule, *Frontiers of Colonialism* (Gainesville: University Press of Florida, 2017), 2.

11. See Federal Writers' Project and Library of Congress, *Alabama Slave Narratives*, 104.

12. Faro, *Evil in Genesis*, 6.

13. Anton Szandor LaVey, *Satan Speaks!* (Venice, CA: Feral House, 1998), 1.

14. Von Rad, *Genesis*, 129.

15. Robyn Johnson, "A World Without Fathers: Patriarchy, Colonialism, and the Male Creator in Northwest Tribal Narratives," *The American Indian Quarterly* 38, no. 3 (June 22, 2014): 343.

16. Gurminder K. Bhambra, *Rethinking Modernity: Postcolonialism and the Sociological Imagination* (New York: Palgrave Macmillan, 2007), 9.

17. As described by Regina Schwartz, cited by Haynes, *Noah's Curse*, location 3167.

18. Stephen M. Wilson, "Blood Vengeance and the Imago Dei in the Flood Narrative, Genesis 9:6," *Int* 71, no. 3 (July 1, 2017): 264–65.

19. Wilson, 268.

20. Jules Ferry, "Jules Ferry (28 Juillet 1885)—Histoire—Grands Discours Parlementaires—Assemblée Nationale," 1885, https://www2.assemblee-nationale.fr/decouvrir-l-assemblee/histoire/grands-discours-parlementaires/jules-ferry-28-juillet-1885, translation mine.

21. Carol Kaminski, *From Noah to Israel: Realization of the Primaeval Blessing After the Flood*, Journal for the Study of the Old Testament: Supplemental Series 413 (London/New York: T & T Clark/Bloomsbury, 2004), 1.

22. LaSor, Hubbard, and Bush, *Old Testament Survey*, 30.

23. Fretheim, "God of the Flood," 22.

24. Cf. Sarah Pulliam Bailey, "'God Is Not Against Building Walls!' The Sermon Trump Heard from Robert Jeffress Before His Inauguration." *Washington Post*, January 20, 2017, sec. Acts of Faith, https://www.washingtonpost.com/news/acts-of-faith/wp/2017/01/20/god-is-not-against-building-walls-the-sermon-donald-trump-heard-before-his-inauguration/.

25. Fretheim, "God of the Flood," 23.

26. Fretheim, 27–28.

27. Fretheim, 28.

28. Fretheim, 30.

Chapter 6

Inverting the Tower of Babel

Postcolonial challenges highlight biblical interpretation's grotesque vein of inequality, rooted in imperial assumptions about authority and identity, running through the biblical texts. Because of defeat to the Assyrians, and even more directly the Babylonian empire, their authors re-imagined an elect community, in a seat of authority, founded upon what they believed their national community *should* be. Perhaps it is better said what they imagined was more the re-institution of hierarchies of authority that benefitted the aristocracy. Many of the biblical authors, as literati, were part of that group. Over time, and with the aid of increasingly institutionalized monotheism (though there remained a great deal of diversity in both Jewish and Christian traditions until at least the latter part of the first millennium CE), this nationalist-oriented desire would become rooted in abstracted, universalized translations of divine revelation and desire characteristic of more complex forms of monotheism. These later became the basis for dominant traditions of biblical interpretation that continue to shape monotheistic traditions of Christianity and Judaism in the modern world.[1] In Genesis, the author's ideals comprised regulating and defining the "other" as someone subordinate, to draw boundaries between insider and outsider. That continuing aspect can be seen in evangelist J. Vernon McGee's description of the UN as America's own tower of Babel: "There is in the United States an organization that I am confident can and will become the instrument in setting up the stage for [the] fulfillment of prophecy. This organization is located in New York City [and] may have a large part in man's final act of the sordid drama of sin."[2] McGee's assumption is rooted in the exclusive definition of community that is characteristic of every monotheistic tradition. The biblical author provided symbolic legitimation for definitions of the "elect" community, which, while originally a political statement, became a theological one in later Judaism and Christianity. The political aspirations of a bygone aristocratic view became translated as the basis for a new community expressing its own sense of identity against the body of the disfigured "other," which it itself fashioned, as though it were an even more

98 *Chapter 6*

grotesque version of Dr. Frankenstein. It saw not the comprehensive diversity and complexity of other cultures and individuals. It saw difference as a threat and responded by corralling everything outside of itself into a singular category of profane, sinner, and outsider. With that done, it celebrated its own generosity because it fashioned a gate through which some individuals could pass, confessing their own inferiority and leaving their profane existence to become members of the "true" community.

Hence the question that motivates, in part, this work must be restated. What would it look like to read stories like that of the Tower of Babel against the grain? To challenge the correlation that dominant modes of interpretation have made between election and power? To challenge the binary assumption about bodies that permeates monotheistic thinking: the insider as the true, saved individual and the outsider as the profane, monstrous "other"? Does God *really* empower one community and justify the eternal annihilation of others? Should interpretations even be based on the assumption that God *is* an active agent in human affairs? Or, is God only a symbol that communities project as a symbol of their own highest ideals?[3] And in this, we see the truth of what I exposed in a previous work, while recognizing that restoration remains an anticipated event for monotheism. "The unspoken fear of monotheism . . . is that there is no object, no shared collective symbol, no God that can adequately support the monotheistic identity. That restoration will never happen, that it has all been a façade, that there will never be any reward for suppressing individual desires. That is why monotheism needs a mysterious God that both liberates and oppresses."[4] God embodies the self-sustaining confidence in the community's desired outcome. The fear that it may *not* happen is projected, in a gross attempt to ease internal cognitive dissonance, upon the outsider, the profane sinner, the infidel, and ultimately Satan. Monotheism cannot exist outside of a radical dependence upon binaries. If God symbolizes cherished values, Satan symbolizes the face of what may be the truth about the communal, collective self. Monotheistic emphasis upon restoration, which entails the refactoring of networks of power, necessitates both. Power must have something to exercise power over. If God is the symbol of our most cherished values, Satan symbolizes what we are afraid is actually the truth about ourselves.

What would it be like, as postcolonialism demands we do, to see the Bible as a criticism of the dominant traditions and communities that claim it? To subvert monotheism's belligerent dependence upon binaries? This demand is one that has motivated this work to *challenge* prevailing colonialist presuppositions and tendencies, whether they be physical or ideological. In response to that challenge, this chapter analyzes how Gen. 11 might be productive for postcolonial strategies, as well as to challenge tendencies to subordinate minority reading strategies and perspectives to dominant trends in biblical interpretation. That is especially important in areas where biblical interpretation informs sociopolitical engagement, loyalties, and behaviors.

To be sure, this reading is experimental. I recognize that reading against the grain often reads a text different from how an author intended it. But where interpretations and translations have provided ideological justifications for inequalities, oppressions, conquests, and more, we must learn to read in ways that dismantle and subvert hegemonic interpretations and traditions that fabricated the body of the idealized antithetical "other" as the foil against which to celebrate the cherished values and ideals insiders imagine are true for themselves. *Isn't that the foundation of how God is understood and defined?* Failure to do so preserves the dichotomy between insider and outsider upon which oppressive institutions build an ideological rationale for expressions of power and prejudice. My focus is on challenging dominant reading strategies to expose possible presuppositions of a colonial consciousness that have helped keep postcolonial perspectives on the margins. For this chapter, I chose the story of the Tower of Babel because we can read it as a struggle against authority from several angles.

> For that reason Yahweh called it Babel because he confounded the language of all the earth there, and from there he scattered them [the people of Babel] throughout the earth. (Gen. 11:9)

One can interpret that passage as a statement of God's (Yahweh's) power and influence over the natural world, and that God also imposed limits upon human potential. But if such limits were God-imposed, then a particular narrative, including its host culture, embodies that narrative. It is the basis for, in a word, election. Under the auspices of an elect community, divine limits, as expressed in monotheistic traditions, benefit a particular community. Monotheistic communities have made defense of that idea—emphasizing their own proposed election—a primary strategy for navigating and responding to the world around them. Take, for example, the following rather common view, "The demonic tower signifies the aspect of history known as imperialism, the human effort to unite human resources by force that organizes larger and larger social units, and eventually exalts some king into a world ruler, a parody representative of God."[5] Biblical stories are almost always read from the crystallized perspective of the dominant community as the chosen of God and God's literary actions as historical accounts of divine world formation to ease the ultimate salvation of the "righteous community." In that vein, stories like the Tower of Babel, the subject of which is cast as antithetical to divine will, are read as contests between good and evil. Such a reading strategy not only reinforces the identity of the believer, it contributes legitimation to divine actions that conducted by any human being would be

100 *Chapter 6*

deemed selfish and atrocious. And, it demonizes any articulated or practiced resistance to what it has defined as the divinely ordained normative.

If history is the narrative in which we tell "our" stories, then the story that is presented to us in the Bible, if we read it as literal or objective history conveying divine revelation, becomes the history we must adopt. And *that* is precisely the struggle that postcolonial critics have with the dominant traditions in biblical interpretation. The histories of colonized bodies and their cultures are overwritten by the narrative of a dominant power. Is it surprising that divine revelation, once it has been institutionalized in religion, never seems to happen in colonized or potentially colonized cultures? That divine revelation, which becomes the paradigm for the world, is controlled by "civilized" cultures and even world powers in the modern context? Otherwise, in the possible absence of such a (rooted) culture, revelation's very ideological position demands that it be *dis*-embodied. *If God didn't reveal God's self to us, and we're wrong, God didn't reveal God's self to any community, right?*

Postcolonialism challenges the colonial assumption that truth is possible only at the expense of a minority body's identity.

In saying that, I am reminded of Sugirtharajah's assessment of postcolonialism, that its focus is not simply about looking for liberating readings, although it entails that.[6] It is also about challenging the dominant status quo rooted in center-periphery dichotomies. It is there, in the eye of challenge, that my reading of Gen. 11 focuses. With biblical studies, the dominant status quo reads the biblical texts in positivist ways. It reads biblical texts as conveying something true about Israelite society, on one hand, and about God as a positive cause, on the other. Both subjects are elevated by readers from believing communities into the status of a universal ideal. God is assumed to be objectively real, and Israel his prize, which Jews have made a core tenet of their belief and Christians seek benefit by interpreting themselves as the "new Israel" (cf. Heb. 8:1–13). Such readings also accept the biblical presentation of God as an agent involved in directing and influencing history. Even that the Yahweh of the past is *the* monotheistic God. In isolation, that is not a problem. When those readings become the basis for attitudes of superiority, they risk legitimating ideological colonialism. One can see the stress of that, for example, in the Israeli-Palestinian tensions, in which modern Israel justifies its policy of land acquisition based on its interpretation of God and revelation.[7] The monotheistic connection modern Israel maintains to God, regardless of its democratic claims, ideologically limits the tolerable identities of minorities, a point that many citizens of Israel also argue in contrast to the political apparatus and its conservative or orthodox supporters. For instance, "The attempt to reconcile the Jewish nature of the state with the political rights of the Arab minority force serious challenges."[8] Note the conflation of a religious identity with a political one, such that "Jewish" appears synonymous with "Israeli." Similar is the correlation between "citizen" and "Christian" made by members of the Christian Right and by Christian Nationalists in the United States. Making political claim to religious universals in justifying political strategy reflects the actions of empires and colonizers of the past. Political claim over the religious heritage of Judaism seeks to link modern Israel's political claim over the land with the ancient biblical claim that God gave the land to Abraham and his descendants (cf. the discussion in chapter 7), which was itself part of the nationalist narrative of ancient Israel. Moreover, the designation of the modern nation-state as "Israel" claims that heritage.[9]

Even the act of *translating* is not immune to what Kinyua describes as the discourses of colonialism.[10] Frequently, in the fields of many academic disciplines, translators are those whose native affiliation or educational background is rooted in cultures traditionally associated with colonization. For that reason, in part, "the Bible has the potential of becoming both a solution and a problem, both an oppressor and a liberator."[11] The Bible may offer hope, but how it is interpreted is frequently regulated by dominant traditions. I would refine Kinyua's warning: biblical interpretation and its legitimation have that potential. The meaning of the Bible is an object of Western ideals rooted in divinely legitimated colonial and imperial aspirations. While some colonized cultures have adopted the Bible as their own, that they have done so is frequently a consequence of colonization. The framework by which biblical meaning is known is *still* rooted in the cultures of historical oppressors. How often, in other words, has the Bible been interpreted outside of Western meaning and value systems?

Biblical studies can put itself at the forefront of change. It can break free of the shackles that confine it to rooting around in fabricated binaries that only serve to further abjectify, make monstrous, the body of "other." To break free from that is to see others with whom it may enter dialogue. Rather than merely echoing voices of protest within culture, it can *lead* the conversation that includes the diverse voices of "scattered peoples" (regarding Gen. 11:8). But it can't do that siloed in its own echo chamber. It must step outside and engage the voices of those who are actively struggling against a dominant majority. Our conversations must adopt the strategy described by Sugirtharajah, in which postcolonial criticism challenges the context, contours, and procedures of biblical scholarship, enabling us to criticize the totalizing tendencies of Western reading practices by "scrutinizing and exposing colonial domination and power as they are embodied in biblical text and in interpretations, and as searching for alternative hermeneutics while thus overturning and dismantling colonial perspectives."[12]

I would argue that intent should be what embodies the sentiment of Pope Francis when he warned:

102 *Chapter 6*

> These are the new forms of cultural colonization. . . . One effective way to weaken historical consciousness, critical thinking, the struggle for justice and the processes of integration is to empty great words of their meaning or to manipulate them. Nowadays, what do certain words like democracy, freedom, justice or unity really mean? They have been bent and shaped to serve as tools for domination, as meaningless tags that can be used to justify any action.[13]

Likewise, how much so have the concepts of Bible, God, revelation, divine law, and righteous community served as tools for domination that justify actions against others who remain on the margins of a monotheistic world? If the Bible is something that we engage with as a source of meaning, as well as a basis by which we define dominant cultural attributes within and for the communities in which we live, then the relevance of such stories for the contemporary context is something we must explore. What does it mean to maintain that Yahweh, transformed into the God of Judaism and Christianity, has the power to make or break cultures? In making such claims, are believing communities implying their own relatively superior positions? Engaging with such questions and readings exposes presuppositions about the social world, our prejudices, our values, and even our attempts to build relationships in a manner befitting pluralism. These are strategies that should help us better navigate not only reading the text itself, but understanding what role the Bible should fulfill, and how that translates into intercultural engagement.

We should seek to understand how not only a reading strategy exposes a particular set of meanings but also how it might translate to other types of engagements with the Bible, by different communities, in society and in politics. How can we as readers be challenged, not on a theological level but on a social or political one? How can we recognize that the ways we interpret the Bible frequently reinforce the dominant traditions that have shaped its reception history? In what ways has the very concept of "Bible" reinforced the ideals of particular communities?

This type of reading emphasizes the importance of understanding inequalities in power and how dominant traditions of interpretation have reinforced them. It focuses on how one narrates identity and how one navigates the sociopolitical world based on that identity. It also tries to avoid an obsession with blaming, though it recognizes the role that cultural indictments can have. It recognizes that colonialism, as Kinyua reminds us, is a practice and not a theory. That in many cases, it has been pervasive enough that the historical consciousness of colonized cultures cannot be fully decolonized. Instead, we must analyze how power relationships have been established at economic, political, and cultural levels in ways that continue to subordinate, materially and ideologically, colonized cultures in relationships to a colonizing power.[14]

Theophus Smith is another scholar who sought to do that and break the rooted nature of biblical translation in binaries while keeping the importance of the Bible and stripping it from the clutches of a dominant majority. He views the Bible as a type of conjuring object, that the meaning that should be derived, and the reading strategies that are most important for the preservation of community and the articulation of identity, are found not in the biblical text. For him, there is no essential meaning that exists within the biblical text. It is open to interpretation by *all* communities, who might find there meanings that are culturally relevant and not externally imposed. Therefore, no interpretive strategy can hold any dominant claim over biblical meaning. It is a direct challenge to the colonist assumptions inherent within the advancement of a singular, universal interpretation. To embody any hegemonic interpretive tradition is to be a victim of what Kinyua describes as a "colonizing of the mind," in which the reading subject assimilates the values and assumptions of a colonizing power and projects them upon the bodies of others. Yet we must also acknowledge that because interpretations have been historically rooted in those values and assumptions, it may not be possible to get away from them entirely. How often, for example, do Bible readers automatically see Babylon in negative terms? For Christians, it has become a code word for the domain and assumed authority of Satan (cf. Rev. 17:5–6).[15] Yet even if that is deeply rooted in the dominant traditions of Bible reading, it is possible to react to that reality, developing interpretive strategies that highlight the readerly position of critique. Such strategies challenge a singular reading and embrace colonized voices as equal expressions of what it means to be human. "Come, let us *too* make a name for ourselves." For the modern world, as Smith alludes, the Bible may be a common point of intersection, but a single interpretive strategy is not.

Practicing that, however, is easier said than done. The Bible as a common point of intersection *and* the concept of "Bible" itself are products of a dominant tradition colonial powers have preserved. Thus, what the Bible *is* is consistent with their experiences and values. Take Gen. 11:1, for instance: "And it was that all the land was of one tongue and spoke the same words." The tendency is to read this as a condemnation of a shared goal. That God was making it impossible for human beings to work together because their inclination was only to create power that rivaled God, as though a substitute for eating from the Tree of Life in order to overcome existential limitations imposed upon human beings. And in that sense, the story of the Tower of Babel provides the culmination of the Primeval History (Gen. 1–11). "It describes," as Neal Blough observes, "the last great judgment that befell humanity, in a sequence that begins with the fall in Genesis 3 and the 'sons of God' episode in Genesis 6:1–4, both of which triggered divine judgments of great and enduring consequence."[16] Yet we often forget that immediately

104   *Chapter 6*

following the story of Babel, Gen. 11:10 picks up with the descendants of Shem (whose name can be translated as "name"), a lineage that will eventually lead to Israel through Abraham. Yahweh's actions must be interpreted while considering the intended outcome. The singular "language" that was not Israelite was disrupted, creating a chaos out of which Israel emerged as a reflection of order and divine favor. What then can we conclude but that the stories we tell reflect the histories we preserve to build the image of ourselves and the world we project upon others. Babel becomes the backdrop to Abraham's emergence.

According to midrashic tradition, Abraham "discovered" Yahweh in the year of the "Babel incident" (cf. *Ber. Rab.* 64:4). He distinguished himself by rejecting the prevailing "Nimrodic theology" of human oneness.[17] While in the land of Shinar this tower was thwarted, in Ur of the Chaldeans, the seed of an idea, a particular people, Israel, was emerging in Abraham. The shared goal of peoples in Babylonia was a problem for the author. The shared goal of Israel was not.

Some early commentators suggested that the common language spoken at the tower was the language of Eden, which would seem to be east of the people's settlement, based on Gen. 3:24, and also 2:8.[18] The sense of a universal, or pure language, isn't that unique. It reflects a utopia in which all people speak the language of the particular community. It also ideologically supports colonial aspirations and is frequently found in cultures for which such practices are known. For the biblical author, this language was Hebrew, as Zeph. 3:9 would also seem to confirm in its implication of the importance of the Israelite language: "Then I will restore for the peoples one purified speech." And even the idea of a paradisal garden finds a parallel in what is now described as a "wonder of the world," the Hanging Gardens of Babylon. The biblical author re-appropriated Babylonian achievement to highlight the cultural aspirations of his own community. The concept of one language is rooted in beliefs about one primary culture against which differences are measured as sinful, profane, and threatening.

In the land of Shinar, where all people shared a collective identity and purpose, expressed through the idea of a common language, Yahweh, the god of Israel, broke that identity. Linguistic differentiation became that basis for alienation and division.[19] Yet, as traditions of biblical interpretation have shown, the differentiation became the space for election, of mapping out the contours of the idealized body through a rejection of difference. Ezra-Nehemiah portrays how that might happen with an emphasis upon divine election, in which knowledge of Hebrew became the basis by which the community accepted individuals into the community (cf. Neh. 13:23–25). That sense of election also became part of the self-identity of Christianity, which largely adopts either an euhemeristic or literal approach to interpreting

Inverting the Tower of Babel

the story, and through that influenced Western definitions of what a civilized, moral society looked like.

Postcolonial strategies are politically and socially sensitive, and colonialism is not just an event of the past. If the Black Lives Matter movement of the 21st century has shown us much, and I believe it has, it emphasizes that there continues to be ideological colonialism in the United States and around the world. Racism is but a perceivable manifestation of that. Bhambra, for instance, calls us to see racism and prejudice not simply as domestic issues but as part of the colonialist formation of nation-states, "The racialized hierarchies of empire defined the broader polity beyond the nation-state and, after decolonization, have continued to construct inequalities of citizenship within states that have only recently become national."[20] When biblical interpretation and translation are wrapped up in cultural identities rooted in nation-states, it perpetuates the colonial frameworks that bolster racism and prejudice.[21] "An authoritative text such as the Bible, which remains (it is assumed) unchanging as the Word of God, can produce the myths, memoirs, values, and symbols, that help define and promote an identity."[22] It can, but under the influence of a colonial past, dominant traditions of biblical interpretation have preserved a singular identity against which the bodies of a diversity of others are suppressed into a hegemonic idea of a singular "other." This "other" becomes transformed into the antithesis of the idealized identity and its collective body. Differences, when properly categorized within the meaning system of monotheism are celebrated as testimonies of God's expansiveness. That, for example, is one of the main reasons parables such as of Jesus speaking to a Samaritan woman are popular among believing communities of Christians (John 4:5–30). My hypothetical protestor would likely respond that the story highlights the appeal of the "truth of Jesus," because even a "loose Samaritan woman" who had five husbands and at least one lover could recognize the anticipated messiah. *Even the lowly non-Israelite sinner finds the savior!* Perhaps, but the assumption that informs interpretations of that parable is that the Samaritan woman is different, but she can be *transformed* into an acceptable body. Not only that but that sexual proclivity is for men only, as the stories of Abraham, Jacob, Lot, and more imply.

HOW WE READ REFLECTS WHO WE ARE: SO UP THE TOWER WE GO!

Initially, Gen. 11:5–7 seems to be friendly to a postcolonial perspective, in that the dispersion of the peoples can be interpreted readily as a strike against empire.

106 *Chapter 6*

Then Yahweh saw the city and the tower that the sons of man (*adam*) had built. And he said, "one people with one language have done all this! They have caused profanity by doing this because now nothing will be inaccessible to them in all that they devise to do. Come! Let us [*Who? Other gods in Yahweh's court?*] go down there and confuse their speech so that each man will not be able to understand his friend [or 'companion']."

One should be able to hear a reflection of imperial strategy in that passage. The Assyrian Empire, for example, did something similar. It was well known among historians for displacing peoples throughout its empire. It "confused" the languages of the peoples by mixing peoples who spoke different languages. Unencumbered, however, by the burden of historical realities, many Bible readers read the story from the perspective of divine intent–the divine being the same monotheistic God of their own monotheistic-oriented cultures who has been granted in the monotheistic value system eternal and universal authority. Neal Blough for example, argues that the canon of stories, including Gen. 11, belong together as Scripture, which is a theologically laden term meant to separate historical texts from the limits of history by linking them to assumptions about God and God's "plan" and authority. He interprets the Bible as a "map" to salvation, the concept of which has been translated in Christian tradition.[23] Even academic perspectives have a difficult time avoiding that perspective. One of my own favorite writers, Blenkinsopp, for example, wrote of Gen. 11:5: "This is the *peripatea*, the turning point, when the project of the new humanity is viewed from a perspective independent of their own devices, desires and decisions."[24] The turning point of the narrative corresponds to the powerful action of Yahweh, interpreted as God, which creates space for a new definition of humanity fashioned in the words of the biblical literati literati. And more, Matthew Michael's argument that the tower reflects a general human desire to build tall buildings as a challenge to an assumed divine-human dichotomy is entirely unconvincing.[25] Yet why if we take all of these examples together is there a tendency to read it as something more universal? What is the underlying motivation? Take, for further example, a passage written by Wulfstan (11th century CE), archbishop of York:

O! It is long ago that through the Devil many things went astray, and that humankind so greatly disobeyed God, and that so very widely did paganism greatly injure and continues to injure widely. Yet we do not read anywhere in books that anyone raised up any heathen idol anywhere in the world in any of that time which was before Noah's flood. But afterwards it happened that Nimrod and the giants wrought that astonishing tower after Noah's flood, and then as many languages came upon them as were those workers of which the books speak. Then afterwards they dispersed to far off lands, and humankind then immediately grew greatly, and then at last they were deceived by that

Inverting the Tower of Babel 107

ancient Devil, who previously before led Adam astray, such that they wrought wickedly and impiously heathen gods for themselves, and forsook the true God and their own creator who created and wrought them as humans.[26]

Major also notes that by invoking the account of the Tower of Babel, Wulfstan "signals the need to recognize and conform to the religious values of his congregation, which point to wider Christian identities within Europe." For Wulfstan, that concern was heightened by the invading "heathen" Vikings.[27] These laid the foundation for later theologies, such as those that "mark importantly for Anglo-Saxon Christians, the linguistic implications of Babel." Those implications were "informed by the events at Pentecost, during which the Holy Spirit sanctifies the use of all languages of the world for spreading the church abroad . . . Together, Babel and Pentecost are primary starting points for understanding the worlds (and Anglo-Saxon England's) linguistic and ethnic situation."[28] We know from history, of course, that that situation was motivated by imperial and colonial concerns. It is hard to reject the possibility of a similar (theological) motivation behind many interpretations of the Babel story, those cherished by readers seeking validation of divine authority and evidence of a divine plan, and action toward that plan in the world.

In Genesis, the power of the Babylonian Empire is subordinated to the generative powers of Yahweh. According to Gen. 10:8–12, Nimrod (perhaps in direct contest to Marduk), a valiant warrior and builder of cities, created a kingdom that included Babel, Erech, Akkad, and CalNeh (a term that might not refer to a location but to "all of them") in the land of Shinar. But he wasn't done. He went from there to the territory of Assyria and built Nineveh, Rehoboth-Ir, Calah, and Resen. The classical Jewish proposal that Nimrod incited the people against God correlates Nimrod and Babel with the actions of the Babylonian Empire, as well as the anti-Assyrian story of Jonah. The tower, Weisner, claims, "constituted the central tactic and goal."[29] But again, here is an example of how translation hooks an idea to a particular cultural body. Jewish tradition, as does Christian tradition, sees itself reflected in the unfolding of the Bible, both claiming knowledge of that plan, though perhaps only in its rough contours. The tower is translated as the antithesis to what God, as the god of a particular religious community, desired. Many in stating their position often overlook the important counterpoint that rarely does any monotheistic community successfully acknowledge that the subjects in the biblical texts were defined by ethnicity and not religion. There were no Jews, Christians, or even Muslims in the Bible. Translation from those religious bodies, however, finds them there, making the contours of their communities synonymous with divine expectation and desire in the textual "revelation" of the Bible.

108   *Chapter 6*

As a possible parallel, Micah claims that seven shepherds and eight princes will rise in defense of Yahweh's community (Micah 5:5). If Herodotus's account of the temple tower is correct, which I will discuss below, would that equal one symbolic individual (prince) for each tower section? Micah's shepherds and princes will rise against the ruler of the land of Nimrod and take the land, ruling over it with a sword. In Micah 5:5, the authority of the victor coalesces in the figure of a coming messianic ruler. One could read that as a postcolonial aspiration, something like the type of proto-apocalypticism expressing a millennial hope for restoration.[30] It certainly fits a linear view of history, in which a community perceiving itself under oppression desires a reversal of its fortunes through world-altering action. But to read it in only that manner overlooks an important element. The literati, while under occupation, have not lost their sense of community, tradition, and identity. In fact, their messianic ruler symbolizes the embodiment of their imagination of a re-instituted Israel.

As Blenkinsopp observes, the scattering in Gen. 11 is like the expulsion from the Garden of Eden in Gen. 3, where divine intervention redirected humanity from its desired aim.[31] In Gen. 3, Adam and Eve were prevented from attaining eternal life. In Gen. 11, the people are prevented from "making a name for themselves" or defining their own collective body and identity. Perhaps instead of the tendency to read the desire in Gen. 11 in negative terms, as though the people were self-centered in their pursuit of human accomplishment and power, and here I offer a new type of postcolonial reading, we should read it in more sociological terms: to make a name for oneself may also be to give identity and structure to one's community; to be known and named as something distinct and not consumed under the consciousness of another dominating culture. In this reading, the act of scattering is itself a type of colonizing act because it breaks the cohesion of another's identity.

In both Gen. 3 and Gen. 11, God's redirection resulted in creating a space for God's people. We shouldn't read the Israelites, or their ancestors, as victims in this sense. Rather, divine action in creating chaotic social and political situations was what became the basis upon which their own cultural identity could be built. That sense of election, of God working through history to build the society of his people, is at the heart of all monotheistic religions. God is the symbol of the highest values of the community, and that reinforces the belief that monotheistic identity is linked to a power that supersedes any other power that does not uphold the monotheistic God as its dominant symbol. As vv. 8–9 tell us, because Yahweh scattered (*parats*) the people, they ceased building *and* they began speaking different languages, *that* is why the location was called Babel, which can be translated as "gate of (the) god" (*bab-ilu* in Babylonian literature). Yahweh confused (*balal*) the speech of the people. Jonathan Weisner's interpretation that Yahweh's actions dictated this meant

Inverting the Tower of Babel 109

societies should adopt an individualistic model that acknowledged diversity of thought and intent among cultures is not convincing. It makes individualism and an obsession with boundaries divine intent.[32] More importantly, anytime one speaks of God as an active historical agent, God becomes translated and defined according to the perspective of the benefitting community; a transformation of "God" that must be resisted, postcolonialism maintains.

In terms of a historical and archaeological perspective, the tower may be a reference to the Babylonian Etemenanki temple tower. While Sennacharib, the Assyrian emperor (705–681 BCE), claims to have destroyed the temple complex, Esarhaddon restored it, and his son, Ashurbanipal, reintroduced the cult of Marduk. Of more direct relevance to the biblical author, perhaps, is that Nebuchadnezzar II restored the complex and its cult after the Babylonian Empire defeated the Assyrian Empire.[33] That would be consistent with the idea that Gen. 11 was intended as a 6th century commentary by Judean literati on the Babylonian Empire and the diasporic hope for a restoration of the kingdom. That idea is preserved even still in the Jewish tradition of a Palaga generation, the deprivation of which, through the action of Yahweh, established "a metric of normative models for successful societies."[34]

Herodotus describes the tower temple or structure as a series of eight towers stacked upon each other, with an ascent wrapping around them. In the middle there was a stopping place with seats to rest. At the top was a cell with a couch and a golden table. A woman, native to Babylon, who was chosen by the god, spent the night as though in *flagrante delicto* with the god, who also reclined there on the couch (*Histories* 1.181–2). Such a structure would be a clear statement of power and authority. And the offering of a virgin to the god as a prerequisite for the benefit of an elect community is something with which even Christianity is familiar. After all, was not the virgin Mary ravished by God to produce a son who would be the savior of all who converted? *At least the Babylonians offered the couple a couch!*

The biblical claim (cf. Gen. 11:5–9) that Yahweh came down upon the tower and imposed his will, scattering the people, is a clear reference to a political claim. Because in that, with an awareness of the tower as a Babylonian symbol of power, the author asserts that the god of Judah was a stronger authority than the gods of Babylon. Not only that, but that the people would be scattered and would speak their own tongues, rather than a common imperial language, which was imposed by Babylonian culture as the *lingua franca*. In that is the deconstruction of empire.

I also wonder if the biblical author knew about the woman at the top of the tower. When he imagined Yahweh coming down onto the tower, did he have in mind a type of sexual conquest, the metaphorical type of which the biblical prophets are often keen on adopting in their oracles? For example, "I passed by you . . . Your breasts were formed and firm. Your pubic hair sprouted, and you were naked and bare. . . . I watched you . . . you had reached the age for love . . . I spread my skirt over you" (Ezek. 16:6–8).[35]

While we can only speculate, the author's presentation contains an accusation of the Babylonian attempt to create a world in its own image, which the author viewed as being in stark contrast to Yahweh. If the Babylonian strategy succeeded, then the desired restoration of Israel, as promised by the prophets, would fail. Even more dramatically, the identity of Israel, and the power of Yahweh as the political god of Israel, would be lost. To prevent that, the god of Israel must respond to the Babylonian threat. That response is found in Gen. 11:8, in which Yahweh scatters the people across the face of the earth, stopping them from building the tower and city. That is why, the author tells us, the place is called *babel*, which may have been a linguistic play on *balal* ("to confuse"). Yahweh confused the language of the entire world and scattered the people (see v. 9). Symbolically, the power of the Babylonian Empire and the world that it created was broken (but the path was set for Israel/Judah).

And while the biblical literati may not view themselves as making imperialist claims for the kingdom of Judah, or Israel, they talk about Judah's capital city as a beacon, especially in the book of Isaiah (cf. Isa. 60:1–3), to the known world, which becomes clear with the power and authority of Yahweh demonstrated in the restoration and success of the kingdom. Aspirational, to be sure, and aspirational along lines that are similar to what an emperor might say.

This is a type of political propaganda claiming that Yahweh, as the symbol of Israel (Judah), would break the power of the empire because Yahweh's power is greater than that of the Babylonian Empire. There is a self-serving element in that claim. If it is true, which the author wants to believe it is, then Yahweh can easily restore the "grandeur" of the Judean kingdom. The construction of a tower refers not only to the political power the empire is building, such as the institutions of society, it also referred to the political hierarchy in the imperial political system and structure. Empires build "towers" of imperial power and structure, enforcing their authority upon conquered peoples through laws, taxes, required labor, and a type of universalizing of an imperial language. Or take Blough's bold assertion: "The common language does not facilitate communication; rather, it represents an attempt to impose a universal point of view and way of speech upon humanity. It is a totalitarian ideology, enforced through political, moral and religious centralization—a city with only one way of thinking and talking, reaching heavenward under the authority of a single power."[36] If that is a criticism of Babel, what are monotheistic traditions if not guilty of the same practices and assumptions? The difference is who gets to translate the unifying symbol (God) and define the dominant contours of the collective body. In contrast to

Inverting the Tower of Babel

a foreign power, Yahweh would exercise authority over those empires and "confuse" the foundation of Babylonian culture and identity. His actions, according to Christian theology, will, through salvation, unify peoples under a single culture and authority.[37] Call it "heaven," "paradise," or "shalom," the paradigm remains: from empire to empire, what changes is the face of the body in authority.

The political nature of this claim is confirmed as well in the statement by von Rad:

> The saga about the confusion of language is concerned with the historical phenomenon that was made concrete in the cosmopolitan city of Babylon; but the story certainly does not originate from Babylon; rather, it shows ideas that were strange to Babylon. Babylon in ancient times, especially in the second millennium B.C., was the heart of the ancient world and its center of power (Hammurabi, 1728–1686), and the rays of its culture went out far into neighboring lands. Thus even in Palestine there was legendary knowledge of gigantic cultural achievements, especially the mighty stepped towers in which the united civilized will of this strong nation had created an enduring monument.[38]

THE MYTH OF COLONIZATION?

Even within Babylonia, there seems to have been sufficient freedom granted conquered peoples to live together in cities (cf. al-Yahudu)[39] while preserving some sense of their shared cultural identity. There was little in the way of colonization, as modern Western empires and cultures perfected. This leads me to hypothesize that while conquered and displaced, the Judeans in Babylonia were not colonized, in contrast to what many biblical scholars assume based entirely on a limited number of biblical passages. More generally, and modern biblical readers are often guilty of making this assumption, the Judeans in Babylonia did not make up the entirety of Judah, or Judean culture. People remained in the land of Judah. We can argue about numbers all day, but we cannot avoid this conclusion: the people who were taken into Babylonia were from Judah's aristocracy.[40] To conclude that they alone made up Judah and Judean culture is the type of classist tendency found in ideological colonization, by which I mean the type of writing and appropriating of others' culture for the benefit of the majority. It was not the people who lived in the land, making ends meet under a fractured economic system, whose histories we remember. Those who are described in Jeremiah and Kings simply as the "poorest of the land" (cf. 2 Kgs. 24:14–17; Jer. 52:16). The "histories" that modern readers and interpretive traditions ritualize and canonize as divine revelation are those of small vivisection of an aristocratic elite.

112   *Chapter 6*

Reading the Judean perspective as a colonized one is a positivist reading of the Bible. In fact, reading any biblical text as a portrayal of what Israelite or Judean culture and identity were in their entireties relies on an overly positivistic assumption. Moreover, it presents the Judeans as wholly dependent upon the salvation of Yahweh. From a modern theological vantage point, that tendency does not seem all that threatening. Yet even into the 1st century CE, when Yahweh symbolized the ideal of restoration around which different communities organized, there was no uniform, institutionalized Judaism. To conclude that there was expresses the story of one community *and* relies upon modern theological sentiments about God and God's favor toward Israel. Such sentiments belong to later interpreters not the biblical authors.

What this discussion of the tower has shown so far is that one can read the symbol of the tower and the consolidation of people and language both as attesting to the destruction of culture *and* as cultural inclusion. A common language does not have to be a specific linguistic pattern, such as one might use to distinguish between English and German. The story does not appear to be about the factual existence of one language. Cross-cultural communication is something that humans have done since language existed. Rather, the emphasis on one language appears to be upon people working together and speaking a common language of purpose and ideal in constructing (shared) institutions within a singular society.

One might even read into the account something more mundane, like a mutual recognition of cultural differences and validity. Such needs are pressing even in the modern context, in which there's much to do about differences between insiders and outsiders. One difficulty in reading that way is that from the authorial perspective, Gen. 11 is not a story celebrating diversity. It issues a warning about trying to find one's identity outside of a relationship with Yahweh. Consequently, for every generation of interpreters, the divine plan for the world was cultural division and divine election. Within Judaism, God chose the Jews. For Christians, the members of the Body of Christ are the "universal Church." Difference was a divine plan. And those differences separated the elect community from all others, as the switch to Shem's lineage shows. We had already seen in the story of Noah (cf. chapter 5) another literary cooption of Babylonian myths, that Noah's sons embodied a hierarchy of authority. Japheth was Shem's helper ("may he live in Shem's tents" [Gen. 9:27]), dependent upon his authority, and Ham was Shem's slave.

The story of the tower of Babel tells us, at least from a postcolonial reading, that there is benefit and strength in unity on the level of being able to work together across cultural differences. "[T]he city arises as a sign of . . . self-reliance, the tower as a sign of will."[41] Though compare that idea with Weisner's argument that the story prohibits "oneness" because "a human cannot and must not perceive, or feel, oneness, as that perception harbors the

Inverting the Tower of Babel   113

prospect of leading to the assumption of an adversarial position in relation to G-d."[42] As Gen. 11:3–4 states, "Then each man said to his companion, 'Come! Let's make a mold for bricks and bake bricks thoroughly.' (They only had brick and mortar instead of stone and bitumen.) Then they said, 'Come! Let's build for ourselves a city and tower that reaches the heavens so that we make a name (*shem*) for ourselves, otherwise we will be scattered over the face of the earth.'" I find it interesting that following the statement about making bricks, the author adds a parenthetical statement that the people used bricks instead of stone and tar instead of mortar. Clearly, the author highlights a distinction between his culture, in whatever form it was, and that of the story. The society that uses stone and mortar he is strongly suggesting is more technologically advanced. I can't help but wonder if the author implies that a less developed society is both clearly self-deluded to think it could accomplish such feats and one easily defeated–a perception that would be shared by later colonizing cultures. In fact, in the story Yahweh, the god and symbol of the culture of stone and mortar, does just that.

I also can't help but hear in the people's given rationale the voice of a colonized community. "Let us build, or we will be scattered." What does it mean to build? Is it only about dominating power? Or is it about building a society capable of withstanding the colonizing and imperialist tendencies of others? Is it like the indigenous peoples of Andes and America who told Pope John Paul II to take his Bible back?

> [I]n five centuries it has given us neither love, nor peace, nor justice. Please, take your Bible and give it back to our oppressors, because they need its moral precepts more than we. Since the arrival of Christopher Columbus the Bible was imposed upon America with force: European culture, language, religion, and values. The Bible came to us as part of imposed colonial change. It was the ideological arm of the colonial assault.[43]

Maybe the tower should not just symbolize colonial conquest or imperial conquest within the spheres of interpretation and translation. Maybe from the historical position of the Bible as a *fait accompli* it symbolizes a radical middle finger to the ideological conquest of monotheism, with its singular universalized notion of "God" and "truth" as artifacts of divine revelation interpreted solely within a single particular religious tradition. *Yahweh came down to see . . .* (Gen. 11:5). "We should not apologetically weaken this very ancient way of speaking, when the Yahwist without embarrassment has let it stand. The God of the whole world and of mankind is meant here."[44] Maybe. But maybe the point is that we *should* challenge traditional ways of reading and speaking about God and the Bible.

Chapter 6

WHAT TO DO NOW? LEAVE THE TOWER AND GO WESTWARD TOWARD OR PAST A NEW "ISRAEL"?

What that means for us, then, is that we should be attentive. There may be times for a common language, but there may be others when the dominant narrative, or language, must be rewritten for relational dialogue focused on diversity, where each community can speak its own language, its own words, and express its own identity. I would argue that modern monotheistic traditions are now at a time in which they must relinquish their dominant narratives to diversification. *The very nature of monotheism is colonizing!* They must embrace the narratives of minority communities they have historically ostracized or of which they demanded conformity. As even Pope Francis stated, "Authentic social dialogue involves the ability to respect the other's point of view and to admit that it may include legitimate convictions and concerns. Based on their identity and experience, others have a contribution to make, and it is desirable that they should articulate their positions for the sake of a more fruitful public debate."[45]

Could we say that the scattering and confusing of people was also the creation of grounds for prejudice? That God broke the unity of humanity and created the foundation for prejudice. That is certainly consistent with a god who curses a son and his descendants to be slaves while ignoring the plight of women. It is consistent with a god that destroys an entire world and all living things. More importantly, the same sense of ideological justification of the priority and centeredness of the collective self is also found in justifications for war, slavery, economic oppression, and more. Communities divided. Lines of identity drawn. Suspicions of outsiders as threats to internal stability perpetuated. Against that possibility, I like the idea of reading the story differently. Rather than seeing the desire to make a name for oneself as a negative expression of power, we might see it as an expression of a common identity, the self-articulation of body, in both its collective and individual senses. One that was not threatened by the existence of others. Working together to build a tower need not be interpreted as a contest between humanity and God. It need not be interpreted as symbolizing the negative consequences of human empires while, for Christians, Christ hastens a new empire as a ruler who replaces any preexisting unity with that of one defined by God's exclusive commands and laws.[46] Instead, it may be interpreted as denoting the importance of a relational dialogue, one in which all peoples may cherish their own identities, but one that still allows us to achieve more than what may be otherwise possible. Together.

NOTES

1. For more on the distinction between compact and complex forms of monotheism, see Cataldo, *Breaking Monotheism*, 1–4.

2. Cited in Dochuk, *From Bible Belt to Sunbelt*, location 3367.

3. Cf. Cataldo, *Biblical Terror*, 54–55.

4. Cataldo, 151.

5. Frye, *Words with Power*, 163.

6. Cf. Sugirtharajah, *Voices*; Sugirtharajah, *Still at the Margins*; Rasiah S. Sugirtharajah, ed., *The Postcolonial Bible*, The Bible and Postcolonialism 1 (Sheffield: Sheffield Academic Press, 1998).

7. Cf. State of Israel, "The State of Israel as a Jewish State," Constitution for Israel, 2014, https://knesset.gov.il/constitution/ConstMJewishState.htm, "Jewish and democratic in Israel's basic documents."

8. State of Israel.

9. See also the discussion in Shlomo Sand, *The Invention of the Jewish People*, ebook (London; New York: Verso, 2010).

10. Johnson Kiriaku Kinyua, "A Postcolonial Analysis of Bible Translation and Its Effectiveness in Shaping and Enhancing the Discourse of Colonialism and the Discourse of Resistance: The Gikuyu New Testament—a Case Study," *Black Theology* 11, no. 1 (2013): 58–95, 59. On the oppressions of translation, see also Brian James Baer and Klaus Kaindl, eds., *Queering translation, translating the queer: theory, practice, activism*, Routledge Advances in Translation and Interpreting Studies 28 (New York London: Routledge, Taylor & Francis Group, 2020).

11. Kinyua, "Postcolonial Analysis," 61.

12. Sugirtharajah, *Postcolonial Bible*, 16.

13. Pope Francis, "Fratelli Tutti," Encyclical, Vatican, October 3, 2020, sec. 14, https://www.vatican.va/content/francesco/en/encyclicals/documents/papa-francesco_20201003_enciclica-fratelli-tutti.html.

14. Kinyua, "Postcolonial Analysis," 62–63.

15. For but one example, see also the sermon, S. Lewis Johnson, "Babylon and Lucifer: Isaiah 13:1–14;23," SLJ Institute, December 5, 2013, https://sljinstitute.net/the-prophets/isaiah/isaiah-babylon-and-lucifer/.

16. Neal Blough, "From the Tower of Babel to the Peace of Jesus Christ: Christological, Ecclesiological and Missiological Foundations for Peacemaking," *The Mennonite Quarterly Review* 76, no. 1 (January 2002): 8.

17. See also the discussion in Jonathan Weiser, "Collectivism or Individualism?: The Tower of Babel as a Sociolinguistic Metaphor with Implications for the Theory and Practice of Messianic Redemption," *JES* 57, no. 1 (2022): 147.

18. As stated in Blenkinsopp, *Creation*, 165.

19. As described by Blenkinsopp, 165.

20. Gurminder K. Bhambra et al., "Why Is Mainstream International Relations Blind to Racism?" *Foreign Policy*, July 3, 2020, https://foreignpolicy.com/2020/07/03/why-is-mainstream-international-relations-ir-blind-to-racism-colonialism/.

116   *Chapter 6*

21. See also the discussion of ethnic separation in Late Antiquity and the Middle Age of the Christian Empire in Major, *Undoing Babel*, 11–12.

22. Major, 10.

23. Blough, "From the Tower of Babel to the Peace of Jesus Christ," 8.

24. Blenkinsopp, *Creation*, 164.

25. Matthew Michael, "The Tower of Babel and Yahweh's Heavenly Staircase," *HBT* 39, no. 1 (2017): 31–45. Moreover, his parallel between the Tower of Babel and Jacob's ladder at Bethel is no more than grasping at metaphors showing upward trajectory.

26. Wulfstan, *De Falsis Deis*, 1–15, cited in Major, *Undoing Babel*, 3–4.

27. Major, 8.

28. Major, 6.

29. Weiser, "Collectivism or Individualism," 142.

30. Cf. the discussion of apocalyptic groups in Stephen L. Cook, *Prophecy and Apocalypticism: The Postexilic Social Setting* (Minneapolis: Fortress Press, 1995), 19–54.

31. Blenkinsopp, *Creation*, 168.

32. Weiser, "Collectivism or Individualism," 135.

33. Cf. the discussion in Blenkinsopp, *Creation*, 167.

34. Weiser, "Collectivism or Individualism," 135.

35. See also the discussion in Cataldo, *What the Bible Says about Sex*, 204–5.

36. Blough, "From the Tower of Babel," 10.

37. See also Blough, 11–12.

38. Von Rad, *Genesis*, 150.

39. Cf. F. Joannès and André Lemaire, "Trois Tablettes Cunéiformes à l'onomastique Ouest-Sémitique," *Transeuphratene* 17 (1999): 17–33.

40. On the debate about demographic size, which includes the Babylonian returnees, cf. Charles E. Carter, *The Emergence of Yehud in the Persian Period: A Social and Demographic Study* (Sheffield: Sheffield Academic Press, 1999).

41. To borrow from von Rad, *Genesis*, 148.

42. Weiser, "Collectivism or Individualism," 138.

43. Pablo Richard, "Hermenéutica Bíblica India: Revelación de Dios En Las Religiones Indígenas y En La Biblia (Después de 500 Años de Dominación)," in *Sentido Histórico Del V Centenario (1492–1992)*, ed. Guillermo Meléndez (San José: Cehiladei, 1992), 45–62, cited in Elsa Tamez, "The Bible and Five Hundred Years of Conquest," in *Voices from the Margin: Interpreting the Bible in the Third World*, ed. R.S. Sugirtharajah, 25th Anniv (New York: Orbis Books, 2016), 3–18, 10

44. Von Rad, *Genesis*, 149.

45. Francis, "Fratelli," sec. 203.

46. Contra Blough, "From the Tower of Babel," 16.

Chapter 7

Father Abraham Sentenced a Son, or Two

[T]he ethical expression for what Abraham did is, that he would murder Isaac . . . [1]

Abraham's story illustrates another example of what can become, through interpretation, ideological colonialism. Here, the bodies of the many are defined by the dominating ideology of the few.

I recognize the rather blanket nature of that statement. Explaining it in more detail is part of what I will do in this chapter. To be clear, I am referring to reading and translation strategies that celebrate Abraham as an "exemplar of faith" and the ancestral patriarch of God's chosen people, this last which is embodied in the translating community, the chosen people as the divine elected community, which is also the basis by which it distinguishes itself from the abject "other," who is embodied in the figure of the non-member or outsider. That ideology hides in Abram's name, which means "father of many," or even "exalted father," as Phyllis Trible interprets.[2] His revised name given by God, Abraham, means "father of many peoples" (cf. also Isa. 51:2). Abraham becomes the patriarchal face of the body upon which the desires of God are mapped out, to the fate of the majority of the historical, present, and future worlds. This fosters the belief, as I argue, that social identity and group membership stem from Abrahamic ancestry. And this belief has been universalized and internalized in Judaism, Islam, and Christianity—compare also the theological implications of Matt. 1:1–17, which begins the genealogy of Jesus with none other than Abraham.

Put differently, "Abraham" denotes a dominant ideology anchoring the individual and his loyalty to the collective community, in the same way that the citizen of the state or empire commits to the dominant ideology of the state; and sometimes, that might be represented in the emperor's form. In the

118   *Chapter 7*

naming of Abraham, a singular identity preeminent above all peoples asserts itself. Those in power are those connected to Abraham's son who received the birthright and blessing (cf. the implications of embodied personhood and inheritance in Rom. 4:1–25). Later, building on theological treatises such as Romans and Hebrews, Christians will make this both a doctrine and having the quality of being universal, claiming that God has chosen specifically the descendants of Abraham, from which Christianity emerged, to be the recipients of God's blessing. Not only in terms of identity but expectation, as Jerry Falwell, confident in his epistemology, put it, "I happen to believe that God deals with nations in relation to how those nations deal with Israel. . . . I do believe that America has been the protector of the Jews in these past many years and God has honored us because we have honored Abraham."[3]

In all of this, God is conceptualized as an invisible emperor who, through Jesus according to Christian belief, is hastening a new empire, the citizens of which will be the "elect" community of God. Membership in this community, at least for Christianity, which during different historical epochs held imperial favor, requires commitment to the dominant ideology. Even, or especially, Paul (Rom. 4:11), who more so than Jesus may be considered the "father" of Christian theology, describes Abraham as the father of all who believe. Belief expects commitment to a dominant ideology that defines a body of people over other competing ideologies and concomitant identities.

There has been countless ideological strife wrapped up in beliefs about Abraham. And each monotheistic tradition struggles to lay claim to the figure, and the inheritance wrapped up in the symbolism of him. Marvin Wilson writes, "God's sovereign place in history was to establish his covenant through a man called Abraham."[4] Linking Jesus or Muhammad to Abraham, as Christians and Muslims do, privatizes that covenant to a particular monotheistic community. The faith of Abraham, and God's "blessing" of him, is the face of the faithful body. I recall a time in which I was presenting to a mixed group of Muslims and Christians in Turkey. Part of that presentation was questioning the historical nature of Abraham. It shouldn't be a surprise to say that the Muslims present became angry. One challenged me, demanding to know why Western scholars thought it was OK to question Abraham's legitimacy, but not that of Jesus. The Christians in the group sat back, comfortable with the idea that the reality of Jesus protected the universalizing claims of their own monotheistic ideology. I told him the historical veracity of the biblical presentation of Jesus should also be questioned. Somewhat appeased, my Muslim challenger accepted the fair nature of my academic position. Several of the present Christians, however, rose in protest. Neither group could accept the possibility that the foundation of their beliefs was wrong or prejudiced toward a specific ideology of body and the symbolic lineage that expressed its identity. When the meeting ended, I had earned the respect of a few but the apprehension of others. One Muslim participant, however, told his colleague not to let me talk about the Quran, and several of the Christians avoided conversation with me. Therein lay the problem of monotheism and its elevation by colonial and imperial cultures. It thrives upon marking out and rejecting the body of the inferior or profane "other."

That is why subordination and supersessionism are woven into the ideological sinews of the monotheistic body.[5] So much so that even how Christians, for example, interpret the Bible as God's revelation reflects a belief that it was intended for them and that they alone represent the saved community. The tradition's theological underpinning *depends* upon the ideological subordination, as the primary relationship to revelation and law, of the Old Testament to the New Testament. It reflects the monotheistic binary of power marked on the bodies of insiders and outsiders that bolsters the Christian worldview. To invert or challenge that hierarchy threatens the foundation of what Christians believe Christ to be. Note also Wilson, who writes,

> The two testaments exhibit a strong continuity, but also a discontinuity. Many Old Testament institutions and themes are radically reinterpreted in the New Testament, often in ways—despite the foreshadowing—that the majority in New Testament times were unable to discern. In addition, the embodiment of the Torah in Jesus created a major tension. Jesus subordinated many of the central symbols of Judaism to himself, and the New Testament writers continued that subordination.[6]

Those subordinated symbols are the basis for the Christian theology of "law," by which I mean the divine law built upon the commands of the Old Testament that are replaced or revised in the "fuller revelation" of Jesus, which also reinforces a network of power coalescing in Jesus, the new (imperial) ruler. Clearly, the attempt by the community to coopt dominant symbols of another community was met with resistance. Historically, this was a later development than Jesus, who practiced Judaism, but was projected back into history later by the later, increasingly anti-Semitic or supersessionist Christian community. Christ's elevation as a dominant symbol and figure was not, however, a simple process. "Opposition to Christianity first arose not against Jesus' followers but against Jesus himself."[7] It began not with a universalizing theology about Jesus, or the "body of Christ." It began with the belief that Jesus was trying to replace Rome and liberate Judaea. He was, but he failed in that regard. That is why his followers, authors of the Gospels and later Christians, who owe a greater debt to Paul than Jesus, transformed that victory into a spiritual one. Undeterred by any perceived failure to overthrow the Roman Empire, they and their spiritual descendants argue Jesus is still working toward victory in the spiritual world, which remains

120   *Chapter 7*

unseen by human eyes. Not only that, but despite the continued existence of world empires, those empires would inevitably fall before the might of an unseen empire internalized in the bodies of the "righteous" community as the body of Christ. Passages instilling anticipation in a historical audience (cf. Mark 13:32; Matt. 24:35–37; John 14:2–4) took on more abstracted spiritual natures. For example, Matt. 3:9 confidently proclaims, "God is able from these stones to raise up children to Abraham," a statement that was attributed to John the Baptist, directed at the Pharisees and Sadducees, and may have been a reference to the stones of the Jerusalem temple or even the architecture of the city, which would be connected to the collective aspiration for the restoration of Judah/Israel. The core of the kingdom would come from God, not from the communal shaping of the Pharisees and Sadducees, who were given cultural authority at various points by the Greeks and Romans.[8]

Abstracted and universalized, because the empire of God is unseen, believers are expected to live in a constant state of anticipation even millennia after the initial claims were made. The fragility of that and the anxieties about it that Christians suppress beneath evangelism and loving one's neighbor, however, is part of the reason Christianity leans so heavily on an insider-outsider binary. The only physical confirmation of the "truth" of God's promised rule is the collective body of those who believe it to be forthcoming. Disappointment, frustration, and fear it may not happen are projected upon the outsider, the sinner. More directly, they are projected upon Satan, who must in this case become evil incarnate, and who has become the ultimate antithesis to God, where both represent what the community desires most and its opposite. This desire enjoys a direct connection to how power is understood. God, the symbol of what Christians value and desire most, represents ultimate power. Satan, while powerful when God doesn't act directly, represents the ultimate antithesis of that monotheistic ideology upon which his identity ultimately depends. "All incarnations of the Devil," write Wray and Moby, "the supreme opponent of God in the monotheistic religions . . . can be traced to a character in the Bible and to stories and lore in early Jewish and Christian writings."[9]

This binary is at the heart of Christian activity, especially evangelism, which emphasizes conversion to an ideological commitment to God as the ultimate power, even if the exercise of that power is long in coming. Michel Foucault correctly noted that there is a network of power, in which those in power create binary structures to secure their own claims to it.[10] But that power can be mediated and expressed in a variety of ways and has different influences. Religion (monotheism) reduces any awareness of that network into the simplified structure of good-evil, god-human, saved-profane, as the criteria by which God's authority is known, translated, and the distinction between those in power and the powerless reinforced. The binary that we feel but do not always articulate is the foundation by which control and authority are imposed over us: those who can direct and benefit from that power and those who cannot. In Christianity, the figure of Jesus is doggedly guarded because he symbolizes the access to membership into a community of power over the "other" who must remain perpetually an outsider. That stranglehold over power is at the heart of historical imperialism, colonialism, and current ideological colonialisms in western, Christians countries. The relevance of this discussion to this point should be clear: it emphasizes the need to expose the ideological assumptions behind dominant interpretations and translations that stand as vanguards to dominant conventions, traditions, identities, and values. That is the very essentialist assumption that postcolonialism, like queer theory, ideological criticism, newer feminisms, and more challenge.[11]

Even without actively trying to promote those senses of colonialism, dominant traditions of biblical interpretation preserve notions of power and the colonizing experience, doing so by imposing order upon a foreign territory and culture and "civilizing" its people under the excuse one is saving them from evil and from themselves. This ideological assumption lays behind theologies and doctrines rooted in the Bible and universalized for all people. Who, for instance, are the beneficiaries of Abraham and the so-called Abrahamic Covenant (cf. Gen. 12:1–9; 15:1–20; 17:1–27)? How we answer that question, as well as how we respond to the moral ambiguity that permeates the biblical texts, depends upon the community to which we belong. Postcolonialism demands that we subvert or challenge the traditional interpretations that have prioritized the identities and cultures of one community over others, and that the binary of power and authority weighted toward the dominating community be dismantled.

Both Christians and Jews claim that the biblical account of Abraham and his descendants, especially, inaugurate the unfolding of God's plan for creation, which should separate them from other peoples and communities, thereby identifying them as the collective body within which the "truth" of God was revealed–a truth that is synonymous with power.[12] The community is called to embody that plan by becoming its manifestation and image of what the plan should attain. Anything outside of that community represents the plan's antithesis. For instance, "While the Jerusalem elite, who presumed on their lineage from Abraham, Isaac, and Jacob, find themselves cast out, the restored people from east and west, north and south, will gather in the banquet of the kingdom of God (Q/Lk 13:28–29), which is now happening as the renewal of the people in its ideal twelve tribes. Thus, in a series of speeches, a presentation very different from the sequence of episodes narrated in Mark but one that has many overlaps with it in both subjects and issues, Q presents a very similar and parallel portrayal of Jesus as prophet pursuing the renewal of Israel in opposition to the rulers."[13]

122   *Chapter 7*

Such has frequently been the historical justification for imperialism and colonialism. Note, for comparison, Alexander Crummell's assessment of "Africa's" need for western missionaries:

> Africa cannot be redeemed by her own unaided energy and agency. . . . . The superior and more enlightened peoples are always the founders of a new faith, or the pioneers of a fresh civilization, in rude and pagan countries. . . . Nothing can be more glorious than the heroic, almost god-like self-sacrifice of [West Africa's] missionaries, for nigh forty years, to introduce Christianity among the natives; nothing, on the other hand, more discouraging than the small results which at first followed their efforts. But by-and-by, one native then another, and another was raised up, fitted and prepared to be preachers of the Gospel. The Christian faith had been engrafted upon the native stock. It swelled with the inspirations of their breath; it coursed along the channels of their veins. Then the truth began to spread; it had lodged itself in a new race and began to assert its authority in a new land. The new soil as genial; and the Divine principle, although transplanted, put forth all its original vitality.[14]

Crummell was an African-American Episcopalian priest, missionary, and scholar. Such an impact was the physical and ideological colonialism of white Christianity in the United States that despite advocating for the abolition of slavery and his promotion of African-American culture, he believed in the colonialist ideology that Africa (presumably the entire continent) needed "saved" by a superior, and presumably Christian, civilization. Add that to the observation of Musa Dube, "[M]issionaries of colonial times did not have to regard themselves openly or consciously as advancing the rule of their countries to be part of the colonizing squad, although many did. Missionaries of colonial times were inevitably colonizing agents. That is, we agree that missionaries were people who 'set out to save Africa [and other continents]: to make people the subjects of a worldwide Christian commonwealth.'"[15] And in that, they established new frontiers of European consciousness.

Such is the power in the claim (and privatization) of divine revelation as *the* source of truth that its purveyors often ignore or are willfully silent about the subjective cultural ideologies they are promoting. Did Abraham exist solely for the benefit of Judaism and Christianity by extension? Both religious traditions make that very claim. "When Yahweh brings Abraham's descendants into the land of others, he not only dispossesses them, but he also kills them or allows the Israelites to kill them. Yahweh carries out this removal systematically and slowly, in a sadistic manner—almost as a sport, allowing the Israelites to give birth and increase in number to be able to control the land resources. Yahweh is categorical about Israel living an exclusive life on the lands of the others."[16] What an act of interpretive cooption that religious traditions have turned what was more likely a political, or *nationalist*, text into

Father Abraham Sentenced a Son, or Two 123

one that justifies their own existences as universal and absolute! Moreover, those assumptions can be seen in *how* the stories about Abraham are told. They established a hierarchy of meaning that faithful interpreters would later internalize. Such stories center on Abraham because he is the symbolic representative of what the biblical author and the interpreting community want, land and authority over it. In that regard, Benjamin Ziemer's questions call the telling and preserving of Abraham's stories into account (translating the quote): "Where is Lot, when Abram and Sarai are in Egypt? Where is Sarah, when Abraham and Isaac go to the land of Moriah? The answer in each case is: they have no contribution to the stories."[17] Without utility for the satisfaction of a desire for land and authority, their bodies are abandoned.

Let us not forget there were people already in the land that was promised to Abraham (cf. Gen. 15:1–21 for a description of the Abrahamic covenant). The Christian imperative to "make disciples of the world" (cf. Matt. 28:19), which can be read either as conversion or as something more political along the lines of creating imperial citizens, together with the condemnable nature of profanity and sin, provides a justification for destructive and even genocidal actions. "The Great Commission (Matt. 28:18–20) is a command incumbent upon the entire church. It includes both a responsibility . . . and a method."[18] For instance, "Regarding the cities of these peoples which Yahweh your god gave you as property (or inheritance), don't let anything remain breathing. You must completely exterminate them—the Hittites, Amorites, Canaanites, Perizzites, Hivites, and the Jebusites—according to the command of Yahweh *your* god. Do this so that they do not teach you to do any of their abominations, which they do for their gods, leading you to sin against Yahweh your god" (Deut. 20:16–18). How close is that command in Deuteronomy, which instructs the Hebrews on how to gain control over the land as part of the Abrahamic Covenant, with Crummell's position on mission work in West Africa! Christianity, perhaps more so than any other monotheism, has linked divine land promise and evangelism, which is unabashedly posed as "saving" a "degenerate" culture and people. But instead of that promise being limited to a specific geographic space, it is linked to wherever the community and its representatives reside. For example, Christians in the United States do not have to go to any land. They believe themselves called to create a moral society wherever they live. They wait patiently for the establishment of the permanent authority and the new paradisal land fashioned by God, specifically for them and over which they will exercise authority along with Christ.

It is all too easy to forget that genocide and colonialism have been justified with interpretations of a divine imperative, but given only to an "elect" community, that permeates the biblical texts. God's community is called to fight against evil, which roots itself in peoples and cultures that are not Christian or who are, in a more general term, "outsiders."

124   *Chapter 7*

If we ever took some time to consider the ramifications of passages such as that from Deuteronomy (above), how can we avoid seeing it as anti-humanitarian colonialism? Even Christian theology, which is generally thought to emphasize "love," tends toward that idea in its reframing of divine commandments in the Old Testament. God's new plan, symbolized in Jesus, leads toward empire building. But because that empire needs members, there is no irredeemable sin. What is it that 1 John 1:9 claims? That if we confess our sins, God will forgive our sins and cleanse us from *all* unrighteousness. As one recent Christian website promised, "The Christian life is marked by the pursuit of righteousness, and yet for our failings there is still forgiveness—a forgiveness grounded in Christ's redemptive work."[19] The worst of humanity could be redeemed, theoretically, if he or she or they converted, and confessed their sins, committing themselves to upholding the dominant traditions, values, and identity of the community of members. *Well, maybe not "they." Christianity is still struggling to maintain the historical gendered binary. Such that many believe one cannot be "practicing" anything along the LGBTQIA spectrum and be a Christian.* And yet, there *is* irredeemable sin by default. None of the inhabitants destroyed by God and God's followers in the Bible are clearly ever given a chance to convert, such as in the flood, Sodom, Gomorrah, Jericho, and so on. And yet, the justification that they were wiped out *because* of their sins is a commonly held one. And let's be honest, the genocide and ethnocide included pregnant women (*divine abortion!*), toddlers, babies, and more who could not be ascribed any sin based on the biblical author's understanding of the concept. With the overwhelming weight of divine atrociousness and "nationalist" extreme, the line between irredeemable and redeemable sin is little more than that which reinforces the dominant expectations and boundaries of the group. And if the Christian adage that "God is love" is true, then that means that God's love, which saves or judges, also reflects the dominant expectations, boundaries, and values of the believing community. *God's love will save you if you are part of God's community and kill you if you are not.*

How we interpret the text and justify its violence, oppressions, inequalities, and prejudices as expressions of divine morality, love, and judgment says something about the traditions of interpretation which have become dominant. As Green, who is frightened of critical thought as a challenge to belief, put it, "Belief in God is a way of protecting conscience from reason's own assaults."[20] But what is conscience among the ignorant if not the instinctual whim and motivation to isolate and protect the group? That is why Dube argued we must focus on what perspective or position a text advances.[21] For instance, missionaries from a colonial culture are frequently either woefully ignorant or belligerently unmoved by how routinely a colonial agenda gets wrapped up in spreading the "good news." And if we are not attentive to that,

Father Abraham Sentenced a Son, or Two 125

then our interpretations will only aggrandize those positions, justifying them within our own cultural contexts and our own values.

The story of Abraham, so foundational to the ideologies that I have been describing, begins with an implied rejection of Babylonian culture as inferior. While portions of Genesis may have existed before the 6th century BCE, scholars generally accept that if it was heavily redacted by scribes who had been taken to Babylonia by the Babylonian empire. Abraham's story details what many Judeans in Babylonia would have wanted: the reclamation of the land along with a re-instituted kingdom, both of which are symbolized in the figure of Yahweh. Consequently, one can also see a correlation to the story of Deut. 20:16–18, which calls for the people in the land, the "Canaanites," to be wiped out before Israel can be established. Upon the altar of national ideal is sacrificed the monstrous body of the "other," reinforcing the boundaries between insider and outsider.

According to his story, Abraham was called out of Ur of Chaldees because of his righteousness. There is a Jewish legend that describes Abraham having an argument with his father about idols. The implication was that Ur was polytheistic and that Abraham's father was an idol maker. But have an argument they did and in a fit of youthful outburst, Abraham broke the idols that his father had made. Like many youths, of course, he did this away from the seeing gaze of his father. When his father returned and saw the broken idols he asked, "What have you done?! I made those!" Abraham responded, "precisely" (*Ber. Rab.* 38:13, paraphrased). Apparently, even Abraham's outbursts, to the joy of Jews and Christians alike, were made in defense of monotheistic faith. Such is the righteousness and faith attributed to Abraham that he is identified in Jewish tradition as the first prophet, "who," according to Stephen Spector, "has the power to save lives with his prayers." And further, "He is also the first human in the Bible to show compassion for others, the first to call for justice for the innocent, and the first to have the courage and diplomatic skill to bargain with God."[22] I cannot help but wonder, if all that is true, then in what way does, *should*, rather, that change how we read the story of Noah, who by implication did not show compassion for anyone outside his family (see again chapter 5) and let the world drown? Or Lot who cared nothing for the innocent in Sodom and Gomorrah or even about his own daughters (which I will discuss further in chapter 8)? What about Hagar and Ishmael?

The Jewish addition to the Genesis story presents an argument that Babylonian society was inferior, a collective body of uncivilized worshipers of stone and clay (like Crummell's Africa?). Abraham's accusation of idolatry, but really the author's in the mouth of Abraham, should be read in that vein. The Genesis account itself establishes a national narrative, something akin to the doctrine of Manifest Destiny in the United States. "Abraham crossed the land as far as Shechem, to the terebinth Moreh." If we follow the literary

126   *Chapter 7*

chronology, the Canaanites were still in the land; yet "Yahweh appeared to Abram and said, 'I will give this land to your seed.' So he [Abram] built an altar there [near the terebinth?] because Yahweh had appeared to him" (Gen. 12:6–7). Shechem was one of the oldest Canaanite cities, possibly mentioned by Pharaoh Sesostris/Senusret (1887–1849 BCE).[23] It was also the location of a significant cultic center. That Yahweh gave the land to Abraham's descendants implies that a "new flag" had been planted in "conquered" territory and that the Canaanites living there were rejected from the community of Yahweh (see Deut. 7:1–3). *Like the East India Company before Colonial Britain?*

At its heart, that is a nationalist statement. In practicality, Yahweh was the god of a kingdom, not the universal God that Judaism and Christianity have pushed. He went into the domain of a different god, or gods, to retrieve Abraham and lead him to yet a different geopolitical domain and promised that to him. (*Imperialism, anyone?*) We cannot dismiss Thomas Thompson's claim that there was never an ethnically distinct Canaanite population whom the Israelites displaced. Nor was there ever a true united monarchy centered in Jerusalem. The idea of the united monarchy, which is the assumption of the Abrahamic covenant, suggested in the biblical texts, was rooted in aspiration, not fact.[24] If this sounds eerily similar to what biblical texts such as the prophets and Ezra-Nehemiah expressed, that Yahweh would call out the people and establish a kingdom, or even promises of deliverance made by Jesus in the New Testament (cf. John 14:1–13; Revelation, the latter on Jesus's behalf), it should. That is why Mark Throntveit wrote, "It serves the practical purpose of assuring the restoration community that they had not arrived upon the scene from out of the blue but were in fact solidly established upon their ancestral roots as emphasized by their family pedigrees and upon their ancestral home as emphasized by their territorial situation. *They were thus not cut off from the ancient promise of land and posterity made to Abraham (Gen. 12:1–3), but rather they were the raw material from which God would now bring forth further fulfillments of that glorious promise.*"[25] There is implied a rejection of Babylonian society in favor of an "Israelite" identity, which will be realized through the lineage of Abraham. The body of the "other" exists as a reminder: unable to translate divine will within its own culture and language, its grotesque body reflects the alternative in the author's assumed binary between insider and outsider that later monotheism would adopt as the foundational division of divine order. Babylonian policy supported the restoration of peoples and their cultural practices, so long as they didn't threaten imperial stability.[26] What the biblical texts portray of the Babylonian Empire, however, is a self-absorbed diabolical power bent on world domination. One should avoid the temptation to read it as objective historiography, which is a more modern expectation about historiography.[27] While the Babylonian Empire certainly sought to remake the world in its own image, as empires are wont to do, it did so by incorporating different advisors that reflected different cultural environments in which the empire had dominion. The story of Abraham, however, is rooted in a rejection of Babylonian culture as a body symbolizing the antithesis of Yahweh's power. Dan. 3:1–31 (4:1 ET) portrays that idea fantastically with its description of a statue of Nebuchadnezzar piercing the heavens at ninety feet that all peoples were expected to pay homage to. Of course, three Judean men refused and were thrown into a fiery furnace, only to emerge miraculously unharmed. For the biblical author, the context of political power is meted out in the divine arena.

That sets the stage for the wandering patriarch finding the land of Syria-Palestine, with Yahweh's promise that the land would be given to his descendants. *Can we forget Abraham placed his own son on an altar to burn him (cf. Gen. 22:6–18)? Is there a connection here to the fiery furnace?* While the land was promised to his descendants, it would not be given to the descendants of Ishmael, Abraham's firstborn son. It would be given to Isaac, the father of Jacob, whose sons symbolized the twelve tribes of Israel. After all, "God chose the Hebrew patriarch Abraham. His election and the election of the land come together."[28] These are the real indigenous to Palestine, the biblical author claims, one that will be echoed by generations of later Jews and Christians. Implied in this promise to Abraham is a rejection of the land's inhabitants as outsiders.[29] The story is like the colonial conquest of Native Americans–a story which would also factor in the nationalist narrative that gave power to American civil religion.[30] How often was heard justification for land conquest that the Native Americans were savages and did not understand the legality of private property? Does not the Bible have a similar view of the Canaanites?[31]

During his sojourn, Abraham established altars and memorials throughout the land that Yahweh promised him. Like a blend of colonialism and Western missionary activity, which I described previously, this act was like planting a national flag. Abraham's actions symbolized the confirmation of Yahweh's presence in the land—a presence in contrast to the peoples already there. That must be read assuming Yahweh as the god of Israel. In other words, Abraham's story was mapping out a vision for (a re-instituted) Israel. This understanding of the story should not surprise us. Abraham's is the story of *Israel's* patriarch. It is the "national" narrative of how the Israelites and Judeans should have dominion over land. Such stories can be found in numerous cultures. As I have already alluded to previously, the United States, for example, tells the story of an oppressed people finding a "new" land and, by the grace of God, establishing themselves as a functioning nation. Forgotten, however, and it is here postcolonialism shouts in protest, are the stories of those already in the land, as well as the slaves whose labor did much to carve

128   *Chapter 7*

out the economic base upon which a national economic and political infrastructure could be raised.

But like the ultimate sacrifice narrative, the story of the nation demanded a test of faith. After driving Ishmael out of his home (cf. Gen. 21:14–16), Abraham was called to sacrifice his remaining son, Isaac (Gen. 22:9–14). It is worth noting that Yahweh's encounters with Abraham isolate him (Abraham) as subject, which ushers him into a function of privileged status above the other members of his own family.[32] Not only that, but as Trible notes, "By the command of God, a single family has become two families, one living with the father, and the other, apart from him. The outcome settles the question of inheritance to favor Isaac over Ishmael, but it does not come to terms with the inequities between them. The putative unity of family and faith, located in the man Abraham, spawns disunity and disparity between his two wives and their respective children."[33] To this day, Muslims, Jews, and Christians see conflict between each other, in part, based on this traditional heritage. Where Jews, and by extension Christians, see themselves as the beneficiaries of God's promise through Isaac, Muslims see themselves as the beneficiaries of God's promise through Ishmael. Jewish and Christian interpretation sees Ishmael as an intersection between citizen and foreigner, an impurity that would replicate prohibitions on marriages with foreign women, which led to "unfaithfulness" to Yahweh (cf. Ezra 10:2). Such unfaithfulness was seen by many biblical authors as the reason that the kingdoms of Israel and Judah were defeated by the empires.

But faithfulness should not be read as the romanticized theological conviction for a universal deity upon which modern religions depend. It should be read more as a conviction to the ideals of the nation symbolized in the deity. Scholars generally accept that deities symbolize ideals, and hopes, of cultures throughout the ancient Near East. However, too many hold Israel and Judah to a different standard, treating the kingdoms as uniformly monotheistic and *dedicated* to God, or an early concept of the monotheistic deity. It's far time that theological shackles be shed in cultural nuances of language and the idealization of some direct connection between historical Israelites and modern Israel. Instead, scholars must treat ancient Israel's concept of Yahweh similar to the ways Marduk, for example, is interpreted.

That is also why the binding of Isaac, which is the story of Abraham's near sacrifice of Isaac, should be read as a story *not* of an individual's faith, but as a threat to the future of Israel. It holds nationalist sentiments. Von Rad notes that "when Israel read and related this story in later times it could only see itself represented by Isaac, i.e., laid on Yahweh's altar, given back to him, then given life again by him alone. That is to say, it could base its existence in history not on its own legal titles as other nations did, but only on the will of him who in the freedom of his will in history permitted Isaac to

Father Abraham Sentenced a Son, or Two   129

live."[34] Abraham binds his son after leading him to the place of sacrifice and puts him on the altar. It's hard to miss the parallel to the displaced Judeans led by the Babylonian military to a place of sacrifice and trial before they were delivered. It is similar to the story of Shadrach, Meshach, and Abednego in the fiery furnace (Dan. 3:22–27). They entered the flames, which are both of sacrifice and judgment, and left unscathed. Isaac is bound but delivered in the moment before death. Likewise, the people, according to the biblical author, will be delivered and restored.

There is a moment in the story where Isaac asks his father about the lack of a sacrificial animal. Abraham knowing he was going to sacrifice his son to Yahweh (the ultimate sacrifice I discussed earlier?) lied to his son. He told him not to worry about it and that God would provide. Modern interpreters motivated by theological conviction frequently claim that Abraham acted in faith believing that God would provide an alternative sacrifice, connecting him with Noah and Enoch as "exemplars of moral rectitude."[35] And also,

> Abraham, the highly renowned patriarch, who had not his equal in honor, as Sirach writes, believed God and trusted upon his word with the whole heart, and thus manifested obedience and power as the result of his faith. . . . Faithful readers, observe, if we had a firm faith and a sure confidence, like this godly man, and dare trust from the heart upon the living God, O how little should we trouble ourselves with such heathenish cares, concerning dwelling, eating, drinking, and clothing, for we well know, that Christ, God's own Son, has promised that if we seek the kingdom of heaven, and his righteousness, and turn our hearts to some honest labor, he will not forsake us to all eternity, but will supply all our necessities, for he cares for us. (*Abraham*)

But there's no indication that Abraham wasn't lying to his son because he was too afraid to be honest. Moreover, the story loses its power even for the theologically convicted if Abraham did not think he *would* have to sacrifice his son. Some Christian theological interpretations claim that Abraham's drama foreshadowed the crucifixion. Kierkegaard maintains that any moral justification of Abraham's actions expects a religious teleological suspension of the ethical for the sake of God's will.[36] Interpretation is full of the monotheistic assumption that human individuals are called to a universal morality that can be suspended for the sake of God's will. What would otherwise be deemed "evil" breaks down the barriers to God's plan. It is a clever bit of theological interpretation, but it does not fit the historical text of Genesis. Otherwise, we must maintain that the authors of the biblical text wrote with some sense of Jesus, and that God was directing the hand of the authors to preface the coming of Jesus.

130   *Chapter 7*

Of note, there is some Jewish speculation that Isaac died and was resurrected, which some scholars consider to have been influenced by Christian speculation (cf. Heb. 11:17–19).[37] If we accept the story as literal historiography, which many who hold Abraham as an exemplar of faith and a foreshadowing of God's plan through Jesus do (compare Heb. 11:8–19), we must somehow explain the child abuse God legitimates; that is, we not only have to come to terms with Isaac's condoned abuse but also the larger symbolic ramifications of nation-building: that according to the Bible God justified genocide (cf. Gen. 6:11–7:24), infanticide (cf. Ps. 137:9), ethnocide (cf. Deut. 20:13), the annihilation of little children, and more for the sake of a single kingdom. Hardly is there ever any discussion by interpreters (and none by the biblical author) of Isaac's internal disposition or fortitude. Isaac is not the focus of the account. His body functions as a confirmation of "nationalist" sentiment. Nor is there any discussion of how the act could do not but change the father-son relationship. I can only imagine what the authorities would do to me if I hogtied my son, threw him atop a bundle of wood, and held a knife to his throat to bleed him. *"You'll be fine, son. I'm doing this to show my faith in God, like Abraham."* The process of sacrificing an animal was to bind the legs, put it on the altar, and slit its throat so the blood would pour out the severed jugular vein. Once the animal was dead, it was burned. In a context in which sacrifices were relatively normal, the son, Isaac, would have known that, so would the author's intended audience. *How can we not give Isaac, or what he symbolizes in the story—the confined and suppressed body underneath the expectations of Abraham and Yahweh as authoritative "others"—the freedom to say, "Fuck you both! I want to tell my story!"* Rabbinic sources try to get around this moral tension of an abusive father by interpreting Isaac to be in his 30s, which would make it unlikely that Abraham could overwhelm his son, forcing him onto the altar. They see Isaac as complicit in the act, freeing Abraham from moral responsibility, in theory.[38] *Maybe.*

But God called out at the last minute, my hypothetical protester will say. Yes, and according to the story, it happened at the moment Abraham was about to slice his son's throat. At that point, it would have been better for the father-son relationship to complete the act. Because now, the son must grow up with the image of his father holding a knife to his throat and conviction in his eyes. No amount of theological justification eases that inevitable psychological trauma. After all, for the story to work on a theological level, *Abraham must believe he had to kill his son.* When God was satisfied with Abraham's "faith," God (actually, Yahweh's messenger [Gen. 22:11]; Yahweh couldn't be bothered to participate) called out in a booming voice, "Stop! Don't sacrifice your son. I am providing an animal." And many interpreters, both Jewish and Christian, celebrate this moment as a testament of faith (see also Rom. 4:2–3). But I argue Abraham and Isaac should be read as functions and not historical personages. In building altars in Canaan, Abraham made a political claim over the territory for Yahweh. His commitment to the national ideal must exceed even the life of his son—like parents who see their sons sacrificed in wars fought on behalf of their country. Isaac symbolizes the perceived dependence upon that ideal—like a colonized body that must accept what the authoritative "other" defines about that body's essence. That ideal is embodied in the symbol of Yahweh as the national god of Israel (in contrast to his other iterations as a more localized deity).[39]

While Isaac is saved, and the lineage of Israel and Judah preserved, we should remember that Ishmael and his mother were abandoned in the wilderness. For the author, it could be justified. Their lineage was that of the Egyptians, and there would be constant strife and between Egypt and Israel. That strife was also the backdrop to the story of Joseph, who was taken into Egypt as a slave (see chapter 11). Through the machinations of Yahweh, the god of Israel manipulating Egyptian politics, Joseph would become second-in-command of Egypt and the intellectual power by which Egypt was saved. It was a temporary staging, Exod. 1:8–10 tells its readers, because there came a time in which a pharaoh in power did not know "what Joseph had done for Egypt." To control the growing size of the Hebrews, he oppressed them with slave labor. They worked as slaves until Moses led them out of Egypt after he and Aaron competed on behalf of Yahweh with Egypt's political and religious authorities. But lest we assume that Yahweh's liberation of the Hebrews means the deity hated slavery, hear the words of 19th century pro-slavery apologist John Henry Hopkins, the eighth presiding bishop of the Episcopal Church in the United States: "For Hopkins, Abraham's ownership of slaves, and the command to the 'fugitive' Hagar, is 'proof that slavery was sanctioned by the Deity,' and, he adds: 'If the philanthropists of our age, who profess to believe the Bible, had been willing to take the counsel of that angel for their guide, it would have preserved the peace and welfare of the Union.'"[40]

Here, we must read the story as a subversion of traditional interpretations, as postcolonialism expects, and read it from its margins, or silences. What would Isaac's response have been to his father? The peripheral body to the power center oppressing it? What would Ishmael's response have been to his father? By modern conventions, Abraham is abusive (*symbolic of colonial power?*) if we assess him based on how he treats *both* of his sons. And yet believers celebrate him as an archetype of faith and as a confirmation of their own connection to divine authority and blessing. Christian children no older than Isaac would have been, for example, sing about how loving and bountiful Abraham is (*Father Abraham / had many sons . . . I am one of them / and so are you*).

132   *Chapter 7*

Let's also not forget that he pimps his wife to the kings of Egypt and Gerar to gain more material wealth and to save himself (cf. Gen. 12:10–13:2; 20:1–16).[41] Her body becomes the vehicle not only for Abraham's self-preservation but also his gaining of material riches (cf. Gen. 12:16; 20:14–16). In neither account is Sarah's wellbeing taken into consideration. In *both* accounts, the authority of Abraham and his god are asserted not only through the taking of material resources but through asserted authority over other life. In Egypt, after pharaoh traded Abraham for Sarah, the pharaoh and his household were struck with plagues. In Gerar, Abimelech and his household were made barren and threatened with death. He returned Sarah to Abraham along with an "offering" of riches. Neither the pharaoh nor Abimelech were inhospitable in their actions. In fact, both kings ask something along the lines of "why did you lie to me?" Yet to fit the author's agenda, their bodies and households become the canvases upon which the superiority of Abraham and his god are written. Even Isaac, the chosen son of Abraham, profits from Abimelech's city. When he settled in Gerar, he told the men of the city that Rebekah was his sister so that his life would be spared (cf. Gen. 26:7). It worked. Until, that is, Isaac had lived in Gerar for a "long time," Abimelech happened to look out a window and see him fondling Rebekah (Gen. 26:8). Such was the nature of the fondling that Abimelech was immediately convinced Rebekah was Isaac's wife and not his sister. *Maybe he forgot about the amorous siblings Abraham and Sarah?* As readers, we can only assume an answer to that question. What we can conclude, however, is that like Abraham, Isaac profits from all this (cf. Gen. 26:10–14).

Defenses made of Abraham's ethics by modern readers, that Sarah really was his sister, and so he wasn't really a liar, are not convincing. Yes, according to Gen. 20:12 (see also 12:13; 20:2), Sarah was Abraham's half-sister. She was also his wife, and his motivation was clearly to deceive the kings for his own benefit, using Sarah's body as a tool in that deception. Moreover, was it acceptable to marry one's half-sister? Not according to Lev. 18:9: "You shall not expose the pudenda of your sister, the daughter of your father or the daughter of your mother, whether born in the household or outside it. Such sexual activity is improper." Would not Sarah be included in that (compare again Gen. 20:12, "she is my father's daughter")? My hypothetical protestor would likely respond that Abraham lived before the law was revealed. Let me entertain the whole fragile assumption about historical objectivity in that statement for but a moment: OK, but the law was revealed by Yahweh, and Yahweh was directing Abraham (cf. Gen. 12:1). Did Yahweh not know the law that the divine would later reveal? Such that the divine would excuse human behavior if the people didn't know any better? What, then, about those annihilated in the flood due to their ignorance of divine law and commandments? Why were they not given a free pass? We should also not overlook

Father Abraham Sentenced a Son, or Two 133

the fact that Abraham didn't know, and doesn't seem to care, if either king slept with Sarah, putting his lineage in jeopardy especially if they were that excited to take her. *Oh, how blind theology is toward the sins of its heroes!*

Spector defends the heritage of Abraham by saying that Abraham was subject to "same frailties as other human beings" and that he was responding to an overwhelming sense of dread.[42] That that act was intentional is clear from Abraham's referral to Sarah as his sister rather than his wife (cf. Gen. 20:2). But her body, like a colonized territory to its colonizer, is Abraham's to use. Through his manipulation of it, his wealth and stature are increased. Perhaps not unlike the bodies of slaves who made fatter the purses of some Christian landowners in the United States.

To read this from a postcolonial perspective is to read it from the perspectives of the sons and the women. Because in that, we might see some similar occurrences or ways in which colonized or marginalized peoples suffer under cultures in colonial or imperial positions. Could it even be said that in gross imperial fashion, God raped a woman (Mary) and sacrificed her son (Jesus)? To read for the perspective of women, children, slaves, and other marginalized bodies means one recognizes they have been mistreated for the benefit of those in power, and have suffered without recourse to retribution. Even that God justified their suffering. Recall the claim of ex-slave Charlie Aarons, who said that God had deemed slavery a necessary step in the evolution of humanity, but which was ultimately remedied through the evangelical wake of European and American Christians.[43] Such a claim assumes that the marginalized find their self-worth in the success of an authoritative "other." It adopts a colonizer's mindset *par excellence* and frames the marginalized voice as a testament to the profound and pervasive impact of ideological colonization.

Read simply as a straightforward narrative, the story of Abraham presents a challenge in identifying a postcolonial position. Given its emphasis upon establishing a claim over land already occupied, it does not offer a strong or direct critique of colonial or imperial power. Its dismissal of Babylonia is simply an attempt to aggrandize itself. Its strength as a postcolonial story comes from the margins, where individuals are walked over by Abraham and Yahweh, and whose trampled bodies lay the groundwork for the economic and political prosperity of two male figures and symbols. And in that sense, this story is still very much about the preservation of the aristocracy and its position of authority. Recognizing that can help us see where it cannot acknowledge the existence of other people or at least give them space to tell their own stories. After all, how would Isaac, Ishmael, Hagar, and even Sarah tell their own stories? Or even the leaders of other people who sought love and companionship but who were terrorized by Yahweh because of Abraham's deceit and not any sinful act of their own (cf. again Gen. 12:10–13:2; 20:1–16)?

NOTES

1. Kierkegaard 1947, 61; taken from Ronald M Green, "Abraham, Isaac, and the Jewish Tradition: An Ethical Reappraisal," *Journal of Religious Ethics* 10, no. 1 (1982): 2.

2. Phyllis Trible, "Ominous Beginnings for a Promise of Blessing," in *Hagar, Sarah, and Their Children: Jewish, Christian, and Muslim Perspectives*, ed. Phyllis Trible and Letty M. Russell, Kindle (Louisville: Westminster John Knox Press, 2006), 33–70, location 1086.

3. Jerry Falwell, "Speech Given to the 'Strengthening Families' Seminar of the Christian Life Commission Conference" (Falwell Archives: FAL 4: Speeches and Sermons (FAL 4:1–3 Box 1), April 1982).

4. Wilson, *Our Father Abraham*, 3.

5. For more on the definition of "monotheistic body" see Cataldo, *Breaking Monotheism*, 565:13–18.

6. Wilson, *Our Father Abraham*, 56.

7. Wilson, 58.

8. See Cataldo, *Social-Political History*.

9. Wray and Mobley, *The Birth of Satan*, xiii.

10. Cf. Michel Foucault, *Discipline and Punish: The Birth of the Prison*, trans. Alan Sheridan (New York: Vintage Books, 1995).

11. Cf. José Santaemilia, "Sexuality and Translation as Intimate Partners? Toward a *Queer Turn* in Rewriting Identities and Desires," in *Queering Translation, Translating the Queer: Theory, Practice, Activism*, ed. Brian James Baer and Klaus Kaindl, Routledge Advances in Translation and Interpreting Studies 28 (New York London: Routledge, Taylor & Francis Group, 2020), 19.

12. Cf. Wilson, *Our Father Abraham*, 3–5.

13. Richard A. Horsley, *Jesus and the Politics of Palestine* (Columbia: University of South Carolina Press, 2014), 14–15.

14. Alexander Crummell, *Africa and America; Addresses and Discourses* (Springfield, MA: Willey, 1891), 435, 436, 438.

15. Dube and Wafula, *Postcoloniality*, 12.

16. Dube and Wafula, *Postcoloniality*, 202.

17. Benjamin Ziemer, *Abram—Abraham: Kompositionsgeschichtliche Untersuchungen zu Genesis 14, 15 und 17*, BZAW 350 (Berlin: De Gruyter, 2005), 13.

18. Wilson, *Our Father Abraham*, 307, translation mine.

19. Bradley Green, "Confession of Sin," The Gospel Coalition, accessed December 14, 2022, https://www.thegospelcoalition.org/essay/confession-of-sin/.

20. Green, "Abraham, Isaac, and the Jewish Tradition," 18.

21. Cf. Dube and Wafula, *Postcoloniality*, 12; see also Nayar, *Postcolonialism*, 4.

22. Stephen Spector, "Abraham and Isaac: Human Frailty and Trauma in Genesis," *JBQ* 50, no. 4 (October 2022): 212.

23. Cf. von Rad, *Genesis*, 162.

24. See Thompson, *Mythic Past*, 190.

25. Mark A. Throntveit, *Ezra-Nehemiah*, Kindle (Louisville, KY: John Knox Press, 1992), 19, emphasis mine.

26. Cf. Thompson, *Mythic Past*, 193–95.

27. See Thompson, 194.

28. Wilson, *Our Father Abraham*, 262.

29. Compare Thompson, *Mythic Past*, 40.

30. See also Robert Neelly Bellah, "Civil Religion in America," *Daedalus* 134, no. 4 (2005): 40–55.

31. Cf. how their comprehension was challenged in Johnson & Graham v. M'Intosh (1823), Article 1, Section 8, Clause 3 (Indians).

32. See also Dube and Wafula, *Postcoloniality*, 200.

33. Trible, "Ominous Beginnings," location 130.

34. Von Rad, *Genesis*, 244–45.

35. Haynes, *Noah's Curse*, location 441.

36. Soren Kierkegaard, *Fear and Trembling*, trans. Walter Lowrie (Princeton: Princeton University Press, 1947), 70; cited in Green, "Abraham, Isaac, and the Jewish Tradition," 3.

37. See Green, "Abraham, Isaac, and the Jewish Tradition," 13.

38. cf. *Ber. Rab.* 56:4–8; Green, "Abraham, Isaac, and the Jewish Tradition," 9.

39. Cf. Mark S. Smith, *The Early History of God: Yahweh and the Other Deities in Ancient Israel*, 2nd ed. (Grand Rapids: William B. Eerdmans, 2002).

40. Cited in Andrew Judd, "Hagar, *Uncle Tom's Cabin*, and Why We Cannot Agree on What the Bible Says about Slavery," *BBR* 31, no. 1 (2021): 4.

41. See also Trible's bitter description of Abraham in "Ominous Beginnings," location 956.

42. Spector, "Abraham and Isaac," 213.

43. Federal Writers' Project and Library of Congress, *Alabama Slave Narratives*, 5.

Chapter 8

A(n Incestual, Pedophilic) Cave-Dwelling Lot

The story of Lot and his daughters has been so enthusiastically linked to Sodom and Gomorrah by conservative Bible readers that much of its atrocities have been overlooked. It has been so in favor of divine condemnation of homosexuality and, for Christian readers generally, symbolically reading Lot as a body saved through Abraham's righteousness, as though a foreshadow of Christ's body as the vehicle of salvation for the "children of Abraham."[1] The story begins, at least as it is concerned about Lot and his journey with his virgin daughters to a cave—*the Freudian imagery is hard to miss!*—with the events in the bustling twin cities of Sodom and Gomorrah. According to the author, the overall character of the populations of both cities is a problem for Yahweh, so he destroyed them with fire. As part of a national foundation myth, this destruction is not the end of the story because its aim is the denigration of the Ammonites and Moabites, foreigners who maintained a consistent presence in the histories of Israel and Judah as a foil to highlight the biblical author's community. Yet that aspect is often ignored by interpreters; instead, the author's justification is frequently made the central core of the story, which confirms, for many interpreters, God's unwavering *hatred* for homosexuality (see Gen. 19:1–13).[2] My analysis, then, must address both the given authorial intent and the dominant interpretive tendency. So egregious was men wanting to have their way with the divine messengers in God's eyes that God wiped out the cities in their entirety: women, children, babies, servants, slaves, and animals included. But like the divine did in the story of Noah, God saved a family. It should also perhaps no longer seem odd that in both stories drunkenness would result in the condemnation of generations of people. In the end, codified in interpretation traditions, upon the destruction of non-Israelite cities, the voices of the marginalized fall upon the deafened ears of a supposedly loving God and of later biblical interpreters, who sing

138   *Chapter 8*

quasi-erotically about laying in God's arms, the same metaphorical arms that slaughtered untold numbers (compare Mal. 3:6; Heb. 13:8).

> What a fellowship, what a joy divine,
> leaning on the everlasting arms;
> what a blessedness, what a peace is mine,
> leaning on the everlasting arms.[3]

But I am getting ahead of myself. The belief that the biblical story of Sodom and Gomorrah was evidence of divine condemnation of homosexuality is one that has enjoyed a preeminent place in dominant traditions of interpretation for centuries. Note, for example, the fiery Jonathan Edwards: "That Sodom is a city full of filthiness and abominations. It is full of those impurities that ought to be had in the utmost abhorrence and detestation by all. The inhabitants of it are a polluted company, they are all under the power and dominion of hateful lusts. All their faculties and affections are polluted with those vile dispositions that are unworthy of the human nature, that greatly debase it, that are exceedingly hateful to God, and that dreadfully incense his anger. Every kind of spiritual abominations bounds in it. There is nothing so hateful and abominable but that there it is to be found, and there it abounds" (*Looking Back*). While that or similarly theologically nuanced interpretations have enjoyed a preeminent place in dominant traditions, a careful reading without theological agenda, I argue, shows the story itself is not so much about homosexuality in the sense that we understand in the modern context. Terms, Mary Douglas explained, like "filthiness" and "abomination," which are frequently attached to the story by interpreters, are rooted in cultural value and meaning systems.[4] With that understanding, we may conclude that the previous example of Edwards reflects his own cultural concerns projected as being universal and absolute. It is easy to use such terms when describing the outsider, who does not conform to the norms and patterns of our own culture. This again is what monotheism does. It maps out and reinforces through ritual and doctrine the boundaries separating member and nonmember. Certainly, it is community building because the ultimate aim of the monotheistic body, which is the foundation for all monotheistic traditions, is the attainment of power and authority over the world by and within a sanctified community.

Despite the hasty interpretation of readers who seek to find in the destroyed bodies of Sodom and Gomorrah confirmation of divine hatred for what threatens their own assumptions about the nature of the status quo, it is not an address of LGBTQIA communities, same-sex marriage, or even a sexual and loving relationship between two members of the same gender.[5] The story is about the transgression of hospitality, namely in the grotesque expression of gang rape as part of a national foundation that prioritizes a singular ethnic

A(n Incestual, Pedophilic) Cave-Dwelling Lot   139

body—the author's assumption here seems to be a unified Israel and Judah as symbolized in the relationship between Abraham and Lot.[6] When we lose that element, when we read it as a diatribe, not just a diatribe but a *genocide*, portraying God's disdain for homosexuality, our interpretation relishes in translation stemming from the perspective of the center, in which difference, which is associated with the peripheral and marginal body, is rejected as profane, uncivilized, and in need either of acculturation or destruction. Such bodies become decentralized in our own narratives, pushed beyond the margins where exists the line between tolerable and intolerable deviances—defined from the perspective of the dominating subjects. Doing so perpetuates the illusion of biblical tradition that the elect community of God is the basis by which *all* peoples should conform. Judgment becomes excusable with the assumption that the punished had a choice to eschew what was "right." Monotheistic traditions such as Christianity refer to this with the vocabulary of "conversion." But what is conversion, from a sociological perspective, if it is not making others like us, as though we were the arms of a colonial empire transforming the world into our own image?

And this is true, generally speaking, of colonial interpretations and the colonialist enterprise. Anything that is rooted in the colonialist position for the basis of morals, interpretations, ethics, values, and mores reinforce the dominant normative and power structure where a centralized power, such as a State (which can also be symbolic in ideological colonialism) asserts itself over distant or peripheral territories or communities.[7] That is the nature of the colonial position, which is separate from colonization, and which communities in the postcolonial, or colonized, position are pushing back against.[8] They seek the free expression of their own identities unencumbered by categorical limits imposed by the linguistic and meaning structures of a dominant normative or power.

The problem with using biblical interpretation rooted in monotheistic claims to absolute and universal truth to justify modern and culturally contingent social and political agendas and ideologies is that it elevates a singular community's narrative into the status as an objective "revelation" that must be internalized by all others. Its ideology is colonial. Concomitant with that is the expectations of the new dominant community that the (em)bodied "other" animates the categorical form constructed within the meaning and value frameworks of the "central" culture. Questioning them, as I can attest to from personal conversations, and even some readers of this book may assume this about me, is equated with questioning the existence and will of God, and to be seen as casting one's lot with the outsider, the sinner who does not advance the monotheistic aim of bolstering or witnessing to the absolute authority of God. And once one does that, it's easy to dismiss the person raising the question as a heathen. Labelling others as heathen, skeptic, anti-Christian, or the

140   *Chapter 8*

like, dominant interpretations (traditions) highlight the contours of what the "true" community is, whose pristine image is cast against the monstrosity of the (em)bodied "other." Doing so offers justification on behalf of the "righteous" body for destructive actions or responses that can be directed against outsiders in the name of God's will and its manifestation in the world. Sodom and Gomorrah is one such story.

In that story, Yahweh should not be read apart from the deity's role as the national god of Israel.[9] Setting aside any monotheistic conviction about a universal, absolute God that transcends time and space, intervening every so often to sprinkle blessings on believers and destruction on non-believers, "god" is little more than the symbol of the national aims of the biblical authors. Later Christian and Jewish traditions would transform the nationalist aims of historical authors into justification for imperial and colonial conquest in which the god of the kingdom "cleaned" out the land of peoples who did not fit the dominant categories or attributes that identified a citizen. It is a necessary strategy. Reading Yahweh as the monotheistic God whose revelation is universal and absolute necessitates a rejection of "outsiders," who embody competing centers of power and collective ideologies. That monotheistic need is how later interpreters can justify biblical passages that call for the annihilation of others, from unborn children to the elderly (cf. Deut. 7:1–6; 13:15–16). *After all, can a god that represents the aristocratic culture of a particular ethnic group be translated as an accepting representation of all people?* Yahweh, and even Elohim (who was co-opted from Canaanite religions[10]), was linked to the kingdoms of Israel and Judah, which became the blueprint for the community of believers as the core of Jewish and Christian traditions.

It's hard to avoid the conclusion that references to Yahweh in the Bible are connected to a vision of Israel imagined by a literati writing primarily during the 6th century and later. Their presentation of history was for prescriptive, or constructivist, purposes. Ezra-Nehemiah may be an example *par excellence* of that (compare the genealogical roster [Neh. 7:4–73], the concern over intermarriage [Neh. 10:28–33], and the tradition of conquest [Neh. 9:5–35]). This description of Yahweh and community emphasized the contours of a "righteous" community and the antithesis of the monstrous profane body of the outsider. These, or similar ideas, are among the assumptions in the author's, or editor's, narrative about Sodom and Gomorrah. The story of Sodom and Gomorrah occurs within the larger literary framework of Abraham's sojourning through the "promised land." As I discussed in chapter 7, his building of altars and memorials where he encounters Yahweh along the way was a type of mapping out the land. A more modern equivalent might be inflected in the mapping practices of the British and Napoleonic Empires. Abraham's acts were political statements, planting the flag of a future kingdom. His story was part of Israel's foundation myth, at least the "Israel" as the literati re-imagined it after the falls of Israel and Judah to the Assyrian and Babylonian empires, respectively.

As mentioned, and the point is important enough to return to, perhaps one of the best ways to understand what gods stood for in the ancient world is to consider what flags symbolize in the modern world. As flags represent the national ideal, national gods, selected by the ruling authorities, represented the ideals that the ruling aristocracy thought should define the kingdom. Their role, for instance, is one reason rulers might replace a previous national deity. In political contexts, before the modern mapping of nation-states, rulers would change a collective people's flag, banner, or crest to represent the rulers and their own values. Solomon did that by replacing Yahweh with other deities (cf. 1 Kgs. 11:31–33; 2 Kgs. 23:13–14; Neh. 13:26). Nabonidus did that in the Babylonian Empire, replacing Marduk with Sin. Akhenaten did that, replacing Amun with Aten. Darius did that in the Persian Empire with his Behistun Inscription, describing the elevation of Ahuramazda over all other deities as he defeated political contestants to the imperial throne. One could even say that Jesus did that in speaking for a community distinct from the Roman Empire. When a community's god is imposed upon outsiders, the act decentralizes the values of an outsider's community, replacing it with those of the invading or oppressing community.[11] In that sense, Abraham's actions are consistent with what the literati imagined Israel should be.

It is with this background of interpretive assumptions that we should read the redacted form of the story of Sodom and Gomorrah, and its part in Genesis. When the messengers commissioned by Yahweh visit Lot, their presence coupled with the destruction that follows can be read as part of a land claim over Canaan. The people who lived there were portrayed as sexually aggressive and unaware of what moral responsibilities lay with hospitality. *How frequently have colonial powers justified their colonizing of others on similar ideas!* Their purpose was to remove Lot from the city before Abraham's god wiped out its citizens, granting the body of God's community life while slaughtering the bodies of outsiders. While the men of Sodom tried to assert their power over the messengers of their doom, perhaps even to provide a counter resistance to the imperializing claim the messengers of Yahweh, god of Israel, represented, they were ultimately powerless to stop the destruction, according to the biblical author.

With their purpose as their guide, the messengers meet Lot, Abraham's nephew (cf. Gen. 12:5), in the city of Sodom. And as they are trying to enter Lot's house, the men of the city glimpse them. Licking their wounds from recent military defeat (cf. Gen. 14:8–12), the men of the city approach Lot, bang on his door and demand that the visitors be brought out so that the men of the city could "know them" (Gen. 19:5). The political motivation is set,

142   *Chapter 8*

though often ignored by conservative interpreters, even though this story too
is part of the larger Israelite foundation myth. The city lost a battle, and its
destruction was being proclaimed. Lot's refusal to release his visitors to the
men highlights ethnic tension, "the one who came here to live as a foreigner
among us now thinks he's our judge" (19:9). This moment often gets overlooked in biblical interpretations of the account in favor of reading the story
solely as a condemnation of homosexuality. Lot is identified as a foreigner
among people whose land has been promised to Abraham's descendants. He
has been made an outsider, separated from the actions of the monstrous body
of men outside his house, its walls and demarcated spaces being a symbolic
representation of community, banging on his piqued door.

As an additional counterpoint to prevailing interpretations, at this point in
the story no mention is made of these individuals being divine messengers,
which Christians often interpret as angels. Yet because biblical interpreters
often want to see this story as a literal condemnation of homosexuality, let me
be literal in my critique: were the divine messengers men? Can angel-human
sex even be said to be homosexual? Most Christian theologies do not impose
human gender, a theological concept that does not distinguish between gender and sexuality, on angels. In any event, wouldn't that be interspecies sex?
Perhaps something along the lines of bestiality? If one is going to interpret
the text as a literal condemnation of homosexuality, then one should read the
text literally. But if the messengers were not human, then the basis for this as
a universal condemnation of homosexuality is lost. God, who is the supposed
source of divine revelation, would have known better.

Undeterred, conservative interpretations marginalize the gay body; rather,
this is not merely marginalization but outright rejection. To avoid doing that,
we might observe that this story is more about hospitality and resistance to
annihilation or conquest than it is about relationships between men. The men
of the city don't demand a relationship. They don't even demand a particular
sexual activity. They simply say "we want to *know* them," and "we want to
have our way with them." In the traditional sense, the Hebrew term, *yada*,
"to know," frequently refers to the type of sexual activity that would produce
children. It also implies a hierarchy of authority. Men know women, not the
other way around. In the story of Sodom, men wanted "to know" men, or
angels. If we keep this issue to the parameters of physical interaction, interpreting *yada'* as sex, then it refers to sexual penetration. But that was not
for the sake of pleasure alone. Its public expression would entail a political
motivation such as has been so pornographically portrayed on the Eurymedon
Vase, which shows an aroused Greek soldier approaching from behind a
Persian soldier (or perhaps a Scythian squire) bent over.[12] This was not gay
pornography for any solicitous purpose. It was a political statement: the bug-
gered soldier was a symbol of a culture's military defeat. The men's request

transgresses the mores of hospitality by advancing political aspirations for authority and dominance. *Let us know them as subordinate bodies before ourselves.*

This is not a consensual act, and that is the interpretive problem. It is about the assertion of will and power over another. *Like rape.* It is about the idea that a patriarchal male could be subordinated to another patriarchal male similar to how women are in the biblical author's cultural context. Women were objects used to assert masculine authority, not men. If anyone doubts what I am saying, recall that Lot tries to convince the men of the city to take his two virgin daughters and do whatever they wanted with them, so long as they left the visitors alone (Gen. 19:8). The demand for hospitality was so great that Lot offered to give his own daughters for its sake. But the daughters were, by cultural and legal definition, Lot's property to do with as he saw fit. Does anyone doubt the high probability his daughters would be raped to death if the crowd of men was as big as most biblical interpreters want to imagine? After all, the *entire* city was wiped out.

Most readers, however, pay little attention to that part of the story. They often will see Lot as a desperate man trying to do right. Their belief that God hates homosexuality with such passion inevitably leads to the conclusion that Lot offering his daughters was OK with God. *Another account of a great biblical father! To save men, men, it's OK to prostitute your daughters!*

It is also worth noting that Lot's wife does not appear in the story yet. Her "five minutes of fame" came when they were fleeing the city of Sodom, when she "looked back" and was turned into a pillar of salt (Gen. 19:26). *Why salt?* Who knows? Maybe she symbolized the Dead Sea, and this was a legend describing the origins of its high salt content. (One proposed location for Sodom and Gomorrah is the southern bank of the Dead Sea.) Was the location prone to salt pillars, or salt domes, at some point? I don't rightly know. What the biblical author tells us is that she is not a factor in the story until her death, which sets up Lot's nocturnal activities with his daughters. Salt is also a mineral used for destruction of crops as well as the preservation of food. Perhaps his wife's body, whose skin is transformed, functions as a metaphor denoting two potentialities: death and life. She is killed (and I'm not familiar with the process of becoming salt, but it sounds painful). Salt is also used for preserving food, which is critical for life. But note when she even thinks about choosing or prioritizing a different value than what is imposed upon her, her body is destroyed. She cannot be who she is, she must be who she is told to be—like the colonizer's assumption that the body of the colonized must be "saved." There is no evidence in this text that she did anything else that would warrant her death. Even knowing where Lot will plant his seed—*in the virgin wombs of his underage daughters*—interpreters often interpret his wife as sinful and therefore worthy of being killed by Yahweh. Such interpretations

144   *Chapter 8*

run the range of, "She looked back in desire for the city and its culture." "She had evil in her heart." But those interpretive dances are justifications for what is difficult to avoid describing as Yahweh's murder. Her body as one non-normative functions solely as a symbolic counterpoint or foil of Lot's lot as a normalized body, and the decision he must make. Nothing is mentioned about the culture of the city. The only real description the Bible offers is that men of the city wanted to rape Lot's visitors. Why is Lot's wife conflated with that? All we know about her is conflated into the actions and desires of men. Her body is colonized by author's and interpreter's agendas that seek to rationalize the destruction of Sodom and Gomorrah, her transfiguration into salt, and later fears of homosexuality so joyously linked to the destruction of Sodom and Gomorrah by interpreters.[13] The irony, as I have mentioned, is that this story is *not* about homosexuality. It is about national power.

But what if we read Lot's wife looking back as a yearning for what she is about to lose: the traditions, culture, values of her own community? She was being uprooted and taken elsewhere by the actions and decisions of men (and a masculine god). Who would not have a sense of longing when moving, especially if they are uprooted and taken elsewhere on the whim of someone who exercises power over them? *I cannot help but ask, in that spirit, how often are the experiences and stories of colonized and displaced bodies taken seriously?* Add on to that the rush to avoid destruction that the story seems to show. For a recent parallel, if I were to ask Ukrainians fleeing their homes from Russian bombardment, I would assume that many feel a longing for their homes.[14] Lina Udodenko, for example, who fled Ukraine to the UK, stated wistfully, "It's really nice here but for me it's not my home, and it's hard to imagine how now we can return there."[15] To assume that they are "looking back" because of sexual desire is naïve. It grossly reduces the body of the "other" into a dismissible category, and a sexual category at that as interpreters have confined to women historically: the sinner, the sexual deviant, worthy of annihilation because it undermines conventional assumptions about the foundational roles and relationships by which a society is defined.[16] The possible analogy with individuals forced into slavery should be obvious. Such is the act of ideological colonialism in biblical interpretation!

Lot's wife loses the connection that she had to her past, like a colonized community or people. Under no choice of her own, she will lose that because Yahweh wanted the land, as the figure of Abraham symbolizes, for the kingdoms of Israel and Judah. The annihilation of people for the ultimate aim of forcing them from the land to make space for "Israel" is a common theme in the Bible. Before the technological age of bombs, the destruction of cities was frequently explained as the action or will of gods. Such explanations by the biblical authors sit better with modern readers when it is possible to ignore the atrocities committed in the name of God. *"God's ways are not our ways.*" The elementary insider-outsider distinction reinforces the distinction between sinner and saint. And that offers rationalized justification for divine actions: "God is fighting against evil and has the authority to wipe it out." Now all one need do is attribute evil to Sodom: *the men of the city were flaming homosexuals, and God hates the gays! Satan is alive and well! Sure, God loves the sinner but hates the sin. But **they** were unredeemable. Homosex is so unnatural that God will wipe out those who practice it. Remember AIDS?* Does that commentary sound like hyperbole? It is not within Christian circles. Take, for instance, Peter LaBarbera's frustration over the movie *Love, Simon,* which portrays a young man coming out as gay and falling in love. "We're never going to hear later about the diseases associated with homosexuality that [the main character] would get, mental illness, and of course the judgment of God. . . . homosexual behavior is a perversion like God says it is, it is deviant, it is not normal."[17]

The morning after, Abraham saw a thick smoke rising from what used to be cities in the rounded district (*hakikar*) like a furnace (Gen. 19:27–28). The term for "thick smoke" (*qiytor*) is the same one used in Ex. 19:18 to describe the visual confirmation of Yahweh's presence on Mt. Sinai. God had made a successful claim over the land.

Monotheism wants the Bible to be prejudiced. It wants it to discriminate between insiders and outsiders, to reject homosexuality, foreigners, and to reinforce the subordinate status of women. It wants that comfort and that assurance that there is a sense of hierarchy, place, position, inclusion, and exclusion. It is rooted in that very necessity, that struggle against the other, the Frankensteinian creation of the monstrous "other," the struggle for authority, and the distinction between insider and outsider. Monotheism cannot exist without that dichotomy.[18] That is why Christian traditions like Unitarian Universalism are such threats to mainstream Christian ideals. It poses an untenable ideology for dominant forms of monotheism because it embraces diversity in a more humanistic fashion. But it does so as a reaction to the dichotomization between member and nonmember inherent within monotheism.

So, judged by monotheism's theological vanguard, the "raging homosexuals" of Sodom were annihilated, along with the women, children, teens, toddlers, unborn babies, animals, and vegetation. *Apparently, God doesn't care to discriminate between the guilty and the innocent outside his "preferred" people group or community.* But we know that already based on the flood story. God gets pissed and destroys things. Meanwhile, setting the stage for a great deal more "forgiveness" by the divine, Lot and his daughters fled to Zoar, another city near Sodom. There is some suggestion that Lot's wife made it to Zoar before she was turned into salt (Gen. 19:23–26), but that is

146   *Chapter 8*

not entirely clear in this context. In any event, Lot and his daughters eventually leave Zoar to live in a cave because they were afraid of what we can only assume to be the divine bombardment of cities according to Gen. 19:25, which states that Yahweh destroyed Sodom and Gomorrah and all the cities of the rounded district (*kikar*), or region. Was the "rounded district" a general reference to the shape of a city? Or did it refer to something like a meteor crater? I'm not sure, and it is not helpful to get lost in the weeds lest we overlook the real issues at work in the story. What matters is that God destroyed peoples and cultures in order to elevate one as dominant and (eventually) authoritative. It also matters that the story takes a rather ominous turn as the characters enter a cave.

As readers, we know that this narrative thrives on the leitmotif of sex; not sexuality, but sex as an assertion of power. Understanding that will aid our understanding of what happens in the cave between Lot and his young daughters.

Rather than stick it out in Zoar, Lot and his daughters move "off grid" and into a cave. And at that point, I can't help but be reminded of people who get frustrated, for whatever reason, with bills, city life, other people, or neighbors and decide to move into the wilderness. But the author doesn't want us to spend too much time thinking about the logistics of living in a cave near a land with diminishing vegetation. Rather, the cave takes on a more symbolic tone because the author wants us to gaze voyeuristically upon what happens there. This is Freudian analogy before Freud.[19] The daughters say to themselves, "there's no man to come into us to help us continue the line of our father." The phrase used is not *yada'* because the daughters are strategizing in utilitarian terms. They use the phrase *labo' 'alenu* ("to come upon/into us" [*as in the "missionary" position?*]; Gen. 19:31). According to the story, they took action because they assumed no men were left in the land (again, Gen. 19:31). Clearly, they forgot about Zoar, which they just left. They forgot about their relative Abraham, who lived among other men, or even the men in Abraham's extended family. *Abraham married his sister, so clearly incest rules were relaxed for Abraham and his family. They could have married a cousin.* Likely the reader is supposed to be suspicious. The function of the girls is not who they are—we don't even know their names—but their attempt to overturn and manipulate the dominant cultural normative. Their bodies become subsumed by the monstrous "other" that threatens the nomos of the community. The author does not want us to associate intellectual reasoning with the daughters. The threat that Eve posed by seeking knowledge should be a confirmation of that. It matters only that they are women (girls, in this case) who are manipulating a man after getting him drunk.

Not only that, but if we pay attention to the ages of the daughters, based on what is known about betrothal and marital practices in the ancient world, they were young. If the oldest was 13 or 14, then the youngest would have been 12 or 13, possibly even younger.[20] Thus, early teen or preteen girls were deciding about their father's lineage; a decision they would not have been prepared to make. It is also concerning that it is the same daughters Lot earlier offered to be raped by men in Sodom. Where is any condemnation of Lot for treating his young daughters as sexual objects; offering them to be raped and eventually embracing them in incestual *flagrante delicto*? Where too is any condemnation of Lot in creating an environment of expectation that led his daughters to make such a decision? Interpreters do not seek those answers because those answers do not reinforce what they want from the text. They want stories that show God's engagement with history as *he* (the pronoun is intentional) remakes the world for the benefit of *his* chosen community, which excludes more than it includes.

I am surprised at the amount of my students and even feminist interpreters, more broadly, who see an empowering element for women in the story, that the daughters *did what they needed to do*. Such interpreters overlook the likely age of the girls and how they are redefined as an "other" who needed to be civilized—such assumptions, for example, about "uncivilized" sexual license were common among colonial cultures toward their "tribal colonies." They were of the age that modern societies would call for the incarceration or killing of the older male for sexually violating underage girls, who were also his daughters. I can imagine no court in the modern Western world that would excuse any father for doing that simply because he was drunk.[21] The desire to celebrate the actions of women is a direct response to the very patriarchal weight that biblical interpretation has imposed upon how we read the Bible. But this isn't the place to celebrate the choice of women. This is the place to recognize that something extraordinary is being said: very young girls had sex with their father. And legions of Bible readers have acquitted Lot of any blame while also celebrating God's absolute annihilation of the people of Sodom and Gomorrah. Why? Lot was not an outsider but a patriarchal male who shared lineage with Abraham. *God sure loves the men!*

There are several issues that must be acknowledged if we even entertain this as a possible historical story, which many conservative interpreters are wont to do. If we do not challenge what is being presented, but we see it as a way of reinforcing our own beliefs, then we are guilty of perpetuating the ideological colonialism of bodies. Lot, after all, is exonerated from any wrongdoing by the biblical authors and interpreters because condemnation never springs from their lips. And we perpetuate inequality and immorality within our own traditions of interpretation. That is the very thing that postcolonialism seeks to subvert: the colonialist, imperialist assumptions that continue to perpetuate oppression and marginalization justified by an appeal to an oppressive authority through the weight of a monotheistic God or the overwhelming

148   *Chapter 8*

power of empire. While we should avoid celebrating the audacity of the daughters to take their father's matter into their own hands, we should also cease exonerating Lot. If, for comparison, any man in the United States had sex with a girl under 18, he would be guilty of pedophilia. If a father had sex with his daughters, he would be guilty of incest. Both actions would result in the man going to prison if he was caught and convicted. Interpreters try to get around that tension by highlighting the fact that Lot's daughters got him so drunk he was not aware of anything. *Another Noah!* But that is ignorant. If a man is so drunk that he is oblivious to who is on his penis in a cave with only three people, his body will not perform as necessary. The phenomenon is not unknown. When I was in high school, teenage boys used the term "drunk dick" to refer to the state of being too drunk to have sex. Yet even in that situation, the affected party knew who his potential partner was and could sadly recount the tale of failed sexual conquest, if only by general attributes *and* an unshakeable confidence that the almost-partner was *not* family.

If we accept the story as divine revelation and a historical account, then we also accept that Lot would have *already been favorably disposed toward having sex with his daughters*. All he needed was a little alcohol to lower his inhibitions. Twice. *How can we forget that?! If the first time could even be considered an accident, what was the second?!* Yet before I miss perhaps the most obvious point: where did the daughters get sufficient alcohol in a cave? Did they go back to Zoar and buy wine from a man? But were not they also the ones who naively claimed, "There are no men left in the land"? Did God give them the wine? *Our Father who art in Heaven . . . your will be done?*

With the prize of Lot's semen, the daughters become pregnant, eventually giving birth to sons who would be the ancestors of the Ammonites and the Moabites (Gen. 19:36–38). And here now is another ideological statement that the Ammonites and the Moabites, who may not enter the "assembly of Yahweh" (Deut. 23:3 ET, v. 4 HB), are worthy of oppression, slavery, colonization, and imperializing. They are the products of incest. Like the Canaanites, in Joshua, who are wiped out by God, at least as Joshua tells the story, Ammonites and Moabites may be dealt with in any way necessary to perpetuate the livelihood of the Israelite and Judean kingdoms. *They are bastards and products of incest!*

In all of this, Lot is never condemned. Dominant traditions of biblical interpretation never condemn Lot. The Bible never condemns Lot. Commentators never condemn Lot for being possibly one of the worst fathers in the biblical texts. *Did Lot ever accept his role as daddy-grandpa?* Not only do Lot's daughters, as women and minorities, represent the abject, or objects worthy of marginalization, they are credited with the ancestors of the Ammonites and Moabites. While such credit usually goes to the patriarch, in this case, because the Ammonites and Moabites were traditional enemies of Israel, the credit goes to the monstrous bodies of females who took initiative and threatened nomos. *Those little Eves!* The daughters and their descendants take on the quality of a foreign "other," who in modern Western tradition is often portrayed as sexually deviant and unbounded by civilized mores.

The tendency to link qualities of civilization to sexual practice can be seen even in the more recent history with the concept of the "Oriental." Sexual license, sex outside the control of a regulating power hierarchy, is character-istic of a culture that needs to be civilized. In contrast, "civilized" cultures generally maintain that individuals must clothe themselves properly, not sleep with certain women, or underage girls, not sleep with men, and keep in mind that their sexual activities are foremost about preserving one's lineage. The bodies of Lot's daughters, which represent the symbolic origins of the Ammonites and Moabites and so also the subordination of those peoples to Israel, were not only indirectly colonized by him, they were more so by later interpreters who saw any sin only in the actions of the daughters while exon-erating Lot. It was the monstrous female that tricked Lot into doing what, we are encouraged to assume, he would not normally do. But we know better. As an interpretive strategy, Lot functions in the story as the colonial agenda while his daughters are the uncivilized bodies who inversely carve out the boundaries of acceptability by posing not only as those who must be civi-lized but those whose very tendencies are the reasons death and destruction can be morally justified. "No Ammonite or Moabite shall enter the assembly (*qahal*) of Yahweh" (Deut. 23:4 HB; v. 3 ET). As an additional bearing on interpretation, *qahal* is also used to denote the core people of the kingdom of Israel (cf. Ezra 10:12; see also Neh. 13:1; Num. 16:3 in contrast with *'edah* [congregation]). That understood, the story of Lot's daughters is a political allegory. It is part of the foundation myth constructed by the biblical author re-imagining a post-defeated Israel. Why would the story of Sodom and Gomorrah be any different?

NOTES

1. Faro, for instance, describes the story of Sodom and Gomorrah, and Lot's salva-tion from destruction, as God's actions against evil. At no point throughout Faro's work does the author address Lot sleeping with his daughters (cf. *Evil in Genesis*, 40, 50–52, 125). In fact, the only reference is this, "Lot chooses to listen to the divine voice, but his wife and future sons-in-law do not. Lot is delivered from destruction, even though the deliverance of his daughters produces the birth of two nations that become enemies of Israel" (125).

2. Cf. Tim LaHaye, *The Battle for the Family* (Old Tappan, NJ: Fleming H. Revell Company, 1982), 110; see also Tim LaHaye, *The Unhappy Gays: What Everyone*

150   *Chapter 8*

Should Know about Homosexuality (Tyndale House, 1978); Paul D. Morris, *Shadow of Sodom: Facing the Facts of Homosexuality* (Tyndale House Publishers, 1978).

3. E. A. Hoffman, *Leaning On the Everlasting Arms*, vol. The United Methodist Hymnal, 1887.

4. Cf. Mary Douglas, *Purity and Danger: An Analysis of Concepts of Pollution and Taboo* (London: Routledge & Kegan Paul, 1966).

5. Cf. General Presbytery Assemblies of God, "Homosexuality, Marriage, and Sexual Identity," August 4–5, 2014.

6. Cf. Cataldo, *What the Bible Says about Sex*, 144–47.

7. Cf. Beaule, *Frontiers*, 6.

8. Cf. the discussion of distinctions in Beaule, 4.

9. Gen. 19:29, which describes the destruction of the cities, refers to "god," or *elohim*. However, the story is prefaced by 18:16–33, which describes Abraham's intercession of Yahweh on behalf of the cities and his nephew, Lot.

10. The literature on this is vast.

11. Cf. the discussion of the general activity in Beaule, *Frontiers*, 335.

12. See also the discussion about debates over the vase in Amy C. Smith, "Eurymedon and the Evolution of Political Personifications in the Early Classical Period," *The Journal of Hellenic Studies* 119 (1999): 128–41.

13. Cf. Cataldo, *What the Bible Says about Sex*, 142–47.

14. As of the time of writing in 2023, the war between Ukraine and Russia is ongoing.

15. Jeremy Ball and Samantha Noble, "Ukrainian Refugee Who Lost Home in Bombing Feels UK Welcome," *BBC News*, June 2, 2022, sec. Nottingham, https:// www.bbc.com/news/uk-england-nottinghamshire-61667884.

16. Cf. the larger discussion of this trend in Cataldo, *What the Bible Says about Sex*.

17. Cited in Jared Holt, "Peter LaBarbera Is Upset 'Love, Simon' Did Not Mention The 'Judgment of God' on Gay People," Right Wing Watch, April 5, 2018, https:// www.rightwingwatch.org/post/peter-labarbera-is-upset-love-simon-did-not-mention -the-judgment-of-god-on-gay-people/.

18. Cf. Cataldo, *Breaking Monotheism*; Cataldo, *Biblical Terror*.

19. Cf. Sigmund Freud, *The Interpretation of Dreams* (Mineola, NY: Courier Dover Publications, 2015).

20. See also the discussion in Cataldo, *What the Bible Says about Sex*, 119–22.

21. Note, for example, the arguments made in the case J Schnepp, THE PEOPLE OF THE STATE OF NEW YORK, Respondent, v. KENNETH R. FACEY, SR. (Appellate Division of the Supreme Court of New York, Fourth Department February 21, 1986).

Chapter 9

Sarah's (Colonizing) Laughter and Hagar's (Colonized) Tears

The two women thrust into the story of Abraham, Sarah and Hagar, reaffirm the prejudice of the biblical author's assumed cultural superiority. The symbolic use of their bodies is not unlike the symbolic distinction master-subordinate or colonizer-colonized that reaffirms a unique relational perspective between the center and the margin. In the Bible, their stories are meaningless without Abraham. Take, for example, that, as Phyllis Trible bemoans, Abraham never calls Hagar by name.[1] In addition, while in relation to Abraham they may share similarities they differ in relation to each other. Both Sarah and Hagar bear Abraham's children and initially live "within his tents," however their statuses diverge along the lines of citizen and foreigner reinforcing a prevailing center-periphery dichotomy. One is embraced within the cultural arms of Yahweh's community while the other is cast off as an outsider into the wilderness, the paradigmatic locale of the uncivilized body. *And isn't anxiety over the influence of the "other," which might encourage internal change, at the heart of what is deemed profane?* Not only that, but Hagar's own people, the Egyptians, would be the foil against which Yahweh and Moses would later in the narrative chronology assert Yahweh's power—their collective bodies to become the canvas upon which to highlight the definition and hierarchy of Israelite power. This contrast projects into the past a partial explanation for the historical tensions between the kingdom of Israel and the kingdom of Egypt. More importantly, however, it betrays an ideology of racial purity and land acquisition seen as a narrative strand through the biblical texts, which should be understood in nationalist rather than universalist terms. That fits with the idea that Abraham's story is part of Israel's foundation myth.

Based on the framing of the biblical account and this project's emphasis upon postcolonial analysis, consider Sarah's and Hagar's stories as extensions of Abraham's own quasi-imperialist one. Recall from chapter 7 that

152   *Chapter 9*

Abram/Abraham planted Israel's metaphorical flag, claiming territory, as he wandered about Canaan. His actions on a geopolitical level are mirrored in his sexual activities, the consequences which are meted out on the bodies of his children: one to receive his blessing, the other his rejection. The community insider, such as of the nation, would emerge from the metaphorical loins of the former while the outsider, or foreigner, the author leaves us to presume, would be expelled from those of the latter. The logic of the choice the author and interpreter attribute to God. *God's ways are not our ways (Isa. 55:8).* As von Rad writes, "God has indicated his plan for history, namely, to make Abraham a great people; Abraham 'has firmly assented' to that, i.e., he took it seriously and adjusted to it. In so doing he adopted, according to God's judgment, the only correct relationship to God."[2] There is a problem with that idea, however. With sociological and historical awareness, we can explain the elevation of Isaac over Ishmael on a political level. If, however, we choose to elevate the Bible as divine, universal revelation, then we can only conclude, as von Rad does, that God has a plan. But it is a plan that includes a select few and excludes numerous others. We would certainly not be alone in that belief because that is the very assumption inherent in all monotheistic traditions. Even the Christian emphasis upon "love" does not get around this prejudiced ideal (cf. Rev. 7:4; 14:1, 3). Moreover, it is the same God, and plan, monotheistic theologies must conclude, that oppresses and annihilates people outside his elect community.

Hagar was an Egyptian, which establishes a contrast between the Israelites and the Egyptians in the story. Not only that, but she is described as a menial servant *(siphchah)* to Sarah (Gen. 16:1). It's hard to avoid seeing the orientation of power being made here. The Egyptians, presented in the body of a woman, are subordinate not only to Abraham but to his wife. *A woman subordinate to a woman!* Hagar, bearing Ishmael as Abraham's son, was useful as a proxy mother when Sarah couldn't get pregnant, but she was no longer important when Sarah finally bore Isaac. *What similar stories we see with how enslaved women bore children for the economic and social aims of their white owners in the 17th–19th centuries of the colonial territories of the United States!*[3] Hagar's elevated status, from menial servant to mother of Abraham's firstborn, stirred up jealousy in Sarah. Because Sarah *was* Abraham's wife, she sought to preserve her own status as a citizen-wife and that of Isaac as the sole beneficiary of Abraham's blessing, which we might interpret to include, in longitudinal terms, as many modern Christians and Jews do, the land that Yahweh promised Abraham (cf. Gen. 12:1–9; 15:1–20; 17:1–27). In the hands of the biblical author, her defense starts, and many married heterosexual men claim empathy, by blaming Abraham: "the wrong that has happened to me is your fault" (see Gen. 16:5).[4] The responsibility and consequence of a pregnant Egyptian whose son could receive Israel's birthright are cast upon Israel's (and later monotheism's) archetypical father.

There is another aspect to the story: Abraham is not described as "knowing" Hagar, a sexual euphemism often used to explain births that perpetuate the line of a patriarch. His sexual encounter is described in functionalist terms. He "entered into" her (cf. Gen. 16:4), as though entering a new land and raising a phallic memorial in imperialist political claim. Like a colonized body no longer necessary, she and her son could be cast off, abandoned to survive on their own in the wilderness of a foreign social, political, and economic world.

I don't want to overlook the fact that Ishmael's name poses what could be an interesting dilemma. The covenant that the author ascribes to Abraham is with Yahweh, the national god of Israel and Judah. Abraham names the son conceived with Hagar "Ishmael," which can be translated as "El hears." We should also note the fact that, according to Gen. 16:11, Yahweh's messenger told Hagar to name her son, but it was Abraham who did so (Gen. 16:15).[5] So what shall we make of the distinction between Elohim and Yahweh?

Since at least Julius Wellhausen, a scholar from the 19th century CE, scholars have seen different divine names and typological references as indicative of different authorial or editorial traditions.[6] JEDP (Jahwist, Elohist, Deuteronomist, and Priestly sources), the acronym for editorial traditions associated with different divine names (J, E, JE) as well as the priests of Yahweh (P), for instance, denotes that idea. ("D" refers to an editorial school associated with Deuteronomy.) What is of interest regarding Ishmael is that Yahweh (J), the political god of Israel, is *not* associated with Ishmael. Rather, the god of Canaan that was incorporated into Israelite tradition, El(ohim [E]), was. Even when Hagar is shown water that would save her and Ishmael, it was Elohim, not Yahweh (Gen. 21:17–19). And when Abimelech, a few verses later, declares that "god" is with Abraham, he too refers to Elohim. Elohim, in this situation, seems to be the god of the land as it exists, not the future geopolitical kingdom of Israel. If so, then Yahweh may be the god of Israel as it hopes to be both in the story and the literati's re-imagining of the kingdom. That makes sense on a political level, especially if we accept Genesis was part of a national foundation myth. Yahweh cannot be seen as helping foreign nations. Yahweh judges them, but does not aid them in the same way as he does Israel and Judah. That is why, for instance, some of the biblical prophets use a marriage metaphor to describe the relationship between Yahweh and his kingdom. Elohim, in contrast, doesn't hold the same political status as a national deity. A temple to Yahweh, not Elohim, became the centerpiece of Jerusalem. The vestiges of which are the objects of monotheistic pilgrimage even today. Thus, El (for the E source) may signify the identification of that which can be claimed, while Yahweh may signify

154   Chapter 9

the basis by which that claim can be made. At this point, that contrast is not certain, but its potential is compelling. I raise the possibility to highlight the fact that for the biblical writers, Yahweh and Elohim were not always the same deity, and their references may serve different ideological purposes. In fact, there is some suggestion that their blending did not happen until after the 6th century BCE, during the defeat of Judah to the Babylonians, which also encouraged the beginnings of a strict monotheism.[7]

Abraham left Hagar and Ishmael in the wilderness, a space which is also symbolic of uncivilized chaos. Unneeded slaves—they were still defined by the ideological contours of the Abrahamic Covenant and were not completely free—they eventually moved to the wilderness of Paran, which was part of the east central region of the Sinai Peninsula, northeast of Mt. Sinai. Hagar found there a woman for Ishmael in Egypt, which reinforced the imposed separation between Abraham and Ishmael. Of the narrative to this point, von Rad opined, "It is interesting to see how the materials of this narrative slowly strip off the external historical circumstances not to volatilize into timeless truth but to represent a divine act of typical validity."[8] Part of that, I would argue, is due to the story written originally as a myth. The other part, the expectation of historical legitimacy von Rad assumes, is due to the monotheistic expectation about the Bible as God's absolute revelation. In such a raptured spirit, the intrepid founder of Methodism, John Wesley, wrote, "Hagar was probably one of those maid-servants which the king of Egypt (among other gifts) bestowed upon Abram, chap. xii.16" (*Notes*). His comfort in her rejection has been set: she was the gift of an unfaithful king in a kingdom that would later oppress the Hebrews. Not only does Ishmael marry into Egyptian society, but he lives in the wilderness, which is a space removed from sociopolitical order.[9] That tension also lay behind Yahweh's giving the law to Moses on Mt. Sinai after the Hebrews left Egypt, lived in the wilderness, and emerged from that dusty environ as a nation (cf. Ex. 20:1–23:19). In that account, a new "order" was created out of disorder in the wilderness, but it is one that transformed the collective body into a nation. Once done, that sociopolitical seed could be cultivated in the land of Canaan once its current inhabitants and their cultures were wiped out (cf. Ex. 23:27–33). The foundation of Israel could be celebrated while surrounding kingdoms and peoples were defeated, denigrated, or devalued by Israel's deity and its political myth. The development of this more prejudiced view of the "other's" body reaches an apotheosis in Gal. 4:28–31 when Paul translates Ishmael as an enemy or antithesis of what he believed to be the nature of Christ's idealized body, which was the community of believers.[10]

Even when Egypt is portrayed in somewhat neutral or even amicable terms, such as the Chronicler does in the story Josiah (2 Chron. 35:20–22), it is frequently connected to conflict. Josiah, for instance, assumed that Pharaoh

Necho was coming to attack. According to the Chronicler, when Josiah rode out to confront the pharaoh, the latter stated he was "just passing through" and was on his way to Carchemish to aid Assyria against the Babylonians and its allies, not pose a challenge to Judah. Josiah pressed the matter and ended up losing his life in battle at Megiddo, a site that is preserved in Christian tradition as important in the return of Christ to establish (the foundation of, a connection to Seth?) his kingdom. Necho symbolizes the antithesis to the "life" of the collective body, whether of Israel symbolized in Josiah, who would be elevated to the status of faithful martyr, or the Body of Christ who would be oppressed until the return of Christ. Rev. 16:16, for example, refers to Armageddon, or "mount (of) Megiddo." There, Christ will "make right" the initial defeat as he inaugurates a worldwide conquest against his enemies and establish his kingdom. The time of goodwill and loving one's neighbor will be over. Unyielding conquest will be the order of the day.

Joseph (see also chapter 11), for additional example, was sold into slavery in Egypt. Sold as a slave, he became the second most powerful man in the kingdom. Joseph, as Israel's son, symbolized the future of the kingdom of Israel. It was by his actions that Jacob/Israel and his other sons were brought into the land of Egypt, a land that was also associated with Ishmael. There, they could settle down and multiply with the aid of Egyptian resources, becoming large enough as a body of people to embody the seed of a new nation (cf. Ex. 1:7–9). Exodus 1:7 states that they multiplied (*rab*), swarmed (*sharats*), and filled (*male'*) the land so much that the Egyptian pharaoh saw them as a threat to his own power in his own kingdom.

The intent of the story is not a factual accounting of what happened to the Hebrews. The likelihood is that there was *no* Joseph and the Hebrews were not slaves in Egypt. *But what a great foundation story, from slavery to monarchy!* In fact, there is no archaeological evidence supporting the story. The *only* point of reference is the account in Genesis, the whole of which I describe as a national foundation myth describing the ideological contours of an Israelite collective body. What is the function of such a narrative? If nationalism is "a pervasive cognitive and affective orientation rather than a coherent ideology" then nationalist narratives codify, ritualize in their retelling the expected dominant orientation.[11] The medley of stories in Genesis portrays the emergence, the growth, and the burgeoning of a specific historical kingdom, Israel. National narratives evoke collective pride and reinforce the dominant contours of collective identity, as well as reinforce the dominant distributions of power.

It is helpful to read the story of Sarah and Hagar through a nationalist lens that facilitates an alignment of individual identity with the larger political body.[12] Granted, that would have been the ideal of the biblical author. It is unlikely that the common populace would have known the stories. Instead,

156 *Chapter 9*

it is more likely the author wrote with progressivist intent, telling the story of Israel to describe what it *should* be and why the defeated kingdom of the past failed to fully embody that ideal. As I mentioned earlier, this puts the editorial context of Genesis around the 6th century BCE, likely during the time in which Judean scribes were displaced into Babylonia—a time that is increasingly the consensus among biblical scholars.

Vis-à-vis Sarah, Hagar, who may also symbolize the author's idealization of Egypt, is the colonized body of the minority. She is the marginalized woman whose body is used to perpetuate the lineage of Abraham. She receives none of the benefits of being a wife. In fact, because she is successful, and because her son plays with Isaac as an equal, ignorant of hierarchical divisions, as children are wont to do, Sarah tells Abraham that he must drive Hagar into the wilderness. It is a self-serving demand. If both Ishmael and Isaac are accepted as Abraham's sons, and they are equals in that respect, Ishmael is first in line for Abraham's birthright and blessing. *But the Israelites, not the Egyptians, were Yahweh's people, according to the biblical author.*

Often, when this story is told to children in churches or synagogues, those stories highlight Abraham provided Hagar with some provisions before sending her on her way, as though he were trying to insure her survival but that he had no other choice. That he was torn up about the decision but followed his wife's promptings because they resonated with God's initial command to trust in the divine to make Sarah fertile is eagerly assumed by many interpreters. Ishmael, on that count, was the product of Sarah and Abraham taking matters into their own hands. Yet Abraham's reputation, but probably not Sarah's, could still be saved. As Augustine wrote, "As regards this transaction [impregnating Hagar], Abraham is in no way to be branded as guilty concerning the concubine, for he used her for the begetting of progeny, not for the gratification of lust; and not to insult, but rather to obey his wife." (*City* XVI.25). But to me, the story doesn't sound so amicable. Hagar and Ishmael are abandoned in the wilderness, symbolic of a lack of protection and a lack of cultural support base. Whatever provisions they were given, it does not seem to have been for more than a day or two. Like colonized bodies, they were sentenced to death because they did not fit within the cultural normative symbolized by Abraham's family.

Anybody who has been in the wilderness of Judea and in the surrounding environment knows that without proper food, water, shade, or transportation, there is a high likelihood of death. Oddly enough, Sarah is nowhere near this series of events to witness firsthand the demise of a woman and her child. She demands that they be driven out, but leaves it to Abraham to do it, which he does. In fact, Sarah's action and inaction are not surprising. How she is portrayed in the Bible shows a history of oppressing Hagar, which causes Hagar to run away. Yahweh (not Elohim) tells her to return to Sarah and submit

Sarah's (Colonizing) Laughter and Hagar's (Colonized) Tears 157

(Gen. 16:6–9). Hagar obeys, only to be chased out again by Sarah later on (Gen. 21:9–10).

The reason they don't die, according to Gen. 21:17–19, is that Elohim heard the boy's voice and reveals to Hagar a well of water. He promises her that Ishmael will grow up and become an ancestor to many descendants whose bodies we later Bible readers know will serve as a foil against which Israelite identity will be measured. Even when God promised Abraham that Ishmael will become a nation (*goy*), it is through the figure of Elohim, not Yahweh (cf. Gen. 21:12). Not only that, but Ishmael's descendants would become peoples outside the boundaries of Israel and Judah. Can we, as I proposed earlier, read Elohim as associated with the land, the somewhat unrefined foundation, and Yahweh with the kingdom built upon the land? To reinforce the ideological and ethnic separation between Isaac and Ishmael, the passage affirms that Isaac will be Abraham's "seed" (*zara*), which is the basis of the patriarchal lineage. Monotheistic tradition maintains that Isaac and Ishmael would become the ancestors of Jews, Christians, and Muslims. The story becomes a basis for explaining conflict between these main groups, which has frequently oriented itself around land ideologies: who has the right to the land *and* who is the beneficiary of the revelation of God? That conflict continues to shape relations between the "children of Isaac" and the "children of Ishmael." Take, for example, the following rejection on a Christian talk show of Muslims as diabolical (and how the statement correlates to a national narrative and land ideology). "They want to bring chaos because their mahdi will appear. . . . What if they're nice Islamic people looking to have the American Dream and to make a life for themselves? That's ridiculous. That's absolutely ridiculous! . . . If you're a Muslim looking for a good life, go to Dubai. . . . Why would they want to come to America? . . . It's a plan. They're not coming here for the American Dream, they're coming here to destroy America."[13] Why are Muslims not fit for the American Dream, according to this speaker from the Jim Bakker show? Because they are not Christian, and they do not belong to the tradition of Isaac's children.

To read Sarah and Hagar from a more modern perspective is to read the conflict between them as symbolic of the conflict that continues to exist between the main monotheistic traditions. In fact, the tendency in interpretative traditions has been to avoid reading Hagar and Sarah as women with real struggles and to see them as allegories. "The allegorizing of Sarai and Hagar as ideas rather than women has precedent within the NT, in Paul's use of Hagar as an allegory for the Old and New Covenants in Gal. 4:21–31."[14] This conflict has resulted in a series of wars in the Middle Ages over the land of Jerusalem and surrounding environments. It was a conflict that saw an unfortunate number of crusades, and it is one that continues to exist even in the modern context in debates over the state of Israel and the territories of

158   *Chapter 9*

Palestine. Building prejudices against Muslims also became the background for several papal bulls. For example, *Super Gregem Dominicum* (Eugene IV) forbade Castilian Christians from eating, drinking, living, or bathing with Jews and Muslims. In addition, any testimony of Jews and Muslims against Christians was declared invalid. Pope Nicholas V in *Dum diversas* authorized perpetual slavery of Muslims, pagans, and other unbelievers in Portugal: "invadendi, conquerendi, expugnandi, et subjugandi illorumque personas in perpetuam servitutuem redigendi." In a similar spirit, I have lost count of the times in which I have heard that the United States should uphold an international policy to support Israel and that Palestinians, who are homogenized as Muslim, should acquiesce to Israel's authority.

Hagar symbolizes the marginalized woman, the slave, and the foreigner. "It is a testament to the power of Hagar's story that both sides of the slavery debate [i.e., apologists and abolitionists] have wanted to claim her for themselves."[15] While God promises Hagar that her son's descendants will be numerous, she remains a slave rejected by Sarah. The sense of that lay behind Matthew Henry's comment that Ishmael's descendants will be multiplied for the sake of Abraham but not sanctified (or taken into the covenant; see *Com. Bible* 108). Her story in the Bible ends not with her liberation, but her rejection. While Ishmael may be made into a great nation (*but one still considered an outsider in relation to Israel/Judah!*), Hagar's last act is to procure a wife for Ishmael in Egypt (Gen. 21:20). And Ishmael, she was already promised, will be "a wild ass of a man. His hand will be against all, and the hand of all will be against him" (Gen. 16:12). He will be uncivilized, unregulated by the cultural values, mores, obligations, and institutions that anchor Israel's collective, national identity. *Like Cain's restlessness?* Was not something similar said to justify the taking of black persons to be slaves in Europe and the Americas? That slavery was a type of divine domestication of uncivilized bodies?[16] One could certainly point to passages describing the changed relationship between Hagar and Sarah *because* of Hagar's pregnancy; even claiming, as some theologians have done, that Hagar was kicked out because she acted outside her station. Most English translations highlight a personal element: "Hagar despised Sarai/Sarah" (Gen. 16:4). The Hebrew emphasizes role distribution over personal disdain: *vatere' kiy haratah vatteqal gbirtah b'eyneyha* ("when she saw that she was pregnant, her mistress of servants became contemptible in her eyes"). In the story, Hagar's station changed, opening her eyes to the possibility that she could be more than a slave. She saw Sarah as the symbol of what kept her in her subordinated position. To be free from oppression, she left but was instructed by *mal'ak Yahweh* ("a messenger of Yahweh") to return to her "mistress of servants," or "lady, queen" (*gbirah*) and "be lowly/submissive under her hand" (Gen. 16:9). *The feminized Egyptian was commanded to be subordinate to Israel by Israel's god.* Trible was right to bemoan, "And yet, the messenger has ordered her to return to affliction. Rather than dispelling suffering, divine hearing affirms it."[17] Faced with an appalling narrative, we should avoid reading modern theological sentiments into the story, that Hagar was treated well, that her contempt for Sarah was a sin, and more. Hagar was a slave. Sarah was her authoritative mistress. Hagar interpreted her pregnancy with Abraham's first-born as a change in status from slave to surrogate mother. She saw that the hierarchy under which she lived was not ideal. Sarah saw neither. *And in all of this, where was Abraham?*

Did Hagar harbor disdain for Sarah? Or did she disdain the hierarchy that told her she was only a slave to a woman, who, being a woman, was already a lowered status in a patriarchal culture? Responses to those questions often adopt the perspective of the biblical author. For example, Calvin, in the relative comfort of not being slave, and with what are hard *not* to interpret as lofty colonial ideals, wrote that while Hagar had been "treated with singular kindness and honor begins to treat her mistress with contempt" she behaved in manner worthy of chastisement (cf. *Com. Gen.* 1.16.4). Moreover,

> [Hagar] remained a servant, though she had escaped the hands of her mistress; because liberty is not to be obtained by stealth, nor by flight, but by manumission. Moreover, by this expression, God shows that he approves of civil government, and that the violation of it is inexcusable. The condition of servitude was then hard; and thanks are to be given to the Lord, that this barbarity has been abolished; yet God has declared from heaven his pleasure, that servants should bear the yoke; as also by the mouth of Paul, he does not give servants their freedom, nor deprive their masters of their use; but only commands them to be kindly and liberally treated. (*Com. Gen.* 1.16.8)

Because she imagined herself to be more than a slave, Yahweh commanded her to subject her body to its yoke once again. It is logical that Hagar saw herself as a mother, and as a mother of Abraham's lineage. Yet with Hagar's rise, Sarah saw her own insecurity and lowered position. In the same sense that empires see colonized peoples as slaves, or as inferior individuals and cultures that need to be civilized in a way consistent with the imperial or colonial culture, Sarah assumed the superior cultural identity chosen by Yahweh. In turn, she expected Hagar to fit within the dominant cultural expectations that centralized power in Sarah's relationship with Abraham. While her standing was initially threatened, it was regained when she bore Isaac. Yet because Isaac and Ishmael play together, presenting themselves as equals who might share Abraham's blessing, she took action to reinforce the insider-outsider distinction.

160   *Chapter 9*

And not only do Isaac and Ishmael present themselves as equals, but as children, they represent a potentially altered cultural identity in which some element of the slave-master distinction is broken. Initially, we readers may be tempted to see them as brothers. They represent a future, one that Sarah's character does not appreciate. Why does the text never describe Hagar as fearful of the children playing together, even if that meant her son might get overlooked in Abraham's blessing? Perhaps Hagar was happy in her possibly elevated status, even if it was not on the same level as Sarah's. That sense of satisfaction wasn't shared by Sarah, who becoming jealous, convinces Abraham, who does not seem to need much convincing, to drive Hagar and her son into the wilderness. This act rejects them from "civilization," which entails being beneficiaries of the community, and forces upon them the category of uncivilized bodies. As readers, we are counting on Elohim's promise to transform Ishmael into a nation, but we know also that Elohim has been known to second-guess (cf. Gen. 9:11–17). We are also reminded of Gen. 15:13, which foreshadows the enslavement and oppression of Hebrews in "a land not theirs," which further separates Isaac and Ishmael because it will be Isaac's descendants to whom Yahweh gives the land when Yahweh liberates the Hebrews from the Egyptians.[18]

The Bible justifies the near death of Hagar and Ishmael in the wilderness on the assumption that God had chosen the Israelites, which fits the function of a national narrative. God chose a specific cultural group, a "seed," that would be the beacon on a hill, the representation of Yahweh to all the peoples in the world. They would come to Zion, to the temple of Yahweh; they would come and become enlightened (cf. Isa. 2:3).

Such sentiments can easily reinforce an imperialist ideology. They are, to borrow from Bhabha, performative through the establishment of de-formative structures.[19] Empires assume themselves or present themselves as beacons of light in the world. And they also justify taking land and overriding different cultures. The identities and bodies of Hagar and Ishmael *could* be marginalized because they were not central to the story of Israel. Their importance was in their rejection; it symbolized Israel's power (though certainly idealistic, we know from history) to reject Egypt, which had a history of trying to claim territory in Palestine.

Sarah and Hagar represent these things symbolically, but they also display the inequalities of power built into Israelite culture. Hagar's position is reinforced as subordinate, marginalized, and when she steps outside that position, she suffers consequences that even God condones (in part because she is a foreigner). And that is why Sarah drives a wedge between Isaac and Ishmael, and between Hagar and the rest of the family. To support Israel's uniqueness, Abraham leaves Hagar and Ishmael in the middle of nowhere with "some bread and a waterskin." *Like leaving a toddler in the desert with nothing but a lunch box!*

Sarah and Abraham did this. What Sarah and Abraham represent did this. Hagar symbolically represents the postcolonial, or colonized, position in the modern context. In the struggle over land and birthright, which is spoken of now as a political right, violence against colonized bodies has been justified under the presupposition that a particular community has a divine right to the land. Perhaps it should not be surprising that Israel's Declaration of the Establishment of the State of Israel written in the 20th century CE invokes a similar idea,

> Eretz-Israel [the land of Israel, Palestine] was the birthplace of the Jewish people. Here their spiritual, religious and political identity was shaped. Here they first attained to statehood, created cultural values of national and universal significance and gave to the world the eternal Book of Books. After being forcibly exiled from their land, the people kept faith with it throughout their Dispersion and never ceased to pray and hope for their return to it and for the restoration in it of their political freedom.[20]

Hagar was rejected. And she was rejected in confirmation of everything that stands outside the boundaries of what the biblical author, with his own cultural prejudices, viewed as the idealized national identity of Israel. With the Bible equated with divine revelation in a universal sense, the story of Hagar and Sarah offers justification for preserving racial purity and ideologies of land based on the assumed election of a specific "body" of people. Monotheistic traditions preserve that body in the makeup of their members.

Hagar's and Ishmael's struggle to survive did not earn them liberation from a dominating meaning system and framework. Yet maybe their spirits persist among peoples who continue to struggle for freedom from oppression. Maybe the need for accountability in a world in which disfigured bodies are the foils against which power is measured demands that they be given the freedom to narrate their own stories apart from the colonizing influences that dehumanize them.

NOTES

1. Trible, "Ominous Beginnings," location 1010.

2. Von Rad, *Genesis*, 185.

3. Compare Nikole Hannah-Jones, ed., *The 1619 Project: A New Origin Story* (Random House Publishing Group, 2021).

4. See also the discussion in von Rad, *Genesis*, 192.

5. See also Trible, "Ominous Beginnings," location 1090.

162   *Chapter 9*

6. Cf. the work Julius Wellhausen, *Prolegomena to the History of Israel* (Atlanta: Scholars Press, 1994).

7. See Cataldo, *Breaking Monotheism.*

8. Von Rad, *Genesis*, 234.

9. See also the discussion of the symbolism of "wilderness" throughout Eliade, *Eternal Return.*

10. See also the discussion in von Rad, *Genesis*, 234.

11. Bart Bonikowski, "Nationalism in Settled Times," *Ann. Rev. Soc.* 42 (2016): 428.

12. Cf. the description of narratives in Bonikowski, 432.

13. Zach Drew on "'Jim Bakker Show' Co-Host: Muslim Immigrants Are 'Coming Here To Destroy America,'" *The Jim Bakker Show*, August 1, 2016, https://www .rightwingwatch.org/post/jim-bakker-show-co-host-muslim-immigrants-are-coming -here-to-destroy-america/.

14. Judd, "Hagar," 6.

15. Judd, 1.

16. Cf. Warren, *Southern Slavery.* See also Haynes, *Noah's Curse*, locations 1967–1982

17. Phyllis Trible and Letty M. Russell, eds., *Hagar, Sarah, and Their Children: Jewish, Christian, and Muslim Perspectives*, Kindle (Louisville: Westminster John Knox Press, 2006), 41.

18. See also the discussion in Judd, "Hagar," 12.

19. Bhabha, *The Location of Culture*, 241–42.

20. "The Declaration of the Establishment of the State of Israel," GOV.IL, May 14, 1948, https://www.gov.il/en/Departments/General/declaration-of-establishment -state-of-israel.

Chapter 10

Jacob and Esau

I sometimes find myself "examining my identity," as other people examine their conscience. As you may imagine my object is not to discover within myself some "essential" allegiance in which I may recognize myself. Rather the opposite: I scour my memory to find as many ingredients of my identity as I can. I then assemble and arrange them. I don't deny them. (Amin Maalouf)[1]

The story of Isaac and Ishmael (cf. chapters 7, 9) highlighted brothers who symbolized the process of separation between insider and outsider along the lines of birthright—who has it and who doesn't. The story of Jacob and Esau does something similar. Esau was born first, Jacob second. Both were sons of Isaac, the nearly sacrificed son of Abraham, who is never described as doing much after the event, even that he went blind, which may symbolize his failure or inability to see what Yahweh promised his father. In the end, only one of Isaac's sons would be the symbolic patriarch of Israel's twelve tribes; but it would not be without struggle.

In contrast to those of Esau, Jacob's struggles are portrayed as of a "higher order," rather than the base experiences of a barely civilized barbarian, which seems to be the biblical author's view of Esau. As the patriarch of Israel's tribes, Jacob must engage in a battle of wits with Laban for a wife (Gen. 29:9–28), outwit Laban for flocks (Gen. 30:31–43), wrestle with God (Gen. 32:23–29 ET; 32:24–30 HB), and defeat the men of Shechem for being "uncivilized" (Gen. 34:1–31). As a counterpoint to Jacob's expected intellectual and physical sophistication, Esau was described by the biblical author according to the attributes of his body, "red and hairy." I can't help but think this is the type of stereotypical reduction of body to physical attributes found similarly in more modern cultures emphasizing, in contrast to the idealized body, base attributes and behaviors of a comparatively inadequate body: such as Native Americans as "red," Asians as "yellow," Africans as "black," etc.

163

164   Chapter 10

Reduction of the person to obvious attributes of the body is typical of prejudiced categorization, especially when a center of power expresses it over a
marginalized and peripheral body. It defines the individual body as "other"
by emphasizing its difference from the normative. Wrapped up in a narrative
retelling of social history or within a dominating tradition, it reinforces the
peripheral status of the individual. If identity is "the socially constructed,
socially sanctioned . . . complex of self-significations" having the ability to
reduce those to externally imposed categories reinforces a center-periphery
relationship of power over others: red, black, hairy, foreigner, oriental, sinner.[2]

> Though "othering" and colonialism often go hand-in-hand, as we shall see, the
> discourse of the "other" in Western Europe during the modern period was not
> nearly the intellectual arm of imperialism; equally—as emphasized by Fanon,
> Said, and others—it played a central role in the process of self-definition. Thus,
> while a view of alteritism as a rhetoric of control and domination is surely
> accurate to a certain extent, it is important not to lose sight of the fact that this
> rhetoric "often exists alongside (behind) a rhetoric of more obscure desires: of
> sexual desires or fears, of class, or religious, or national, or racial anxieties, of
> confusion or outright self-loathing."[3]

For Schick, the author of the preceding quote, desiring, othering, and body
all intersect at the level of the individual's definition. The concept is a general
sociological truth: what cultures desire at their most basic levels provide the
foundation for what marks out distinctions between insider and outsider, distinctions which are marked upon the body of the outsider in a reverse image
of what the insider imagines themself to be. Paolo Mantegazza spoke to such
tendencies describing humanity as: "savage and uncivilized tribes, for it is in
these scala that are most easily traced the roots and the infinite divergencies
of the sexual life of humankind."[4] These tendencies deal with the preservation of lineage, society, communal stability, and relations of power, which are
driven by the need to control the social-political definition of the community
and the preservation of its (sense of) internal stability. Even where power is
consolidated in the hands of the individual, it does not entirely shed its concern for preserving the world–though now defined as the individual sees it.
This helps us understand that how the biblical author describes Esau entails
an assumption about power in which Esau's body is peripheral. Esau's actions
revolve around base senses such as hunger and tend to reflect emotional and
physical responses consumed by the instinctual needs of his body. Genesis
25:27, for instance, describes Esau as a man "who knew hunting" who was a
"man of the field" (*yode'a tsayid 'ish sadeh*) in contrast to Jacob as a "complete" (*tam*) man who lived in tents. Here, the walls of a tent, like the walls
of a home or a city, separate Jacob from the chaotic world outside. Until they

are breached, as the threat at Lot's door reminds us, which results in a type of anxiety that is frequently more profound than any other.

All this establishes Esau's downfall from the status of the firstborn son. Rather, his biological placement remains. He was born first, but he loses the birthright and blessing through manipulation. The contrast between the parents is also mapped out on the sons. Isaac loved Esau for "[the taste of] game in his mouth" but Rebekah loved Jacob (Gen. 25:28), presumably for who he was *completely*, given the contrast established with the disjunctive clause in Hebrew between Isaac's love for Esau because he liked the taste of game and Rebekah's love of Jacob without additional qualifications. This contrast also reinforces the biblical view of Isaac (described in chapter 9) as a bit of dolt. He gives love because his taste buds are excited. The comparison reinforces the qualities of the sons. Esau is favored by Isaac only for what he can provide in terms of material resources, which also testifies to Isaac's lack of sophistication. (Perhaps lingering PTSD, or daddy issues, from being nearly sacrificed on an altar by his own father?) But Rebekah loves Jacob, seemingly without restriction, and Jacob becomes a "complete" person.

As readers, we are left to assume that Jacob learns some of the more domesticated acts because of his relationship to his mother. He knows how to cook stew (Gen. 25:29), which becomes an important element in Jacob's taking of Esau's birthright. Like a woman, he manipulates the "seat" of a man. But Esau is more easily duped because of his uncivilized nature. His lack of intellectual sophistication and appearance are reminiscent of a Neanderthal—the qualities of which are also those that mark outsiders unfamiliar with dominant cultural norms. These become the basis for what is an increasing definition of him as an outsider. His body symbolizes in its function the uncivilized, unintellectual (quasi) savage creature. Left to his actions, interpretive traditions will compose assumptions about Esau, that his is an inferiority due not only to an existence defined solely by reflex but also a propensity toward evil, as that which threatens the normative order of those in authority.[5]

When he returns from a hunt, he can't think beyond his senses, which are brought to the fore in his stomach. Incidentally, the lower abdomen was also the reference point for sexual desire, a longstanding conception that may also be at the heart of later aestheticism, which typically included abstaining from sex and extreme forms of fasting and other highly regulated dietary practices. Driven by sensual need and desire, like most individuals who see themselves in a position of civilized authority describe of ethnic bodies they see as inferior and base, he pleads with Jacob to feed him some of the "red stuff" he was boiling for stew because he was "faint" with hunger. The biblical author adds, "for that reason he was called 'Edom'" (Gen. 25:30). Consistent with his birth narrative, Esau was described as red (*admoni*) and "hairy," or *se'ar* (Gen. 25:25), which is a play on the word for goat *and* Mt. Seir, which

166   *Chapter 10*

designated the land of Edom south of the Dead Sea. *Like Asians are yellow, Native Americans are red, and Africans are black?* This act of categorical reduction keeps the colonized body, as Fanon bemoans, halfway between "domesticated man" and beast. With simplified categories that denote the boundary between order and chaos, the colonized body so categorized is always already known by the same character traits. He "lives on nothing and understands only the language of violence."[6] That is how the biblical author portrays Esau. Like the Moabites and the Ammonites, whose birth narratives can also be linked to that general geographic area (cf. chapter 8), the Edomites had an often-tense relationship with the Israelites. Once again, we are reminded that these ancestral narratives are *nationalist narratives. The ancestors of the Israelites are producers and planners. The ancestors of the Edomites, who once celebrated the fall of Jerusalem (Ps. 137:7), will be subordinate to the authority of Judah/Israel (cf. 2 Sam. 8:14; 1 Chron. 18:12–13; Jer. 49:19).* And that "red stuff" that the unsophisticated red man desired so much he'd give anything just to have it? Lentil stew (Gen. 25:34).

But there is a wrinkle in this portrayal: we cannot get around the play on gender and ethnic stereotypes. While the author portrays Esau as a hairy, ruddy, and predisposed toward the masculine role in a non-sedentary society of hunter-provider, the same author presents Jacob in effeminate terms. Is the father of Israel more like a stereotypical woman, or even what many modern readers would associate as the qualities of a gay man? The author's first descriptions of him adopt qualities that can be said of women. He lived in tents (Gen. 25:27). His mother loved him (25:28). He cooked (25:29; like his mother, cf. 27:9). He is named "Jacob" because he "follows at the heel" (25:26), which implies insidiousness and deceitfulness, both of which Jacob uses to gain Esau's birthright and blessing. Is there a connection to Eve and her heel here (cf. Gen. 3:15)? In her story, while the serpent attacks (chews on) the heel of her masculine offspring, he will crush the serpent's head. In the account of Jacob, there may be two reasons for this. It was not uncommon among the biblical prophets, for example, to describe Israel in strong feminine terms to comment, usually criticize, on its sociopolitical function and status. Another reason can be found in deception, which invokes the idea of a feminine technique, such as one might loosely parallel with biblical women such as, Eve, Jael, Esther, among others, as the means by which he gains what he (and his mother, cf. Gen. 27:5–10) wanted over the stereotypical male. Jacob and Rebekah conspire together to deceive Isaac into giving Jacob his blessing (27:15–30). Esau suffers the consequence. With his father being unwilling to "undo" the act, Esau married (*laqach*, "took") an Ishmaelite woman because he heard his father viewed Canaanite women as evil (28:6–9).[7] According to the biblical author, that woman was Mahalath, the sister of Nebaioth (a

Jacob and Esau   167

possible reference to Nabateans) and daughter of Ishmael. Ishmael enters the story again through his descendants who are fit only for what the biblical author portrays as "idiot men" whose intellect is restricted to their "stomachs" (28:9). And did not Ishmael almost die because of an empty stomach only to be saved so that he could use his loins to procreate for the benefit of Abraham, who symbolized the center of power? Are not these descriptions similar to how Esau is described? *Gormandizing and fucking, that's what the savages do!* Even those individuals trying to find themselves apart from the colonial experience frequently see themselves, and their internal anxieties, through the categorical lenses imposed upon them. That, for example, is how Libyan writers Tayib Salih and Ahmad Ibrahim al-Faqih portray their main characters, who seek to know themselves but are haunted by sexual encounters and fractured relationships as they try to define themselves within the framework of a dominating center.[8]

According to Faro, Esau's parallel is Cain, but the former eventually masters his murderous rage, adopting the demands of an ethical model symbolized by Jacob, and "receives" Jacob (and his status), resulting in a happy and "blessed" life. *The beast is civilized by its master?* Prior to that, however, Esau's "uncontrolled inclinations," driven as they were by sense and unbridled emotion, posed a chaotic threat to Jacob, which is why Isaac instructs Jacob to flee (Gen. 27:43–45).[9] Reducing the colonized body to the status of a beast permits a moral route around the quagmire of a human problem. To see the other as a beast permits justification of one's treatment of the other as such.[10] This, to give a broader historical parallel, was perhaps the most common ideological justification of slavery in the European and American territories.

But a transformation that reinforces both gendered and social hierarchies occurs in which Jacob becomes portrayed by the biblical author more as a patriarch than an effeminate character. Once Isaac blesses him, he sends Jacob to Paddan Haram to find a wife. On his journey, he has a vision (at Bethel) in which Yahweh appeared to him confirming his place in the lineage from Abraham to Israel, repeating also the Abrahamic Covenant and adding that the descendants will be known by Jacob's own name, which is later changed to "Israel" (cf. Gen. 28:13–14; 32:27–28 ET [28–29 HB]). He wrestled with Elohim (32:24–30 ET [25–31 HB]), but not Yahweh, the former who could not beat him (32:25 ET [26 HB]). As a result, he became the ancestral "father" to the twelve tribes of Israel.

In his feminine-to-masculine transformation, Jacob learns how to manipulate men and *then* wrestle against them. While Jacob does not manipulate men through sexuality (compare Esther, Ruth, Jael [Judg. 4:18–21], Delilah [Judg. 16]), the location for the sensual manipulation he *can* manipulate is very near that of the location where men feel hormonal stirrings. The concentration of

168   *Chapter 10*

feelings occurs in the lower abdomen. That location is very close to where
one feels hunger pangs. While Jacob does not manipulate Esau through sex,
he manipulates Esau through the seat of masculine decision making. That
may be one reason why the ancient conception of the central core, or "heart,"
of human beings was in the abdomen.[11]

Despite his more "masculine" accomplishments, Jacob is never a consistently strong character in the biblical text. He goes blind after he has sons
(Gen. 48:10) and is easily manipulated by his wife and son. His importance
comes through his connection to Abraham and to his sons, a connection that
is highlighted by his name, Israel, which means "El perseveres," or "fights."
In that, he represents a transitional figure from abject body to desired ideal
under the strength of Elohim.[12]

Perhaps in that process, we see some reference to a cultural process of
"becoming a man." And that process parallels the strengthening of the
ancestral lineage that would lead to the kingdom of Israel (and Judah), from
Abraham, to Isaac, to Jacob-become-Israel, to the twelve tribes. This was
a story of a body *becoming*. And Jacob is the transformative moment of
that process, the culmination of which may be symbolized in his sons, their
descendants, and their taking of the so-called Promised Land (*like one takes
a woman?*). Who he was becomes the abject of who he must be. Like the
collective struggle toward nationhood portrayed in many national narratives,
Jacob undergoes a process of transformation. The intellectual, civilized man
can do this. In contrast, Esau cannot—a contrast possibly also highlighted
by references to his descendants having chieftains rather than kings. Their
political bodies never fully formed, which is reinforced in the claim that Esau
took additional wives from the Canaanites (Gen. 36:2). And, in doing that,
he further seals his fate, separating himself in greater degrees from the center
of power that thrives on the story told in the national foundation myth. In
contrast, Israel emerges from Jacob's loins.

Both brothers determine their fates based on this core: Esau, to satiate his
own individual needs, consumes, while Jacob produces a national lineage.
Jacob's struggles are portrayed as being of a higher order, of becoming or
ascending into his role. His struggles are about the preservation of lineage,
of society, and of communal stability, all manifest in the emergence of a
strong nation (land and people). Esau, on the other hand, becomes relegated
to an ancestor, like Ishmael, of other peoples who inhabit territories near the
Israelites and Judeans but are not fully part of their ethnic identities. Even
the brief list of kings (Gen. 36:31–34) is redefined as chiefs (*'allup*) denoting
a tribe (cf. Gen. 36:15–29, 40). It seems very clear that the switch is intentional for the biblical author. Kings symbolize authority in a civilized society.
Chiefs govern tribes, which would have been seen as something closer to
Bedouin groups than a kingdom. So when Genesis discusses stories of Jacob

as a father, or his living with Laban and fleeing from Laban with Rachel (Gen. 29:10–31:55 ET [29:10–32:1 HB]), these stories are focused on ideas about the preservation of lineage in society and communal stability. Esau's lineage in contrast embodies tribal groups in the area labeled Edom. *A land of red and hairy beasts with a naive understanding of civilized society.*

From a postcolonial perspective, Esau represents the "oriental" of the two brothers. He is a minority character in the sense that he straddles the border between family and foreigner, or insider and outsider. He is portrayed as an uncivilized barbarian motivated more by feeling than intellect. *A common assessment of tribal groups by colonizers.* He struggles with hunger and is prone to emotional and physical responses. In contrast, Jacob develops into the intellectual patriarch, who will father the foundation of the nation of Israel. Esau lives in the hill country like a tribal "savage," giving birth to chiefs who would later coalesce their people into "Edom" (cf. Gen. 36:40–43), which according to the biblical author is a Frankensteinian body of ill-fitting parts forced to function in relation to the civilized man, or patriarch. Perhaps more importantly, how Esau is described by the author, and that description's preservation by later interpreters, speaks to the perspective assumed to reflect authority. Consider the description of Esau alongside Fanon's declaration of the colonized body: "Confronted with a world configured, the colonized subject is always presumed guilty. The colonized does not accept his guilt, but rather considers it a kind of curse, a sword of Damocles. But deep down the colonized subject knows no authority. He is dominated but not domesticated. He is made to feel inferior, but by no means convinced of his inferiority."[13]

The biblical descriptions of Esau and his struggles parallel more modern colonial views of colonized "others." Such can be seen in the traditional ways that cultures of Western Europe and the United States described communities of people outside their own. And they often boiled down to coloration and their assumed lack of civilization; the "other" was frequently described as not being civilized in contrast to the assessing subject, who casts judgement based on their own definition of culture. For example, in the United States, as I described earlier, Native Americans were described as red men, savages, and barbarians who were largely motivated by their senses. "Some are of disposition fearfull, some bold, most cautelous, all Savage."[14] People of the Middle East in French and British cultures were often described in similar terms. Such is the goal of dehumanizing the individual, subordinating them to the whim and will of a dominating and central culture. "No effort is spared to demolish their traditions, to substitute our language for theirs, and to destroy their culture without giving them ours."[15] Can we not see a form of this in the portrayal of Esau as one who does nothing else but accept Jacob and Jacob's claim over the birthright and blessing? All of this speaks to a larger issue.

170   *Chapter 10*

Take, for literary comparison, Joseph Conrad's reductive description of Jim as a peripheral body:

> He was an inch, perhaps two, under six feet, powerfully built, and he advanced straight at you with a slight stoop of the shoulders, head forward, and a fixed from-under stare which made you think of a charging bull. . . . Jim had always good wages and as much humouring as would have bought the fidelity of a fiend. Nevertheless, with black ingratitude he would throw up the job suddenly and depart. To his employers the reasons he gave were obviously inadequate. They said "Confounded fool!" as soon as his back was turned.[16]

Conrad set up a contrast between the citizen, the person who partakes in the intellectual awareness and advancement of the culture and who benefits from the cultural institution and the community and the nation, and the "other" who does not. The marginalized or colonized body is always described in reductive terms defined from the perspective of a dominant, or dominating, community. Huggan describes this as the "anterior" of the imperial perspective, as the base by which the world is categorized and the boundaries of the "subject" are known.[17] The marginalized or the colonized individual is always described as somehow being less than capable, or not fully comprehending what it means to be a citizen in the dominant (civilized) community. Even when they take part within that community, they are still defined first based on their physical appearance, and then assessed by how much they fit the categories expected for participation within the community. This is a human tendency that motivates postcolonial concerns beyond the more simple binary of colonizer-colonized. This assumption is pervasive in how cultures speak about and categorize the world around them. That is the assumption, for additional literary comparison, that lay behind Ahmida's reflection on Al-Faqih's trilogy of novels:

> The trilogy explodes with all of these contradictions and gives no direct clue as to how they can be resolved. According to the author, there can be no happy ending to this complex novel, not until Libyan society itself resolves these conflicts. The author does not apologize for these contradictions, nor does he create a happy ending for his novel. Indeed, these are not unique contradictions; other societies experiencing colonialism, economic transformation, and social and cultural dislocation suffer the same challenges.[18]

And that, incidentally, is one struggle for the African-American community in the United States. Black men and women are often seen first as "black" and the history of that designation is rooted in a subordinated status, first as slaves, then as three-fifths (note the Three-Fifths Compromise) of a person, and then finally as individuals emerging from segregation but still giving voice to inequalities that oppress them. That cultural history still weighs upon how "black" is defined within a dominant white culture. And it was one reason why George Zimmerman could justify his shooting of Trayvon Martin (in 2012), a "black boy wearing a hoodie." George made assumptions about Trayvon according to the stereotype of someone who existed on the margins of society, denoted as such by his physical appearance and not his intellect. Thus, his body was associated with the "uncivilized" sensual tendencies such as violence. His body was labeled with uncertainty as to whether he would stand in solidarity with the dominant cultural normative or threaten it with chaos. This, as I have been arguing, is like how the biblical author sets up the contrast between Jacob and Esau. Jacob embodied the dominating, "civilized" through its connection to Yahweh, culture over the "uncivilized" and potentially chaotic body Esau represents. That process culminated in his wrestling with God, his dedicating of Peniel, and his encounter of Yahweh in Bethel (cf. Gen. 28:10–22), completing the colonization of the territory Abraham had begun. *Only the manliest of men can wrestle gods and prevail! Did not Gilgamesh, that man-god from Ur, show that?! To them go the spoils!*

THE VOICELESS BODY OF DINAH
AS A STEPPING STONE?

There is a brief but important story in Jacob's novella about his daughter Dinah, born through Leah. Shechem, the son of Hamor the Hivite, who ruled the area in which Jacob and his household were staying, raped her. Shechem became so infatuated with Dinah that he told his father to "take the girl" for him to be his wife (cf. Gen. 34:1–4). When Hamor went to speak with Jacob about Dinah, he offered to pay anything for the bride price. It was Jacob's sons who spoke on his behalf (cf. Gen. 34:13–17), separating Jacob from the coming act of violence. The bride price, they claimed, was only that Hamor and "all his males" (of his city) be circumcised. In a strange turn of events, the men eagerly agreed, debilitating themselves for several days. During that time, Jacob's sons entered the city and slaughtered all the males and retrieved Dinah (cf. Gen. 34:24–29). In addition, they plundered the city of its wealth, children, and women.

At first blush, the story may seem innocent enough. Jacob and his sons (though more so his sons) are angry and seek to defend Dinah's honor. Yet it is not Dinah's own honor that is tarnished, but "Israel's" (see Gen. 34:7). Does Israel here refer to the kingdom or to the patriarch Jacob, who is renamed Israel? I would argue both. While the man bought land from the sons of Hamor, implying Hamor's initial political authority, Jacob also symbolizes the kingdom that would eventually rule the area in the narrative; it is Jacob/

172   *Chapter 10*

Israel's honor that must be restored through vengeance against Shechem, both the son of Hamor and an historically important Canaanite city. Dinah's now disfigured body is but the arena in which the men of Shechem and the men of Israel seek to lay claim over the other. (Part of Hamor's argument to the men of Shechem was that allowing themselves to be circumcised would grant them access to the wealth of Israel [cf. Gen. 34:23].) That this conquest was inevitable was signaled by the biblical author's claim that after Jacob bought land in Shechem, he built an altar and called it *"el elohe yisrael"* signaling both his own status vis-à-vis Hamor (Jacob becomes Israel) and the coming Israelite kingdom (Gen. 33:20).

Dinah's name is a feminized form of *din*, which can be translated as "judgment" in Hebrew. Yet while she is named, it is unlikely for readers to remember her but to foreshadow the coming "judgment" against Shechem, necessary against the man who raped Dinah and the men of the city requesting Israel to intermarry his family with them. Her body is abused sexually by Shechem and ideologically by her brothers, who see her as nothing more than the property of Israel and justification for their own decision to plunder a Canaanite city. While it is tempting to consider the story a *fait accompli* of justice, it is only so for the Israelite male. Dinah's voice is never heard, nor do readers ever get a sense of who she is as a person. In the narrative, she is no more than the value of her abused body defined by the men controlling her. Her fate fits the overall theme that lurks in the shadows of Jacob's story. It contributes to the founding myth of Israel, which like many similar myths, is built upon the broken bodies of others. Her story was not ultimately hers but that of the Israelite conquest of Shechem. Taking advantage of the disfigured bodies of others is a theme in Jacob's story.

Jacob/Israel succeeds because Esau is crippled by his domestication. No longer the virile male whose phallus is a symbol of strength, he is subordinated to Jacob, betrayed by his own stomach. Like the colonized subject, he too will become angry, and that will impact his relationship with Jacob later on. Esau is here at the point of disjunction: "the splitting, or disjunction, between being dominated and being domesticated—the irresolvable tension between the colonized as both subject and citizen from which anticolonial violence emerges."[19] What of Jacob's position in this tension? Perhaps the ultimate trial of Jacob is the loss of his son Joseph to a caravan of Ishmaelites headed toward Egypt (Gen. 37:25–28; see also 28–36).[20] But note the author does not bother with too much of a distinction and refers to the (slave) traders as Ishmaelites and Midianites (37:28), a cultural linguistic reduction that may be like one referring to all peoples from the continent of Africa as "Africans," or East Asia as "Asians."[21] Sold into slavery by his brothers to slave traders, Jacob's sons seem to draw out proto-tribal divisions. This also establishes an explanation for the constant struggle between the northern kingdom of Israel

Jacob and Esau

and the southern kingdom of Judah, which were distinguished by their tribes. According to 2 Samuel, David would tenuously unite the tribes (cf. 2 Sam. 6:15). Yet it would be Solomon who is credited with solidifying that unification and expanding Israel's borders, which was lost under Rehoboam, Solomon's son (cf. 2 Kgs. 12:8–16). Eventually, in the eighth century, the Assyrians would defeat the northern kingdom of Israel, and it would cease to exist as a kingdom. The Babylonians would defeat the southern kingdom of Judah, and it would never again exist as a physical kingdom. But it would gain new life in the re-imagined version of it that lived in the biblical author's vision, which would itself provide a foundation to the nationalist aspirations of monotheistic traditions Judaism and Christianity.

Though no longer a kingdom, the territory of Judah would remain a province, but apart from the Hasmonean dynasty (ca. 140–63 BCE), it would never again be ruled by any Israelite or Judean monarchy. The desire for political rule would be the basis for a claimed land right pervasive throughout history. Assumptions about divine justification for that desire have become common in Western colonial thinking, so much so that one Christian website seeming to conflate Ishmael and Esau as a foil for Jacob offers this without fear of refutation: "Many Arabs are descendants of Ishmael; but since the land of Canaan was promised to the sons of Jacob, Arabs have no biblical claim to the land of Palestine."[22] *Why? Because they are "red and hairy"?*

NOTES

1. Cited in Ali Abdullatif Ahmida, *Forgotten Voices: Power and Agency in Colonial and Postcolonial Libya* (London: Taylor & Francis, 2005), 55–56.

2. Irvin Cemil Schick, *The Erotic Margin: Sexuality and Spatiality in Alteritist Discourse* (London: Verso Books, 1999), 19.

3. Schick, 23.

4. Cited in Schick, 83; See also Paolo Mantegazza, *Gli amori degli uomini: saggio di una etnologia dell'amore* (Milano: Paolo Mantegazza, 1886), 5.

5. See also the discussion of this type of ideological colonialism in Frantz Fanon, *The Wretched of the Earth*, trans. Richard Philcox, Reprint edition (New York: Grove Press, 2005), location 777.

6. See also Fanon, location 769.

7. On the taxonomy of the lexeme *ra'* (evil) cf. Faro, *Evil in Genesis*, 66–78.

8. See the discussion in Ahmida, *Forgotten Voices*, 55–66.

9. Faro, *Evil in Genesis*, 157.

10. Fanon makes a similar point in *Wretched*, location 757.

11. From a personal conversation with Herbert Huffmon.

174   *Chapter 10*

12. Cf. the discussion of "abject" in Julia Kristeva, *Powers of Horror: an Essay on Abjection*, trans. Leon Roudiez, Reprint edition (New York, NY: Columbia University Press, 1982), 1–6.

13. Fanon, *Wretched*, location 489.

14. John Smith, *The Generall Historie of Virginia, New England & the Summer Isles* (Glasgow/New York: James MacLehose and Sons/The Macmillan Company, 1907).

15. Fanon, *Wretched*, location 762.

16. Joseph Conrad, *Lord Jim & Nostromo* (New York: Modern Library, 1999), 7–8.

17. Graham Huggan, "Decolonizing the Map: Post-Colonialism, Post-Structuralism and the Cartographic Connection," in *Past the Last Post: Theorizing Post-Colonialism and Post-Modernism*, ed. Ian Adam and Helen Tiffin (Calgary: University of Calgary Press, 1990), 129; cited in Schick, *Erotic Margin*, 34.

18. Ahmida, *Forgotten Voices*, 66, emphasis mine.

19. Fanon, *Wretched*, location 509.

20. Note also von Rad, "When one observes in addition that in our narrative Joseph says that he was stolen from the land of the Hebrews (ch. 40.15), one sees clearly that this narrative is connected with that report of Joseph's transfer to Egypt which told of a theft by the Midianites and not of a sale to the Ishmaelites" (*Genesis*, 369–70).

21. See also Judg. 8:24 on the conflation of Ishmaelites and Midianites.

22. Staff, "From Whom Are the Modern Palestinians Descended?" GotQuestions. org, January 4, 2022, https://www.gotquestions.org/Palestinian-descent.html.

Chapter 11

Joseph from Lowly Status into Authoritative Body

Joseph symbolizes a split between domesticated body and colonial authority by highlighting two potential outcomes: the first, that of the marginalized or oppressed body sold into slavery for the benefit of others; the second, that Joseph represents the biblical author's idealized vision of Israelite international power. As part of the Jacob story (compare chapter 10), the novella of his body and its function are symbolic extensions of Jacob-becoming-Israel. "[T]he family," as von Rad observes, "and everything that occurred in it, along with the unmarried sons, went by his name."[1] Kim also observes that Joseph symbolizes a hybrid identity as an outsider and an insider, though he ultimately maintains that Joseph is an important diasporic symbol, an interpretation that works within an interpretive framework of Jews having a perpetual divine right to the land.[2] As readers, we are left to assume in that case that Joseph's success was because of his connection to Jacob, the father of Israel, the symbol of the nation that prevailed against the powers of the land to embrace a higher status as Yahweh's "chosen" people. That idea would explain why Jacob links deliverance to Yahweh in his "last-breath speech" (see Gen. 49:18). Joseph's story is important for establishing the "birth" of a nation (imagery for which Exodus will supply the allusion to breaking water and birthing canal with the Hebrews passing through the Red Sea on their way to becoming "Israelite"). Hyun Chul Paul Kim was correct to write,

> Put another way, in the story of the Diaspora communities, Joseph portrays a model life amid the sociopolitical, ethnic, and economic struggles and tensions between the "insiders" and the "outsiders," and between the powerful and the marginalized.[3]

To set the stage, Joseph's initial downfall began with his brothers, who grew tired of his self-centeredness and borderline narcissism. The author is, however, careful not to describe Joseph in base terms similar to descriptions

176   *Chapter 11*

of Esau, Ham, and Cain. Joseph's aspirations, the author maintains, are greater than violence and the senses. The biblical author separates Joseph from his brothers by giving him an *intellectual* skill, interpreting dreams—a reference to intellect that his brother Judah is not granted in his story with Tamar (which I will discuss shortly). While self-serving at first, that skill became critical later. Joseph describes his dreams to his brothers, in which they bowed down to him (Gen. 37:5–11). Alone, perhaps, that might be an ignorable offense. But preceding his dreams, Joseph was given a special coat, or tunic, because Israel (Jacob's new name) "loved him more than all his sons" (Gen. 37:3). The coat, or tunic, was a symbolic item that represented their father's favor for Joseph, who was the firstborn of Rachel but not the firstborn of all sons (Leah bore sons first). This tension of hierarchy reminds me of the conflict between Sarah and Hagar. With his place in the hierarchy known, Joseph's ego challenged the established hierarchy of authority while Jacob-Israel condoned that challenge. Consequently, Joseph's body clothed is associated with authority. There may in that image be a parallel with the practice of early missionaries to encourage converts among tribespeople to adorn themselves in clothing, the image denoting the authority of the values of the dominating culture. Beneath the symbolic domination is felt the weight of the colonizer's assumption that the colonized body is not one endowed with reason. Its nakedness displays its assumed lack of sophistication and tendency toward base desires and violent responses.[4] Such is the portrayal of Cain, Ham, and Esau but not Joseph, whose clothed body consents him to the values of the cultural status quo.

The narrative thread of this sibling animosity woven through the story of Israel's birth goes back at least to the story of Jacob trying to marry Rachel but Laban tricking him into marrying Leah. Laban deceived Jacob into marrying his older daughter who Jacob did not want to marry. According to Gen. 29:23–25, Jacob took part in his nuptial ritual, putting the stamp on his newly contracted relationship by having sex with Leah who, according to the biblical author, he thought was Rachel. It was only the morning after that he discovered he was married to Leah. *Like Lot, apparently the men related to Abraham can be completely oblivious of who they are fucking!* Perhaps that means that within Israelite culture the female body is as good as what it can produce: heirs, or sons. Even the story of Ruth, to compare a literary cognate, despite attempts to interpret her story as one of a heroine, would confirm this. Once she became pregnant with a son, she all but disappears from the story.[5]

Aware of the portrayal of men as walking penises, *Eikhah Rabba*, proem 24, explains how or why Jacob believed Leah was Rachel on his wedding night to Leah. According to that interpretation, Rachel, as part of the deception, lay underneath the bed while Leah and Jacob were having sex. I can only assume this was not to fulfill some sort of fetish but that Rachel's hidden

Joseph from Lowly Status into Authoritative Body   177

body—outside the discernment of the masculine gaze—gave her the opportunity to moan and make other sexual noises, or to answer a chatty Jacob during sex. *Any sexually experienced person will know that this rejects out of hand the possibility of pillow talk. This could only be utilitarian sex without emotional connection! Or, as my high school peers used to say, wham! Bam! Thank you, Ma'am!* To secure the erotic deception, Rachel taught Leah "all the signs" to convince Jacob. What signs? Sexual responses and behaviors? If so, then Rachel and Jacob were having sex beforehand. If *that* were true, then Jacob would have recognized through his senses of smell and touch Leah to be a new sexual partner. Nevertheless, instead of Leah having to answer, Rachel from under the bed would respond. *Did they have lofted beds for this?* Maybe. If so, how could Jacob not tell a difference between a muffled sound and something (not) coming from someone immediately in front of his face? Suffice it to say, I am not convinced by the explanation offered by *Eikhah Rabba. Leave it to the imagination of men! Eikhah Rabba*'s explanation does not convince us to rescue Jacob from accusations of cluelessness. The whole proposal is absurd and serves only, if not intentionally, to reinforce the masculine gaze as discerning (thus men, in the Bible must be tricked), an idea that adds a further element to Jacob's tricking of Laban and Esau, and Isaac. Even if one gave it one more possibility, interpreting Jacob to take Leah "doggy style," so that Leah's face and vocal expressions would be directed away from Jacob, and I am interpreting this situation using elementary physics, moans coming from Leah would still be clearer than any emitted from underneath a bed. And what happens when Rachel moaned at the wrong time? Could Jacob not tell when the moaning and the motion didn't match up? Fantastical, the story shows the lengths that masculine authors and interpreters will go to explain and protect the idea that the Bible is a sacred text. More than that, it shows the lengths interpreters will go to protect their heroes. Here, Jacob, the father of the twelves tribes of Israel who would inhabit Canaan as promised to Abraham, is saved from ignorance. Rather than questioning the text and what it might imply, interpreters create stories that reinforce the framework of the biblical stories. According to the rabbinic tradition, Rachel took part because she did not want her older sister to be shamed if Rachel married first. It is a nice little homage to the patriarchal structure reinforcing the distribution of authority along bodies in relation. Her body and its own desires are subordinated to the patriarchal structure in which the foundation for Leah's possible shame has already been established.

Doing that protects the intelligence of the patriarchs. It would be just as easy, of course, to say that Jacob was an idiot and that he thought with his penis rather than his head. *Get a little drunk. See a woman willing and able. Let's have a little fun and sort this out later!* But the easy explanation is not the one that many people accept. And the rabbinic interpretation is not that

178   *Chapter 11*

far out of the norm with different interpretations, or the different traditions of interpretation that are given to stories such as this. Even Christian interpretations emphasize the elaborate trick that Laban and Leah played on Jacob, exonerating Jacob from any accusation of idiocy or sexual wantonness.

Understanding that story is important. The conflict between Joseph and his brothers is paralleled in the competition between Leah and Rachel. Rachel was the favored wife and Leah the pitied object. Leah was more fertile, which only emphasized her utilitarian role in contrast to Rachel, who Jacob loved. This is meant to explain in part some of the internecine struggles between different tribes in Israel. The competition between the women for Jacob's favor symbolizes the competition between the tribes of Israel (for Yahweh's favor?).

According to the biblical author, the competition to bear children was great enough that both Rachel and Leah gave their handmaidens, or servants, to Jacob to impregnate (cf. Gen. 30:4; 9). Rachel even names Bilhah's son Naphtali because "I have struggled with my sister yet I prevailed" (30:8). Most English translations translate the phrase in 30:4 *vatitten-lo' . . . l'ishah* as "gave to be a wife." While *ishah* can be translated as "wife," it can also be translated as "woman." That Rachel names Bilhah's son rather than Bilhah suggests Bilhah was not a wife in the literal sense with the right to name her own son, but that she was given to Jacob to bear a child who could be adopted by Rachel. The same practice was done between Abraham, Sarah, and Hagar. A parallel, perhaps, that can be seen in the tribes later competing against each other for the authority over Israel. Bilhah and Zilpah (cf. 30:9), the latter Leah's servant that she gave to Jacob, are voiceless pawns in the game between Rachel and Leah for the attention and favor of Jacob.

Joseph, the narcissistic son of Rachel, was sold into slavery and became a slave of Potiphar while in Egypt (Gen. 37:36). There he loses the cultural frameworks that he once benefited from. In Egypt, he must learn to navigate a new cultural context. Like the colonized body, he takes on a different cultural framework, vocabulary, meaning and sense of identity. He must learn to become something "other," to assimilate into a dominant culture. His "maturation is interdependent with that of his brothers" over whom he will still become an authority.[6] Is that not also the struggle of colonized cultures? That in order to survive, in many situations, after being colonized, they must assimilate the cultural frameworks and values of the colonizing culture? Cultural traditions, frameworks, histories, languages, and so on are written over. Even in contexts where immigrants seek to create cultural pockets in a host culture, in order to preserve their own, what they look and behave like culturally differs from where they originated.[7] In Gen. 50:20, when Joseph meets his brothers again after being sold and imprisoned, he claims God had turned his brothers' intent for evil action into good in order to increase the size of a people identified by a particular ethnicity (Hebrew). The focus thus was on a political or ethnic potential, not what Brueggemann sees as an objective reference to divine creation. The biblical author was neither motivated by nor referring to any dualistic assumptions about good and evil as objective qualities defined in Gen. 1–2. "[P]erhaps in this address to the brothers, the 'good' that God had first discerned in creation (1:31) is renewed and reasserted."[8]

It's difficult to say that Joseph himself was a truly colonized body. He spends some time as a servant in Potiphar's household until Potiphar's wife tries to have sex with him (Gen. 39:7–15). According to the biblical text, Joseph cried out, "No," and ran out of the house. But Potiphar's wife held on to his cloak as "evidence." In sexual frustration, she accuses Joseph of trying to sleep with her, claiming that when she screamed, he became frightened and ran off ripping part of his garment. A cloak once set him apart. Now, it is evidence of a crime.

Different theories have been offered attempting to explain why Potiphar's wife wanted to have sex with Joseph. Most of these are by masculine, heterosexual interpreters projecting their own suppressed desires and feelings upon the story, whether of the excitement of illicit sex (and being sexually wanted) or seeing themselves in Joseph's idealized masculine body and what it represents through the coming divine rescue of Jacob's children. Some label Potiphar's wife an adulteress. Others maintain that being a "captain of the guard," Potiphar was rarely home and did not satisfy his wife, or that he was a eunuch and that his wife was seeking sex wherever she could get it. *The assumption that women must be sexually domesticated is very heterosexual and masculine!* In nearly all accounts, however, it is the woman who is described as licentious. This leads one to conclude that upon her body is simultaneously projected the desires *and* the fears of masculine readers of the Bible.

Because Joseph was a slave and Potiphar's wife held a higher social station based on her marriage to Potiphar, Joseph was jailed. We can speculate that if Joseph was not jailed, it would have brought shame to Potiphar. Choosing the slave over the master's family would have created social problems by making a value statement that threatened to undermine the social-economic hierarchy and order.

There is a parallel in how we categorize the bodies of "others" as outsiders and dangerous in relatively modern situations such as the 20th century United States and later for understanding the impact of slavery upon the African-American culture or body, and the place of that body within a culture defined primarily as white, heterosexual, able, and masculine. Who does the majority listen to without question more than the other? The black body or the white body? Who is the majority more likely to believe as being an aggressor,

180 *Chapter 11*

the black male or the white male at any given time? These sorts of prejudices and assumptions are there culturally because of the historical tradition of the United States and the influence that slavery and segregation had upon its culture.[9] That is also what lay behind Malcolm X's statement, "Don't let anybody who is oppressing us ever lay the ground rules. Don't go by their games, don't play the game by their rules. Let them know that this is a new game, and we've got some new rules."[10] Cultural values do not change overnight; it is a long process. That is true because, as Peter Berger wrote, "Men *together* shape tools, invent languages, adhere to values, devise institutions, and so on. Not only is the individual's participation in a culture contingent upon a social process . . . but his continuing cultural existence depends upon the maintenance of specific social arrangements."[11] Once those things have been created and legitimated by a dominant culture, changing them entails changing the manners by which individuals interact with each other culturally along with the distributed relationships of authority and power worked out upon their bodies. As social agents, even though we ourselves may not espouse inequality or consciously exercise prejudice, the cultural history creates situations, values, and assumptions that are rooted in the prejudices of the past. We participate in that until their impacts are addressed, which entails a conscious effort to change them.

In Joseph's situation, society was not self critically analyzing. But we can understand why Joseph was jailed with no apparent trial. The body of the slave was disposable and the canvas upon which the values of the dominant culture were marked out. We do not want to assume the modern sense of innocent before proven guilty, such as in the United States, was a motivation in the past. The judgment that was leveled was connected to the positions of the individuals involved. A slave did not have an equal voice to a master. A woman did not have an equal voice to a man. The colonized body was marginalized and silenced.

Joseph presents such a body in his *dis*-placement, which symbolizes his own culture, into prison in a culture imposed upon him through circumstance (and slavery). But the analogy is temporary. The story changes direction. As Kim puts it, "The empire has been and is still dangerous and seductive, cold and utterly utilitarian. Joseph as the Hebrew-Egyptian ruler thus betrays the conceptual tension between the good and virtuous Joseph (47:1–12) and the bad and oppressive Joseph (47:13–26)."[12] While Joseph remains in prison for a time, he is ultimately liberated into a position of authority and power (according to Gen. 41:46, he was 30 years old when he was released from prison to serve the pharaoh), benefiting from the intellectual skill he was credited earlier in his story. While in prison, he interpreted the dreams of two individuals, a cupbearer and a baker from pharaoh's court. Both had displeased the pharaoh and as a consequence were thrown into prison (Gen. 40:1–4), an account which may emphasize the whim and fickle nature of pharaoh's actions. Both have dreams they cannot understand and ask Joseph to interpret them (Gen. 40:5–19). The cupbearer, Joseph claimed, would be reinstated but the chief baker impaled upon a pole (40:12–13; 18–19). His body became a billboard for any who would dare challenge the order of society that hinged upon the voice of the pharaoh.

Egypt also functions as a symbol with double meaning in the story. It is a rival power against Persia and it was a place of forced settlement of Judeans following their defeat to the Babylonian Empire.[13]

When the pharaoh has a dream that his wise men cannot interpret, or at least their interpretations are unsatisfactory, the cupbearer remembered Joseph and brought him to the attention of the pharaoh (Gen. 41:9–13), who tells Joseph about his dreams. According to Joseph, Egypt will have seven years of plenty followed by seven years of famine. To offset the economic impact, imperial storehouses should buy excess grain and produce. During the seven years of famine, the surplus would provide for the kingdom. There may also have been an economic benefit in selling some of the surplus for profit, such as what Egypt did for Joseph's brothers on their trip to Egypt.

The strategy is not that complex. It is a basic economic theory that was typically understood at least from the time in which agrarian modes of production were prominent. One farms, produces agricultural product, and stores that agricultural product enough to weather both a good season and a bad season. Even in the more modern world, farmers know some years are good and plentiful, while other years are not. Joseph's strategy is not that outstanding or extraordinary. However, the cornerstone of the story is that Elohim (perhaps the same manifestation that spoke to Hagar, the Egyptian?) was controlling the economy of Egypt for the benefit of his people, which was symbolized initially in the body of Joseph (cf. Gen. 41:25). Because of that, Elohim (*but not Yahweh?*) can speak to the pharaoh through his dreams and through Joseph. What this account also suggests is that in the mind of the biblical author, the Egyptians, who were connected to Hagar and Ishmael, were not intellectually capable of thoroughly assessing economic and social need.

We don't want to fall into the trap of theology resting on the presupposed explanation that God was an active agent, manipulating the pharaoh for the benefit of God's elect community, as Kim and Brueggemann do in their emphases upon Joseph as a theological model of justice, humility, and mercy in his "walk with God."[14] That model has been a relic of colonial and imperial assumptions for centuries. We must look instead for the symbolic meaning in what the story presents, which is consistent with the larger narrative arc of Genesis, from Adam and Eve through the patriarchs, into the story of Joseph. This is part of the reason it's difficult to see the story of Joseph as completely a postcolonial account. Facets of it can be—those elements that parallel the

182 *Chapter 11*

experiences of colonized bodies—but it ultimately becomes the story of the victor who would take the mantel of political authority and power.[15] Note also Kim, who describes this in terms of a loving God,

> Reading the Joseph story as a Diaspora narrative, we may summarize the fundamental theme of this novella (Genesis 37–50), in light of the larger framework within the entire Pentateuch, with the following concept: it reminds us of a coherent teaching of the Torah concerning "relationship" in that our love of God (Deut 6:4–5) is best demonstrated by our love of our kin, neighbors, and outsiders as ourselves: "You shall not take vengeance or keep anger against any fellow of your people, but you shall love your neighbor as yourself; I am Yhwh" (Lev 19:18).[16]

As an Egyptian insider, Joseph represents the colonizer's position, because like the basis of nearly every colonial ideology, Joseph's actions *saved* the Egyptians. Joseph changed something about Egypt's mode of production, what they were doing in politics and economics at the direction of Elohim. There's something similar in that to the more modern notion of evangelism that went hand in hand with imperialism, pushing colonized peoples to be baptized in order to be saved. Because Joseph's actions and their reception established the contest between Yahweh and the pharaoh in Exodus. To maintain his own internal stability, the pharaoh must acknowledge the power and authority of Israel's national god (cf. Ex. 6:28–12:28). When Egypt "forgets" (Ex. 1:8–10), Moses will remind them—an account that occurs in the exodus story, which includes the plagues that undermine the economic and political stability of the kingdom.

> Alternatively, Joseph the newly endowed power that-be has to tread the thin line between justice and oppression, between reformation and contamination. Joseph, though once an outsider, has become not only an insider but also a typically authoritative overlord. This tension depicts the duality between the ideal, positive admonition (an insider hero) and the oft-real, pessimistic satire (an insider foe).[17]

In views such as that, there is an assumption that smirks of ideological colonialism in this story. That the world can be stabilized and preserved, that it can be "saved" if things are done according to the perspective of one cultural ideology or body, one that is externally imposed, demands internal change within a subject. It demands a foregoing of traditions and ideas that are not compatible with imposed ideas, if the latter are to be followed. In a broader sense, something similar can be said about US political strategies in the modern world. For instance, President George W. Bush justified the war in Iraq by saying that the United States had a divine right to spread freedom and democracy in the world.[18] The idea of the divine, which was assumed to be universal by US culture, was a concept of God rooted in US culture, and not one shared by all cultures of the world. Should other cultures accept the claim, they also accept the US version of God, which is also rooted in Capitalism—one of the protest points emphasized in the concept of the Global South.[19]

Similarly, Yahweh represents Israel's dominion over Egypt in Genesis and Exodus.

The story of Joseph, ultimately, is the burgeoning of nascent imperial ideology. It is not a message of diasporic unity or universal theology about divine will.[20] Because if we accept Genesis was written and edited during the 6th century BCE, then we can accept that the author was reimagining Israel based on his experience with foreign empires. In the absence of Israel's own independent political structure and institutions after its defeat by the Babylonians, the author's exposure to imperial ideology became wed to religion as the framework that preserves culture and provides the foundation for a quasi-legal and social apparatus. It speaks to the ideological foundation or assumption shared by other biblical authors about God's re-institution (typically read as "restoration" by conservative readers) of Israel as God's chosen community—one that Christianity would later claim for itself. The rudimentary forms of that apparatus would also provide for some communities, along with the myth of the Abrahamic Covenant, the ideological basis for modern Israel's political claim over Palestine, as well as US support for it.

WHEN TAMAR RECEIVED JUDAH'S
STAFF (AND SEAL AND CORD)

After selling Joseph into slavery with the aid of his brothers, Judah left and married the daughter of Shua, a Canaanite man (cf. Gen. 38:2). His firstborn son, Er, married Tamar, but Yahweh killed him because he was "evil" (38:7). Based on the (Israelite) practice of kinsman redeemer, Tamar was given to Er's brother, Onan, who was supposed to sleep with her until she bore a son to carry on Er's name. While Onan did have sex with Tamar, because he knew that the son would not be his he pulled out before ejaculating (from which we get the term English "onanism") so that she would not get pregnant. For that, Yahweh killed him. Withholding his seed of life, Onan lost his life. Suspicious of Tamar, Judah instructs her to live in her father's house until his remaining son, Shelah, is older (38:11). As readers, we will be told that Judah didn't plan on sending for Tamar (38:14). Tamar knows this as well. When Judah journeys to Timnah, she sat at the entrance to Enaim on the way to Timnah dressed as a prostitute (cf. 38:12–14). Judah, not recognizing his

184   *Chapter 11*

own daughter-in-law, sleeps with her, but because he can't pay pledges her his staff, seal, and cord until he can come back with a goat from his flock. Tamar, however, leaves before Judah returns with a goat.

When Judah later hears that Tamar is pregnant, even though he had no plans to give her to Shelah, he becomes angry and demands that she be burned as punishment (38:24). In response, she shows him his staff, seal, and cord, which he must acknowledge are his and leads him to declare her righteous. *Just like Susannah in the eponymous deuterocanonical book (though sometimes also called the Judgment of Daniel), she needs a man to declare her innocent.* She bears twins, Perez and Zerah, the first being part of the lineage of David, king of Judah, and, according to New Testament writers, Jesus. While Zerah's wrist came out of the birthing canal first, Perez "broke through" to become the first born. Tamar's function complete, the biblical author returns to the account of Joseph in Egypt.

According to *Tosefta Berakhot* 4:16, even though Judah slept with his daughter-in-law, he didn't warrant the type of punishment that might normally be applied because his actions saved his lineage. Adelman emphasizes a positivist reading by claiming that Tamar imbues Perez with the spirit to "break through," based on her tenacity in dealing with Judah, who the biblical author and later interpreters never seem to see as guilty.[21] While Yahweh kills Onan for ejaculating on the ground instead of in Tamar, Judah lives a seemingly normal life. Onan withholds the seed of life from Tamar while Judah gives it freely but unknowingly (like Lot?). The former dies, the latter lives, and Tamar disappears from the text.

While one might celebrate Tamar's success as Adelman does, it is not her autonomy the author highlights. Her body remains a colonized one, and she "succeeds" only by giving Judah what heterosexual men stereotypically want, sex. Receiving Judah's staff isn't success, as though she had somehow inverted power relations. What constitutes success for her, according to the biblical author, is her bearing children and fulfilling her role as an owned body within a patriarchal culture. As readers we do not know what she really wanted, what stories she wanted her body to tell. We only know that her story is defined by her body's function within the patriarchal narrative of Israel, the lineage of David, and for later Christians, the earthly lineage of Jesus. The cultural norms and institutions that led to her suppression beneath masculine authority do not change because of her actions; they are perversely reinforced.

NOTES

1. Von Rad, *Genesis*, 350.

2. Cf. Hyun Chul Paul Kim, "Reading the Joseph Story (Genesis 37–50) as a Diaspora Narrative," *CBQ* 75, no. 2 (April 2013): 220.

3. Kim, 220.

4. Compare Fanon, *Wretched*, 23.

5. Cf. the discussion in Cataldo, *What the Bible Says about Sex*, 151–57.

6. Kim, "Reading Joseph," 235.

7. As a cross-cultural study, cf. Liucija Baskauskas, "The Lithuanian Refugee Experience and Grief," *International Migration Review* 15 (1981): 276–91.

8. Walter Brueggemann, *Genesis*, 296; cited in Kim, "Reading Joseph," 237.

9. This history informs the basis of Cone's work, for example. Cf. James H. Cone, *A Black Theology of Liberation: 50th Anniversary Edition*, Kindle (New York: Orbis, 2020); Cone, *Lynching Tree*.

10. Cited in Cone, *A Black Theology of Liberation*, location 166.

11. Berger, *Sacred Canopy*, 7.

12. Kim, "Reading Joseph," 226.

13. Kim makes a similar argument in 221.

14. Cf. Kim, "Reading Joseph," 224; see also p. 225; Fretheim follows a similar trend in "The Book of Genesis," in *New Interpreter's Bible*, vol. 1, 12 vols. (Nashville: Abingdon Press, 2003), 641; see also footnote 354.

15. See also the argument of Kim, "Reading Joseph," 222.

16. Kim, 238.

17. Kim, 227.

18. George W Bush, "Press Conference Held by the President of the United States," 2004.

19. Cf. the implication of Liston Pope, "Religion and the Class Structure," *The Annals of the American Academy of Political and Social Science* 256 (1948): 84–91.

20. Contra Kim, "Reading Joseph," 238.

21. Rachel Adelman, "Seduction and Recognition in the Story of Judah and Tamar and the Book of Ruth," *Nashim: A Journal of Jewish Women's Studies & Gender Issues*, no. 23 (2012): 88.

Conclusion

Taking Stock of the Trajectory of Genesis

If I'm gonna tell a real story, I'm gonna start with my name.

(Kendrick Lamar)

A postcolonial reading of Genesis challenges the rootedness of dominant traditions of biblical interpretation in monotheistic aspirations for power and authority. So how do we take stock of Gen. 1–11, the Primeval History, and Gen. 12–50, the Ancestral Narratives? I agree with Joseph Blenkinsopp's questioning of the common uncritical tendency to see Abraham's actions as linking historical epochs, the so-called archaic period with that of the ancestors. However, we must also treat Genesis as a book redacted as a whole to fit a particular purpose.[1] How then do we take stock of them together under the lens of postcolonialism? Rather, how do we see them as amenable to a postcolonial reading? Or is it better said that we should not be yearning for the goal of a "postcolonial reading" of the text as it is traditionally defined? Instead, that we adopt postcolonialism as a method to *subvert* not only dominant traditions of interpretation but also how much different cultures rely upon them? It's easy to overlook the editorial shaping of Genesis, but perhaps the editorial shaping of it is more important than even the authorial intent, of which there are several in Genesis. Because the text as we have it is a product, in large respect, of how the editors shaped the work to function as a national foundation myth. This included articulating the dominant contours of a collective body as a unique identity, distinct in its forcing of "others," who might exist on its peripheral spaces, into subordinate positions. In saying that, however, I would also emphasize that not *all* people in Israel and Judah understood, or were even aware, of the stories, traditions, and narratives in Genesis. The biblical author wrote with aristocratic sentiments—therefore invested in the dominant power structure—treating the text as a prescriptive

188 *Conclusion*

narrative describing his vision of a re-imagined Israel. That however, is frequently lost in traditions of interpretation in which particular individuals and communities see themselves as the intended audience and recipient. Just such a view was articulated by James Muilenberg:

> The biblical doctrine of creation is a derivative of history, the sacred history of the chosen people. The creation account in Genesis 1 is not only the prologue to the history which follows it and thus to be read in relation to it, but is also a development of the election-historical life, of the redemptive history which has the Exodus as its center. It is a product of the mature reflection of Israel upon the meaning of her history within the purpose and grace of God.[2]

Like many others, Muilenberg treats God as an active agent, universal and absolute, revealing God's self to an elect community that would become the archivists of divine revelation. However, the book doesn't see itself in such lofty terms. It is the story of a nation, the "becoming" of a national body. Yet even though Genesis does not get us to the final goal of a nation, perhaps it does not need to. It is the origin story, the mythic legend, the foundational myth of a people that believed in its own uniqueness, exceptionalism, and superiority. Most countries have stories about how they came to be. Ancient Israel is no different in that regard.

Such a statement will have difficulty being accepted by those invested in the monotheistic body of Judaism or Christianity as the ideal face of the collective human body. Even though they accept that the stories of Marduk, Ishtar, and various other Babylonian deities, for instance, were stories that told the coming of age of Babylon, they dismiss the prospect that the stories of Israel and Judah, such as contained within the Bible, should be read only as the "coming of age" stories of Israel and Judah. One reason for that is that the narrative legends of Israel and Judah have been codified as part of a sacred text, and that this status of "sacred" bestowed upon those texts has become the basis by which those texts are interpreted rather than the basis of their history or cultural contexts. As a reflection of what I am challenging, Spector claims that Genesis, despite its tragedies giving "voice to timeless human experiences of suffering and grief" while adding to it the "cost of being chosen," ends in inclusion and reconciliation.[3] But that is *only* for the chosen community. "God redeems his chosen ones, even when that seems impossible."[4] While translators often link the book, and the Bible as a whole, to the ideological commitments of their own communities, the book is not intended for *all* people. It was intended for a specific image of what makes up the body politick of the kingdom of Israel.

Under the influence of translators who hold the Bible as a central symbol for their own communities, it has been merged with the beating heart

Conclusion 189

of monotheism, which maintains its community will ascend into authority while all others will be subordinated, if not enthusiastically and brutally oppressed. (Hell is the ultimate symbol of this.) Where the tendency has been to romanticize history and to whitewash over its atrocities, let us not forget God (the biblical character) set the pattern with genocide, ethnocide, and utter disregard for the bodies of the marginalized, as I have discussed in previous chapters.

The approach I have been describing in this work reads Genesis through that lens. Genesis is a constructivist set of narratives that tells the story of what ancient Israel was, what it was supposed to be, and what it could become. It is a way of preserving the idealized memory of the kingdom, and it provides a national narrative that presents the ideal to which its people should aspire. If, as Blenkinsopp argues, questions about cosmology, palaeo-anthropology, and related matters belong to their relative scientific disciplines and not to the Bible—and I believe he is correct—a postcolonial reading demands we acknowledge the same for social and political issues and identities in shaping how we interpret the Bible.[5] Not only that, but we must deconstruct the rootedness that dominant traditions have in center-periphery, colonizer-colonized, insider-outsider paradigms. The Bible tells a story, rather, a great many stories. It does not tell us *the* story or provide any un-nuanced, objective historiography. Interpreters who accept that the Bible speaks directly to them should consider how much they can do so because they benefit from their membership within cultures residing at centers of authority. Because in comparison, those that do not see themselves as benefitting from such communities may be identified by their frustration with the text, like the colonized bodies of the Andes and Americas who told Pope John Paul II to take his Bible and give it back to their oppressors. "It was the ideological arm of the colonial assault. The Spanish sword, which by day attacked and assassinated the body of the Indians, by night changed itself into the cross which attacked the Indian soul."[6]

For each sociopolitical body, history frequently begins with its own founding, whether the moment of its founding or an assessment of world forces marshaling realia and reality toward that founding. In that sense, even religions are no different. Anything written prior to such a moment is often considered "prehistory" in relation to the story of the nation, the materiel that supports its coming of age, the chaos from which the idealized body is born.

How we tell our stories, and how we preserve them, the expressions of our identities, are exclusive and limiting. National narratives do not tend to be inclusive of outsiders. Such narratives think in historical destinies. In fact, they treat the outsider, the marginalized "other," as a threat to the internal stability of the culture. Outsiders are the foil against which the collective identity of the citizen-member is defined. The Book of Genesis does that. It treats

190 *Conclusion*

foreigners as sources or symptoms of chaos. If Fanon is correct that a people's dignity and sovereignty are equivalent, then when the authors of Genesis diminish the dignities of other peoples they are also undermining their sovereignties.[7] In fact, the ease with which the authors describe Yahweh's violence and aggression, whether personally or commanded, against foreigners confirms the biblical author saw others as lesser than, that their sovereignty existed solely at the whim of author's national deity, who symbolized the sovereignty of Israel/Judah. When interpreters accept that without question, as many do, they perpetuate this hierarchy of prejudices that reinforce as the monotheistic ideal the rigid distinction between sacred and profane, saint and sinner, member and nonmember.

Seeing religious community formation as something like nation building provides a better understanding of how religions function, as Peter Berger described, as "world building."[8] Early Christianity, for example, modeled itself in contrast to Rome as a type of invisible empire developing in strength until Christ would overturn the powers of the world and establish a divine empire. It imagined itself as such with Christ as the ruler and a new kingdom rebuilt in Jerusalem. *As Abraham built memorials to his god as he traversed the land, the cross of Christ symbolizes a memorial raised initially in a Roman-controlled Jerusalem but more broadly translated as an imperializing statement to the world.* But if we consider religions as a type of imagined nation, drawing from the work of Benedict Anderson, though without necessarily strong geographic boundaries, then it becomes easier to understand how interpretation can favor the elect community and justify the rejection of outsiders.[9] It is in the rejection of those outsiders, of the profane, of the sinner, of metaphorical Cain, Ham, and Esau that the Body of Christ identifies itself.

How do we put this more clearly in terms of postcolonialism? Postcolonialism is a method that challenges dominant translations, interpretations, traditions, values, and systems. It seeks to liberate the voice of the marginalized. It is more than the "critical language of duality," which "is part of the spatial imagination that seems to come so naturally to geopolitical thinking of a progressive, postcolonial cast of mind: margin and metropole, center and periphery, the global and the local, the nation and the world."[10] It challenges the legacies of colonialism and imperialism that are rooted in preserved histories, cultures, concepts of land, politics, economics, and ethnicities. It is a tool belt capable of adapting other methods in pursuit of its overall aim: dismantling oppressive power structures that thrive on erasure. It is, as Ştefănescu writes, a point I cited earlier, motivated by an aim that is "multi-centric and poly-peripheral," which sees "a different, more complex geo-cultural and historical portrayal than the one provided by mainstream postcolonialism."[11] And as Cone emphasized, the dominant traditions of biblical interpretation that have historically had the greatest impact on what

Conclusion 191

people think the Bible and its message are do not favor the marginal position.[12] They do not favor the colonized body. The descendants of Cain and Ham are not beneficiaries of biblical interpretation. They are its monstrous "other." Their bodies bear the scars of the dominating culture whose authority and dominance demanded that they reflect the line between imposed categories of civilized human and beast, reminding their assumed masters that chaos is a breath away. For those "masters" to guard against that, the symbolic order of the world must be brought in line with the values of the dominant community. It must, in a word, be "civilized." That is what the dominant traditions of biblical interpretation have sought to do. They favor those who are in positions of power, or who imagine themselves to be in positions of ideological power, central to the formation of a "national" identity that becomes the basis by which all other countries or peoples view themselves. This imagined sociopolitical body is a city on the hill (cf. Ps. 2:6), as one biblical author put it, that highlights the framework, the vocabulary, and the meaning system by which others should identify themselves. *That* feeds the anomaly of racism, which "finds its historical modularity, and its fantasmatic scenario, in the colonial space which is a belated and hybrid attempt to 'weld together dynastic legitimacy and national community.'"[13]

For the dominant cultural bodies or traditions of interpretation, history begins with their civilization. But that idea, that history begins with civilization, which is peculiarly defined, is colonial. It ignores other types of historiography. Postcolonial scholars have shown that such a view of history rejects those other types by prioritizing the restrictive view of the written word. Monotheistic traditions, such as Christianity, give the written account of history a universal and absolute nature. For them, history begins with the Bible. Consequently, interpretation of an ancient text becomes the belligerent framework of the modern social world and its understanding of what makes up the idealized body.

Such a view prioritizes one body and the gaze through which one interprets and categorizes the world. It legitimates conversion, genocide, ethnocide, as well as infanticide and other types of atrocities when those actions can be justified as protecting the order of the world as it sees fit. Even in the history of the United States there are more examples than I can count, in which the slaughter of people through war, through one-sided conflict, or through other types of means, has been justified on religious grounds by claiming that those individuals are sinners, that they are a threat to the community of Christ and the establishment of the invisible empire Christians hope for in their interpretations of the biblical text. Interpretation favors community, and the community that determines what the dominant form of interpretation is one in a position of ideological power.

192 *Conclusion*

We must return to the question, what does that mean for a postcolonial reading? To read the biblical texts from a postcolonial position means to subvert dominant interpretations and assumptions about the body. It means "we must not merely change the narratives of our histories, but transform our sense of what it means to live, to be, in other times and different spaces, both human and historical."[14] How we interpret constructs and reinforces the narratives of our communities. How we use that knowledge can either permit us to be more aware of what it means to be human or be more despotic about defining the restricted essence of the human body. At the same time, "postcolonial modernity moves forward, erasing that compliant past tethered to the myth of progress, ordered in the binarisms of its cultural logic: past/present, inside/outside."[15] It is to seek those who are marginalized in various forms of interpretation and to highlight their stories in contrast to the stories of those who marginalize them.

It recognizes that how dominating bodies read texts, how they interpret texts, how they preserve traditions and meanings, and values, even morals and ethics, that how they do those things may reflect and reinforce a colonial or an imperial position. It is to accept, in some respects, that there is no truly objective meaning, moral, or value that is accessible through text, that text alone cannot be a container or vehicle with which to pass on objective essence. That any reading of a text is subjective and that in contexts of inequality subjectivity often caters to the position of the dominant authority. To recognize that is to challenge it, to expose the shame of the body marked by blemishes it tries to ignore. This is what postcolonialism does.

The different stories of Genesis, as I have covered, have been used by those who control the dominant forms of biblical interpretation to justify elements and ideologies of a colonial order. If interpreting communities and individuals do not acknowledge the dangers of that, along with the tendency of religions to codify marginalization in preserving the central positions in culture and society of a dominant majority, they risk perpetuating the colonial order and framework for interpretation and meaning that have bolstered biblical interpretation for centuries.

This book has been an exploration into what a postcolonial reading of Genesis might look like because scholarly works treating Genesis through postcolonial analysis are woefully absent. That's true in part because of its difficulties, such as who wrote it and when. Some of that tension may be resolved as I have sought to do in this work by interpreting Genesis as a myth that embodies a nationalist narrative. Another point of tension: Genesis also has, in traditions of biblical interpretation, given credence to a colonial position, especially in the concepts of land right, to Canaan/Palestine/Israel, and divine election of Jews and then Christians. Many Bible interpreters, including scholars, don't know *how* to read postcolonially, nor does there seem to

Conclusion 193

be a strong desire to cultivate that skill. In some cases it is too demanding for those who benefit from the dominant normative. Instead, they rely on a simple dichotomy between those in power and those oppressed as the basis for understanding postcolonialism. But that is not the whole of postcolonialism or its intent. It seeks to *give back* to marginalized and oppressed communities the space to speak for themselves without having to explain their relevance within the dominant cultural institutions and frameworks, which belong to cultures by which they have been colonized, physically or ideologically. Postcolonialism demands subversion, a type of deconstruction that exposes power inequalities and cripples the power of outsiders to define the bodies of others. Like the intent of Black Lives Matter as a movement, it is an attempt to reclaim the power over authoring and preserving one's own traditions, cultural narratives, and identity, no longer to be *given* the vocabularies and frameworks by an oppressing culture through which to express the attributes of the community. Postcolonialism cannot reclaim a precolonized past, but it *can* reject, subvert, and seek to dismantle the oppressions and the colonial frameworks of the present. It can also seek the preservation of a space for which new narratives, cultural and national, may be written. Moreover, it forces us to acknowledge,

> Decolonization never goes unnoticed, for it focuses on and fundamentally alters being, and transforms the spectator crushed to a nonessential state into a privileged actor, captured in a virtually grandiose fashion by the spotlight of History. It infuses a new rhythm, specific to a new generation of men, with a new language and a new humanity. Decolonization is truly the creation of new men. But such a creation cannot be attributed to a supernatural power: The "thing" colonized becomes a man through the very process of liberation.[16]

This analysis of Genesis emphasizes how the different stories discussed in the previous chapters revealed the continuing presence of the legacies of colonialism and imperialism. Biblical interpretation is not free from that. That is why our worlds touched by the Bible still have the need for liberation theologies, postcolonial studies, and studies of the Global South. We are not free from the legacies of colonialism, which means that attention to postcolonial concerns demands that we either respond and help facilitate change, or we sit apathetically back and indirectly (or directly) preserve the legacies of colonialism.

Genesis is the story of *a* beginning, and readers from dominant communities should accept that it tells "your" story and not "mine." The history of assumptions that Genesis tells *the* story of the world, (promised) land, and revelation simultaneously assumes *the* claim to know God as the symbol of absolute power and authority. By extension, and this is monotheism's deeply

194   *Conclusion*

rooted desire, the body of the elect, or "saved," community rises from its lowly position into favored status and authority; much like Joseph. But that also means that everyone outside the elect community, who may be symbolized by the Egyptian or any other ethnicity, is only fodder, worthy only of destruction (*or, Hell?*) in contrast to the elect community. They are the monstrous body of the colonized subject in whose rejection the colonizer is known. No, that is not *what* they are. *That* is how a dominating community has named them. Like Abraham, it has taken nearly everything from them.

> For a colonized people, the most essential value, because it is the most meaningful, is first and foremost the land: the land, which must provide bread and, naturally, dignity. But this dignity has nothing to do with "human" dignity. The colonized subject has never heard of such an ideal. All he has ever seen on his land is that he can be arrested, beaten, and starved with impunity; and no sermonizer on morals, no priest has ever stepped in to bear the blows in his place or share his bread. For the colonized, to be a moralist quite plainly means silencing the arrogance of the colonist, breaking his spiral of violence, in a word ejecting him outright from the picture.[17]

NOTES

1. Cf. Blenkinsopp, *Creation*, 3–4.
2. James Muilenburg, "The Biblical View of Time," *HTR* 54, no. 4 (October 1961): 242.
3. Spector, "Abraham and Isaac," 219.
4. Spector, 219.
5. Blenkinsopp, *Creation*, 11.
6. Cited in Tamez, "Bible and Conquest," 10.
7. Cf. Fanon, *Wretched*, 138.
8. Cf. Berger, *Sacred Canopy*.
9. Anderson, *Imagined Communities*.
10. Homi K. Bhabha, "Foreward: Framing Fanon," in *The Wretched of the Earth*, by Frantz Fanon, trans. Richard Philcox, Reprint edition (New York: Grove Press, 2005), location 147.
11. Ştefănescu, "Complicated Selves," 63.
12. See again Cone, *Lynching Tree*; Cone, *A Black Theology of Liberation*.
13. Bhabha, *The Location of Culture*, 248, citing Anderson, *Imagined Communities*, location 3002.
14. Bhabha, *The Location of Culture*, 256.
15. Bhabha, 253.
16. Fanon, *Wretched*, 2.
17. Fanon, *Wretched*, 9.

Bibliography

19-1392 Dobbs v. Jackson Women's Health Organization (Supreme Court of the United States June 24, 2022).

Adelman, Rachel. "Seduction and Recognition in the Story of Judah and Tamar and the Book of Ruth." *Nashim: A Journal of Jewish Women's Studies & Gender Issues*, no. 23 (2012): 87–109.

Ahmida, Ali Abdullatif. *Forgotten Voices: Power and Agency in Colonial and Postcolonial Libya*. London, UK: Taylor & Francis Group, 2005.

Althusser, Louis. "The Object of Capital." In *Reading Capital: The Complete Edition*, translated by Ben Brewster and David Fernbach, 217–355. London: Verso, 2015.

Anderson, Benedict. *Imagined Communities: Reflections on the Origin and Spread of Nationalism*. Ebook. London: Verso, 2016.

Anderson, Elijah. *Black in White Space: The Enduring Impact of Color in Everyday Life*. University of Chicago Press, 2022.

Ash, Christopher. "A Biblical View of Marriage." The Gospel Coalition, January 14, 2020. https://www.thegospelcoalition.org/essay/biblical-view-marriage/.

Assemblies of God, General Presbytery. "Homosexuality, Marriage, and Sexual Identity," August 4–5, 2014. https://ag.org/Beliefs/Position-Papers/Homosexuality -Marriage-and-Sexual-Identity.

Baer, Brian James, and Klaus Kaindl, eds. *Queering Translation, Translating the Queer: Theory, Practice, Activism*. First issued in paperback. Routledge advances in translation and interpreting studies 28. New York / London: Routledge, Taylor & Francis, 2020.

Bailey, Sarah Pulliam. "'God Is Not Against Building Walls!' The Sermon Trump Heard from Robert Jeffress before His Inauguration." *Washington Post*, January 20, 2017, sec. Acts of Faith. https://www.washingtonpost.com/news/acts-of-faith/ wp/2017/01/20/god-is-not-against-building-walls-the-sermon-donald-trump-heard -before-his-inauguration/.

Baker, Lisa Loraine. "What Is God's Purpose for Our Family?" Biblestudytools.com, September 30, 2022. https://www.biblestudytools.com/bible-study/topical-studies/ what-is-gods-purpose-for-our-family.html.

Baldo, Michela. "Queering Translation as Performative and Affective Un-Doing: Translating Butler's *Undoing Gender* into Italian." In *Queering*

Bibliography

Translation, Translating the Queer: Theory, Practice, Activism, edited by Brian James Baer and Klaus Kaindl, 189–205. Routledge Advances in Translation and Interpreting Studies 28. New York London: Routledge, 2020.

Ball, Jeremy, and Samantha Noble. "Ukrainian Refugee Who Lost Home in Bombing Feels UK Welcome." *BBC News*, June 2, 2022, sec. Nottingham. https://www.bbc.com/news/uk-england-nottinghamshire-61667884.

Baskauskas, Liucija. "The Lithuanian Refugee Experience and Grief." *International Migration Review* 15 (1981): 276–91.

Beaule, Christine D. *Frontiers of Colonialism*. Gainesville: University Press of Florida, 2017.

Bellah, Robert Neelly. "Civil Religion in America." *Daedalus* 134, no. 4 (2005): 40–55.

Berger, Peter L. *The Sacred Canopy: Elements of a Sociological Theory of Religion*. New York: Anchor Books, 1990.

Bhabha, Homi K. "Foreward: Framing Fanon." In *The Wretched of the Earth*, by Frantz Fanon and Jean-Paul Sartre, locations 51–636. translated by Richard Philcox, Reprint edition. New York: Grove Press, 2005.

———. *The Location of Culture*. London; New York: Routledge, 1994.

Bhambra, Gurminder K. *Rethinking Modernity: Postcolonialism and the Sociological Imagination*. New York: Palgrave Macmillan, 2007.

Bhambra, Gurminder K., Yolande Bouka, Randolph B. Persaud, Olivia U. Rutazibwa, Vineet Thakur, Duncan Bell, Karen Smith, Toni Haastrup, and Seifudein Adem. "Why Is Mainstream International Relations Blind to Racism?" *Foreign Policy*, July 3, 2020. https://foreignpolicy.com/2020/07/03/why-is-mainstream-international-relations-ir-blind-to-racism-colonialism/.

Blenkinsopp, Joseph. *Creation Un-Creation Re-Creation: A Discursive Commentary on Genesis 1–11*. New York: Bloomsbury / T & T Clark, 2011.

Blough, Neal. "From the Tower of Babel to the Peace of Jesus Christ: Christological, Ecclesiological and Missiological Foundations for Peacemaking." *The Mennonite Quarterly Review* 76, no. 1 (January 2002): 7–33.

Bonikowski, Bart. "Nationalism in Settled Times." *Annual Review of Sociology* 42 (2016): 427–49.

Brownson, James V. *Bible, Gender, Sexuality: Reframing the Church's Debate on Same-Sex Relationships*. Grand Rapids: W.B. Eerdmans, 2013.

Brueggemann, Walter. *Genesis*. International Bible Commentary. Louisville: Wesminster John Knox, 2010.

Bush, George W. "Press Conference Held by the President of the United States," 2004.

Bustanoby, Andre S. "Love, Honor, and Obey." *Christianity Today* 13, no. 18 (June 6, 1969): 3–4. https://www.christianitytoday.com/ct/1969/june-6/love-honor-and-obey.html.

Byron, John. *Cain and Abel in Text and Tradition: Jewish and Christian Interpretations of the First Sibling Rivalry*. Leiden, Brill, 2011.

Carter, Charles E. *The Emergence of Yehud in the Persian Period: A Social and Demographic Study*. Sheffield: Sheffield Academic Press, 1999.

Cataldo, Jeremiah W. "Biblical Strategies for Reinterpreting Crises with 'Outsiders.'" In *Imagined Worlds and Constructed Differences in the Hebrew Bible*,

127–43. Library of Hebrew Bible / Old Testament Studies 677. London: T & T Clark / Bloomsbury, 2019.

———. *A Social-Political History of Monotheism: From Judah to the Byzantines.* London: Routledge Press, 2018.

———. *Biblical Terror: Why Law and Restoration in the Bible Depend Upon Fear.* London: Bloomsbury T & T Clark, 2017.

———. *Breaking Monotheism: Yehud and the Material Formation of Monotheistic Identity.* Vol. 565. London: Bloomsbury, 2012.

———. *What the Bible Says about Sex: Why We Read It the Way We Do.* Abingdon, Oxon; New York, NY: Routledge, 2023.

Chapman, Michael W. "Catholic Exorcist: 'Transgenderism Is a Full-Blown Attack Against Motherhood.'" CNSNews.com, Mon, 01/09/2023 - 17:09. https://cnsnews.com/article/national/michael-w-chapman/catholic-exorcist-transgenderism-full-blown-attack-against.

Cole, Steven J. "1. Why God Designed Marriage (Genesis 2:18–25; Ephesians 5:31–32)." Bible.org, 2017. https://bible.org/seriespage/1-why-god-designed-marriage-genesis-218-25-ephesians-531-32.

Collins, Patricia Hill. *Black Sexual Politics: African Americans, Gender, and the New Racism.* London: Routledge Press, 2004.

Cone, James H. *A Black Theology of Liberation.* 40th anniv. New York: Orbis Books, 2010.

———. *A Black Theology of Liberation: 50th Anniversary Edition.* Kindle. New York: Orbis, 2020.

———. *The Cross and the Lynching Tree.* Kindle. Maryknoll, NY: Orbis Books, 2011.

Conrad, Joseph. *Lord Jim & Nostromo.* New York: Modern Library, 1999.

Cook, Stephen L. *Prophecy and Apocalypticism: The Postexilic Social Setting.* Minneapolis: Fortress Press, 1995.

Crandall, Christian S., and Amy Eshleman. "A Justification-Suppression Model of the Expression and Experience of Prejudice." *Psychological Bulletin* 129, no. 3 (2003): 414–46.

Crummell, Alexander. *Africa and America; Addresses and Discourses.* Springfield, MA: Willey, 1891.

Deleuze, Gilles, and Félix Guattari. *Anti-Oedipus: Capitalism and Schizophrenia.* Minneapolis: University of Minnesota Press, 2005.

Dochuk, Darren. *From Bible Belt to Sunbelt: Plain-Folk Religion, Grassroots Politics, and the Rise of Evangelical Conservatism.* Digital. New York: W.W. Norton, 2011.

Douglas, Mary. *Purity and Danger: An Analysis of Concepts of Pollution and Taboo.* London: Routledge & Kegan Paul, 1966.

Dube, Musa W., and R. S. Wafula, eds. *Postcoloniality, Translation, and the Bible in Africa.* Kindle. Eugene, OR: Pickwick Publications, 2017.

Eliade, Mircea. *The Myth of the Eternal Return: Cosmos and History.* Translated by Willard R. Trask. Princeton: Princeton University Press, 2005.

Esqueda, Octavio. "Much Ado about Gender Roles." ChristianityToday.com, August 22, 2018. https://www.christianitytoday.com/ct/2018/august-web-only/complementarian-egalitarian-debate-gender-roles-explainer.html.

Bibliography

Falwell, Jerry. "Speech Given to the "Strengthening Families" Seminar of the Christian Life Commission Conference." Falwell Archives: FAL 4: Speeches and Sermons (FAL 4:1–3 Box 1), April 1982.

Fanon, Frantz. *The Wretched of the Earth*. Translated by Richard Philcox. Reprint edition. New York: Grove Press, 2005.

Faro, Ingrid. *Evil in Genesis: A Contextual Analysis of Hebrew Lexemes for Evil in the Book of Genesis*. Studies in Scripture & Biblical Theology. Bellingham, WA: Lexham Press, 2021.

Federal Writers' Project, and Library of Congress. *Alabama Slave Narratives: A Folk History of Slavery in Alabama from Interviews with Former Slaves: Typewritten Records*. Bedford, Mass.; Washington, D.C.: Applewood Books; Library of Congress, 2006.

Ferry, Jules. "Jules Ferry (28 Juillet 1885)—Histoire—Grands Discours Parlementaires—Assemblée Nationale," 1885. https://www2.assemblee-nationale .fr/decouvrir-l-assemblee/histoire/grands-discours-parlementaires/jules-ferry-28 -juillet-1885.

Focus on the Family. "Oral and Anal Sex: Biblical Guidelines for Intimacy in Marriage." Focus on the Family, nd. https://www.focusonthefamily.com/family-qa /oral-and-anal-sex-biblical-guidelines-for-intimacy-in-marriage/.

Foucault, Michel. *Discipline and Punish: The Birth of the Prison*. Translated by Alan Sheridan. New York: Vintage Books, 1995.

———. *The Archaeology of Knowledge and the Discourse on Language*. Translated by A M Sheridan Smith. New York: Pantheon Books, 1972.

Francis, Pope. "Fratelli Tutti." Encyclical. Vatican, October 3, 2020. https://www .vatican.va/content/francesco/en/encyclicals/documents/papa-francesco_20201003 _enciclica-fratelli-tutti.html.

Fretheim, Terence E. (Erling). "The God of the Flood Story and Natural Disasters." *Calvin Theological Journal* 43, no. 1 (April 2008): 21–34.

Fretheim, Terrence E. "The Book of Genesis." In *New Interpreter's Bible*, 1:319–674. Nashville: Abingdon Press, 2003.

Freud, Sigmund. *The Interpretation of Dreams*. Mineola, NY: Courier Dover Publications, 2015.

Frye, Northrop. *The Great Code*. New York: Harcourt Brace Jovanovich, 1983.

———. *Words with Power: Being a Second Study of the Bible and Literature*. New York: Harvest/Harcourt Brace Jovanovich, 1990.

Garvey, Marcus. *Selected Writings and Speeches of Marcus Garvey*. Mineola, NY: Dover, 2004.

Gaza, MC. *From Gaza to Aleppo*. Youtube, 2017. https://youtu.be/ah1nzHJjKzc.

Gerloff, Johannes. "Biblical Borders of Israel (Part 1)." *Christians for Israel International* (blog), July 3, 2020. https://www.c4israel.org/_teachings/biblical -borders-of-israel/.

Giddens, Rhiannon. *At the Purchaser's Option*. Vol. Freedom highway. Nonesuch, 2017.

Ginzberg, Louis, Henrietta Szold, and Paul Radin. *Legends of the Jews*. Vol. 2nd ed. JPS Classic Reissues. Philadelphia: Jewish Publication Society, 2003.

Godelier, Maurice. *The Metamorphoses of Kinship*. Translated by Nora Scott. London; New York: Verso Books, 2011.

Goldenberg, David M. *Black and Slave: The Origins and History of the Curse of Ham*. Berlin: Walter de Gruyter GmbH & Co KG, 2017.

———. *The Curse of Ham: Race and Slavery in Early Judaism, Christianity, and Islam*. Princeton University Press, 2003.

GOV.IL. "The Declaration of the Establishment of the State of Israel," May 14, 1948. https://www.gov.il/en/Departments/General/declaration-of-establishment-state-of -israel.

Green, Bradley. "Confession of Sin." The Gospel Coalition. Accessed December 14, 2022. https://www.thegospelcoalition.org/essay/confession-of-sin/.

Green, Ronald M. "Abraham, Isaac, and the Jewish Tradition: An Ethical Reappraisal." *Journal of Religious Ethics* 10, no. 1 (1982): 1–21.

Griswold, Eliza. "The Unmaking of Biblical Womanhood." *The New Yorker*, July 25, 2021. https://www.newyorker.com/news/on-religion/the-unmaking-of-biblical -womanhood.

Hagee, John. *The Promised Land*. San Antonio: CUFI University Press, 2020.

———. *Why Christians Should Support Israel: The Apple of His Eye*. San Antonio: CUFI University Press, 2016.

Hannah-Jones, Nikole, ed. *The 1619 Project: A New Origin Story*. Random House Publishing Group, 2021.

Haynes, Stephen R. *Noah's Curse: The Biblical Justification of American Slavery*. Kindle. Oxford: Oxford University Press, 2002.

Heffernan, Carol. "God's Design for Marriage." *Focus on the Family* (blog), January 1, 2002. https://www.focusonthefamily.com/marriage/gods-design-for-marriage/.

Hoffman, E. A. *Leaning On the Everlasting Arms*. Vol. The United Methodist Hymnal, 1887.

Holt, Jared. "Peter LaBarbera Is Upset 'Love, Simon' Did Not Mention the 'Judgment of God' on Gay People." Right Wing Watch, April 5, 2018. https://www .rightwingwatch.org/post/peter-labarbera-is-upset-love-simon-did-not-mention-the -judgment-of-god-on-gay-people/.

Horsley, Richard A. *Jesus and the Politics of Palestine*. Columbia: University of South Carolina Press, 2014.

Huggan, Graham. "Decolonizing the Map: Post-Colonialism, Post-Structuralism and the Cartographic Connection." In *Past the Last Post: Theorizing Post-Colonialism and Post-Modernism*, edited by Ian Adam and Helen Tiffin, 125–38. Calgary: University of Calgary Press, 1990.

Hunter, Gregg. "Righteous Noah (Genesis 6:5–13)." *Fort Howard Community Church: Fort Howard, MD* (blog), July 19, 2021. https://www.forthowardcc.com/ blog/post/righteous-noah--genesis-65-13-.

"'Jim Bakker Show' Co-Host: Muslim Immigrants Are 'Coming Here to Destroy America.'" *The Jim Bakker Show*, August 1, 2016. https://www.rightwingwatch .org/post/jim-bakker-show-co-host-muslim-immigrants-are-coming-here-to -destroy-america/.

Bibliography

Joannès, F., and André Lemaire. "Trois Tablettes Cunéiformes à l'onomastique Ouest-Sémitique." *Transeuphratene* 17 (1999): 17–33.

Johnson, Robyn. "A World without Fathers: Patriarchy, Colonialism, and the Male Creator in Northwest Tribal Narratives." *The American Indian Quarterly* 38, no. 3 (June 22, 2014): 342–347.

Johnson, S. Lewis. "Babylon and Lucifer: Isaiah 13:1–14;23." SLJ Institute, December 5, 2013. https://sljinstitute.net/the-prophets/isaiah/isaiah-babylon-and -lucifer/.

Johnston, Jeff. "Male and Female He Created Them: Genesis and God's Design of Two Sexes." Focus on the Family, September 13, 2015. https://www.focusonthefamily .com/get-help/male-and-female-he-created-them-genesis-and-gods-design-of-two -sexes/.

Judd, Andrew. "Hagar, Uncle Tom's Cabin, and Why We Cannot Agree on What the Bible Says about Slavery." *Bulletin for Biblical Research* 31, no. 1 (2021): 1–15.

Junior, Nyasha. "The Mark of Cain and White Violence." *Journal of Biblical Literature* 139, no. 4 (2020): 661.

Kabanda, Marcel, and Jean-pierre Chrétien. *Rwanda. Racisme et génocide: L'idéologie hamitique*. Paris: Belin, 2016.

Kaminski, Carol. "From Noah to Israel: Realization of the Primaeval Blessing After the Flood." *Journal for the Study of the Old Testament: Supplemental Series 413*. London / New York: T & T Clark / Bloomsbury, 2004.

Kemp, Joel B. "Racializing Cain, Demonizing Blackness, & Legalizing Discrimination: Proposal for Reception of Cain and America's Racial Caste System." *Perspectives in Religious Studies* 48, no. 4 (2021): 377–99.

Khalidi, Rashid. *The Hundred Years' War on Palestine: A History of Settler Colonialism and Resistance, 1917–2017*. New York: Metropolitan Books, Henry Holt and Company, 2022.

Kierkegaard, Soren. *Fear and Trembling*. Translated by Walter Lowrie. Princeton: Princeton University Press, 1947.

Kim, Hyun Chul Paul. "Reading the Joseph Story (Genesis 37–50) as a Diaspora Narrative." *The Catholic Biblical Quarterly* 75, no. 2 (April 2013): 219–38.

Kinyua, Johnson Kiriaku. "A Postcolonial Analysis of Bible Translation and Its Effectiveness in Shaping and Enhancing the Discourse of Colonialism and the Discourse of Resistance: The Gikuyu New Testament–a Case Study." *Black Theology* 11, no. 1 (2013): 58–95.

Kristeva, Julia. *Powers of Horror: an Essay on Abjection*. Translated by Leon Roudiez. Reprint edition. New York, NY: Columbia University Press, 1982.

LaHaye, Tim. *The Battle for the Family*. Old Tappan, NJ: Fleming H. Revell Company, 1982.

———. *The Unhappy Gays: What Everyone Should Know about Homosexuality*. Tyndale House, 1978.

LaSor, William S, David A Hubbard, and Frederic W Bush. *Old Testament Survey: The Message, Form, and Background of the Old Testament*. 2nd ed. Grand Rapids: William B. Eerdmans, 1996.

LaVey, Anton Szandor. *Satan Speaks!* Venice, CA: Feral House, 1998.

Bibliography

Levine, Amy-Jill. "Roundtable Discussion: Anti-Judaism and Postcolonial Biblical Interpretation." *Journal of Feminist Studies in Religion* 20, no. 1 (April 1, 2004): 91–132.

Liverani, Mario. *Israel's History and the History of Israel.* Translated by Chiara Peri and Philip R. Davies. London; Oakville, CT: Equinox, 2005.

Lucey, Candice. "Was Jesus Ever Married with a Wife and Children?" Christianity.com, July 27, 2020. https://www.christianity.com/wiki/jesus-christ/why-is-there-a-theory-that-jesus-had-children.html.

Ma'ilo, Mosese. "Celebrating Hybridity in Island Bibles: Jesus, the Tamaalepō (Child of the Dark) in Matatio 1:18–26." In *Islands, Islanders, and the Bible: RumInations,* 65–76. Semeia Studies 77. Atlanta: SBL Press, 2015.

Major, Tristan. *Undoing Babel: The Tower of Babel in Anglo-Saxon Literature.* Toronto Anglo-Saxon Series 25. Toronto: University of Toronto Press, 2018.

Mantegazza, Paolo. *Gli amori degli uomini: saggio di una etnologia dell' amore.* Milano: Paolo Mantegazza, 1886.

Mártinez-Vázquez, Hjamil A. *Made in the Margins: Latina/o Constructions of US Religious History.* Waco, TX: Baylor University Press, 2013.

MEE Staff. "Israeli Doctor Says 'Arab Womb' Overwhelming Country with High Birthrate." Middle East Eye, October 24, 2022. http://www.middleeasteye.net/news/israel-doctor-arab-womb-overwhelming-country-high-birthrate.

Mellinkoff, Ruth W. *The Mark of Cain.* Eugene, OR: Wipf and Stock Publishers, 2003.

Meyers, Carol. *Discovering Eve: Ancient Israelite Women in Context.* New York: Oxford University Press, 1988.

Michael, Matthew. "The Tower of Babel and Yahweh's Heavenly Staircase." *Horizons in Biblical Theology* 39, no. 1 (2017): 31–45.

Mishra, Vijay, and Bob Hodges. "What Was Postcolonialism?" *New Literary History* 36 (2005): 375–402. http://www.newliteraryhistory.org/articles/36-3-mishra.pdf.

Moore, Stephen D. *God's Beauty Parlor and Other Queer Spaces in and around the Bible.* Stanford University Press, 2001.

Morris, Paul D. *Shadow of Sodom: Facing the Facts of Homosexuality.* Tyndale House Publishers, 1978.

Mouriquand, David. "Iran Protests: Why Is Cutting Hair an Act of Rebellion?" Euronews, October 6, 2022. https://www.euronews.com/culture/2022/10/06/iran-protests-why-is-cutting-hair-an-act-of-rebellion.

Muilenburg, James. "The Biblical View of Time." *Harvard Theological Review* 54, no. 4 (October 1961): 225–52.

National Association of Evangelicals. "Theology of Sex." National Association of Evangelicals, 2012.

Nayar, Pramod K. *Postcolonialism: A Guide for the Perplexed.* London: Continuum, 2010.

Nerín, Gustau. *Colonialismo e imperialismo: entre el derribo de monumentos y la nostalgia por la grandeza perdida.* Barcelona: Shackleton Books, 2022.

Ochs, Elinor, and Lisa Capps. "Narrating the Self." *Annual Review of Anthropology* 25 (1996): 19–43.

Page, Jr., Hugh R., Randall C. Bailey, Valerie Bridgeman, Stacy Davis, Cheryl Kirk-Duggan, Madipoane Masenya, Nathaniel Samuel Murrell, Rodney S. Sadler Jr., eds. *The Africana Bible: Reading Israel's Scriptures from Africa and the African Diaspora.* Fortress Press, 2009.

Pagels, Elaine H. *Adam, Eve, and the Serpent.* 1st ed. New York: Random House, 1988.

Pope, Liston. "Religion and the Class Structure." *The Annals of the American Academy of Political and Social Science* 256 (1948): 84–91.

Prager, Dennis. "Why Christians Support Israel." *National Review* (blog), March 6, 2018. https://www.nationalreview.com/2018/03/why-christians-support-israel/.

Puscifer. *The Rapture (Fear Is a Mind Killa Mix).* Conditions of My Parole. Puscifer Entertainment, 2011.

Rad, Gerhard von. *Genesis, Revised Edition: A Commentary.* The Old Testament Library. Louisville: Westminster John Knox Press, 1973.

Raheb, Mitri. *Faith in the Face of Empire: The Bible Through Palestinian Eyes.* New York: Orbis Books, 2014.

Richard, Pablo. "Hermenéutica Bíblica India: Revelación de Dios En Las Religiones Indígenas y En La Biblia (Después de 500 Años de Dominación)." In *Sentido Histórico Del V Centenario (1492–1992),* edited by Guillermo Meléndez, 45–62. San José: Cehiladei, 1992.

Said, Edward W. *Orientalism.* New York: Vintage Books, 1994.

Sand, Shlomo. *The Invention of the Jewish People.* Ebook. London; New York: Verso, 2010.

Santaemilia, José. "Sexuality and Translation as Intimate Partners? Toward a Queer Turn in Rewriting Identities and Desires." In *Queering Translation, Translating the Queer: Theory, Practice, Activism,* edited by Brian James Baer and Klaus Kaindl, 11–25. Routledge Advances in Translation and Interpreting Studies 28. New York London: Routledge, 2020.

Schick, Irvin Cemil. *The Erotic Margin: Sexuality and Spatiality in Alteritist Discourse.* London: Verso Books, 1999.

Schiffrin, Deborah. "Narrative as Self-Portrait: Sociolinguistic Constructions of Identity" 25, no. 2 (1996): 167–203.

Schlegel, William. *Satellite Bible Atlas: Historical Geography of the Bible.* Second Edition. Jerusalem: The Bible Society in Israel, 2016.

Schneider, Tammi J. *Mothers of Promise: Women in the Book of Genesis.* Baker Academic, 2008.

Schnepp, J. THE PEOPLE OF THE STATE OF NEW YORK, Respondent, v. KENNETH R. FACEY, SR. (Appellate Division of the Supreme Court of New York, Fourth Department February 21, 1986).

Schreiner, Thomas. *Commentary on Hebrews.* Nashville: Broadman & Holman, 2015.

Schwartz, Regina M. *The Curse of Cain: The Violent Legacy of Monotheism.* Chicago: University of Chicago Press, 1997.

Scuro, Jennifer, Devonya N. Havis, and Lydia X. Z. Brown. *Addressing Ableism: Philosophical Questions via Disability Studies.* Lanham, MD: Lexington Books, 2018.

Segovia, Fernando F. "Introduction." In *Colonialism and the Bible: Contemporary Reflections from the Global South*, edited by Tat-Siong Benny Liew and Fernando F. Segovia, ix–xxxi. Lanham, MD: Lexington Books, 2018.

Shelley, Mary Wollstonecraft. *Frankenstein; or, the Modern Prometheus*. London: Henry Colburn and Richard Bentley, 1831.

Smith, Amy C. "Eurymedon and the Evolution of Political Personifications in the Early Classical Period." *The Journal of Hellenic Studies* 119 (1999): 128–41.

Smith, John. *The Generall Historie of Virginia, New England & the Summer Isles*. Glasgow / New York: James MacLehose and Sons / The Macmillan Company, 1907.

Smith, Mark S. *The Early History of God: Yahweh and the Other Deities in Ancient Israel*. 2nd ed. Grand Rapids: William B. Eerdmans, 2002.

Smith, Ted A. "The Mark of Cain: Sovereign Negation and the Politics of God." *Modern Theology* 36, no. 1 (January 2020): 56–73.

Smith, Theophus H. *Conjuring Culture: Biblical Formations of Black America*. Oxford: Oxford University Press, 1995.

Spector, Stephen. "Abraham and Isaac: Human Frailty and Trauma in Genesis." *Jewish Bible Quarterly* 50, no. 4 (October 2022): 211–20.

Spero, Shubert. "Was Cain the Father of Civilization?" *Jewish Bible Quarterly* 48, no. 2 (April 2020): 111–16.

St. André, James. "In All His Finery: Frederick Marryat's *The Pacha of Many Tales* as Drag." In *Queering Translation, Translating the Queer: Theory, Practice, Activism*, edited by Klaus Kaindl and Brian James Baer, 84–95. Routledge Advances in Translation and Interpreting Studies 28. New York London: Routledge, 2020.

Staff. "From Whom Are the Modern Palestinians Descended?" GotQuestions.org, January 4, 2022. https://www.gotquestions.org/Palestinian-descent.html.

———. "Most U.S. Evangelical Leaders Expect Persecution in Coming Years." National Association of Evangelicals, November 28, 2016. https://www.nae.org/u-s-evangelical-leaders-expect-persecution-coming-years/.

———. "Why Do Christians Support Israel?" International Fellowship of Christians and Jews, December 5, 2022. https://www.ifcj.org/news/stand-for-israel-blog/why-do-christians-support-israel.

Staff, Al Jazeera. "Israel Says 'High Possibility' Its Army Killed Shireen Abu Akleh." *Al Jazeera*, September 5, 2022. https://www.aljazeera.com/news/2022/9/5/israel-probe-shireen-abu-akleh.

State of Israel. "The State of Israel as a Jewish State." Constitution for Israel, 2014. https://knesset.gov.il/constitution/ConstMJewishState.htm.

Ştefănescu, Bogdan. "The Complicated Selves of Transcolonialism: The Triangulation of Identities in the Alternative Peripheries of Global Post/Colonialism." *Metacritic Journal for Comparative Studies and Theory* 8, no. 1 (2022): 63–83.

Sugirtharajah, Rasiah S., ed. *Still at the Margins: Biblical Scholarship Fifteen Years After Voices from the Margin*. T & T Clark, 2008.

———. *The Postcolonial Bible*. The Bible and Postcolonialism 1. Sheffield: Sheffield Academic Press, 1998.

———, ed. *Voices from the Margin: Interpreting the Bible in the Third World*. 25th anniv. Maryknoll, NY: Orbis Books, 2016.

Bibliography

Tahhan, Zena Al. "Shireen Abu Akleh: Al Jazeera Reporter Killed by Israeli Forces." *Al Jazeera*, May 12, 2022. https://www.aljazeera.com/news/2022/5/11/shireen-abu-akleh-israeli-forces-kill-al-jazeera-journalist.

Tamez, Elsa. "The Bible and Five Hundred Years of Conquest." In *Voices from the Margin: Interpreting the Bible in the Third World*, edited by R.S. Sugirtharajah, 25th Anniv., 3–18. New York: Orbis Books, 2016.

The Christian Missionary Alliance. "Staying on Mission: A Guideline for How Alliance Churches Respond to Obergefell v. Hodges." The Christian Missionary Alliance, November 2019.

Thompson, Thomas L. *The Mythic Past: Biblical Archaeology and the Myth of Israel*. New York: Basic Books, 1999.

Throntveit, Mark A. *Ezra-Nehemiah*. Kindle. Louisville, KY: John Knox Press, 1992.

Trible, Phyllis. "Ominous Beginnings for a Promise of Blessing." In *Hagar, Sarah, and Their Children: Jewish, Christian, and Muslim Perspectives*, edited by Phyllis Trible and Letty M. Russell, 33–70. Louisville: Westminster John Knox Press, 2006.

Trible, Phyllis, and Letty M. Russell, eds. *Hagar, Sarah, and Their Children: Jewish, Christian, and Muslim Perspectives*. Kindle. Louisville: Westminster John Knox Press, 2006.

Verkerk, Dorothy Hoogland. "Black Servant, Black Demon: Color Ideology in the Ashburnham Pentateuch." *The Journal of Medieval and Early Modern Studies* 31, no. 1 (Winter 2001): 57–77.

Warren, E. W. *Nellie Norton, or, Southern Slavery and the Bible: A Scriptural Refutation of the Principal Arguments upon Which the Abolitionists Rely: A Vindication of Southern Slavery from the Old and New Testaments*. Macon, GA: Burke, Boykin & Co., 1864.

Weiser, Jonathan. "Collectivism or Individualism?: The Tower of Babel as a Sociolinguistic Metaphor with Implications for the Theory and Practice of Messianic Redemption." *Journal of Ecumenical Studies* 57, no. 1 (2022): 134–47.

Wellhausen, Julius. *Prolegomena to the History of Israel*. Atlanta: Scholars Press, 1994.

Wermund, Benjamin. "Trump's Education Pick Says Reform Can 'Advance God's Kingdom.'" *Politico*, December 2, 2016. http://www.politico.com/story/2016/12/betsy-devos-education-trump-religion-232150.

Westermann, Claus. *Genesis 1–11: A Commentary*. Translated by John J. Scullion. Minneapolis: Augsburg, 1974.

Wheatley, Phillis. "On Being Brought from Africa to America." Poetry Foundation. February 7, 2023. https://www.poetryfoundation.org/poems/45465/on-being-brought-from-africa-to-america.

Whitelam, Keith W. *Invention of Ancient Israel*. New York: Routledge, 1996.

———. "The Poetics of the History of Israel: Shaping Palestinian History." edited by David M. Gunn and Paula M. McNutt, 277–96. Sheffield: Sheffield Academic Press, 2002.

Wilson, Marvin R. *Our Father Abraham: Jewish Roots of the Christian Faith*. Second edition. Grand Rapids: William B. Eerdmans, 2021.

Wilson, Stephen M. "Blood Vengeance and the Imago Dei in the Flood Narrative, Genesis 9:6." *Interpretation* 71, no. 3 (July 1, 2017): 263.

Wiredu, Kwasi. *Cultural Universals and Particulars: An African Perspective*. African Systems of Thought. Bloomington: Indiana University Press, 1996.

Wong, Jessica Wai-Fong. *Disordered: The Holy Icon and Racial Myths*. Waco, TX: Baylor University Press, 2021.

Wray, T. J., and Gregory Mobley. *The Birth of Satan: Tracing the Devil's Biblical Roots*. New York: Palgrave Macmillan, 2005.

Wright, Kai, ed. *The African American Experience: Black History and Culture Through Speeches, Letters, Editorials, Poems, Songs and Stories*. New York: Black Dog & Leventhal, 2009.

Wright, Stephen C., and Micah E. Lubensky. "The Struggle for Social Equality: Collective Action Versus Prejudice Reduction." In *Intergroup Misunderstandings: Impact of Divergent Social Realities*, edited by Stéphanie Demoulin, Jacques-Philippe Leyens, and John F Dovidio, 291–310. New York: Psychology Press, 2009.

Ziemer, Benjamin. *Abram—Abraham: Kompositionsgeschichtliche Untersuchungen zu Genesis 14, 15 und 17*. Beihefte zur Zeitschrift für die alttestamentliche wissenschaft 350. Berlin: De Gruyter, 2005.

Žižek, Slavoj. *In Defense of Lost Causes*. London; New York: Verso, 2008.

———. *Violence: Six Sideways Reflections*. 1st Picado. New York: Picador, 2008.

Index

Abel, 23, 51, 56–59, 65–66, 90
Abraham, 24, 34, 37, 40, 51, 60, 63, 79, 101, 104–5, 117–23, 125–33, 135, 137, 139–42, 144–47, 150, 151–54, 157–61, 163, 167–68, 171, 176–78, 183, 187, 190, 194
abrahamic covenant, 121, 123, 126, 154, 167, 183
Adam, 23, 29, 31–34, 37–38, 41–46, 51–52, 56–60, 64–65, 87, 89, 106–8, 181
adamah, 45
American Israelism, 40
Ammonites, 24, 137, 148–49, 166
Aquinas, Thomas, 44
Augustine, St., 38, 44, 46, 156

Babel, 98–9, 103–4, 107–8, 110, 112, 115
Bilhah, 79, 178
Black Jesus Movement, 75
Black Lives Matter, 73, 79, 81, 105, 193
Body of Christ, 3, 7, 33, 39, 52, 59, 85, 112, 119–20, 155, 190
British Israelism, 40

Cain, 23, 50–54, 56–68, 71, 90, 93, 158, 167, 176, 190–91

Canaanite, 76, 83, 88, 123, 125–26, 140, 148, 166, 168, 172, 183
colonialism (including ideological), 2–5, 13, 23, 31, 33, 36, 40–41, 46, 52, 68, 72–73, 77, 87, 90, 93, 100–102, 105, 117, 121–24, 127, 139, 144, 147, 164, 170, 173n5, 182, 190, 193
Critical race theory, 73

Dinah, 17, 171–72

Eden, 58, 104, 108
Edom, 166, 169
Eli, 2
empire, 3–12, 13–14, 23, 33, 40, 45, 58, 63, 66, 73, 85, 97, 101, 105–7, 109–11, 114, 116–20, 124–28, 139–41, 159–60, 190–91
equality, 8, 20, 46, 74, 80
Esau, 25, 58, 163–69, 171–73, 176–77
Esther, 166–67
Eve, 23, 29, 31–33, 37–38, 41–45, 52, 58, 64–65, 108, 146, 166, 181
evil, 42, 44–45, 52, 57, 65–66, 71, 77, 84–87, 92–93, 99, 120–21, 123, 144–45, 149, 165–66, 178–79

gender, 4, 12–14, 17, 21, 23, 29, 32, 38, 40–41, 43, 46, 124, 138, 142, 166–67

208   *Index*

genocide, 40, 71, 85, 88, 91–92, 94, 123–24, 130, 139, 189, 191
Global South, 4–5, 183, 193

Hagar, 24, 79, 125, 131, 133, 151–61, 176, 178, 181
Ham, 23, 31, 62, 65, 67–69, 71–72, 74–77, 79–81, 86–87, 90, 92, 94, 112, 176, 190–91
Hamitic Hypothesis, 71–72
human dignity, 77, 194

imperialism, 13, 15, 25, 52, 64, 72, 75, 99, 121–22, 164, 182, 190, 193
inequality, 5, 55, 71, 79–81, 97, 147, 180, 192
interpretation, 1, 3–4, 7–24, 29, 31–37, 39–41, 43, 45–46, 51–54, 56–59, 61–62, 65–66, 69, 72–74, 78–81, 87–89, 92–93, 97–105, 108, 113, 117, 121, 123–25, 128–29, 131, 137–40, 142–44, 147, 149, 176–78, 181, 187, 190–93
Isaac, 24, 63, 117, 121, 127–33, 152, 156–57, 159–60, 163, 165–68, 117
ishah, 33–34, 178
Ishmael, 24, 125, 127–28, 131, 133, 152–61, 163, 167–68, 173, 181

Jacob, 25, 79, 105, 116, 121, 127, 155, 163–69, 171–73, 175–78
Jael, 166–67

Lamech, 60, 63–64, 87, 93
Leah, 79, 171, 176–78
LGBT(QIA), 5, 38–39, 47, 80, 124, 138
Liberation theology, 9–10, 73
Lot, 24, 125, 137, 141–49

Marcus Garvey, 65–66
marginalization (and marginalized body), 1, 5–7, 9–10, 14–15, 17, 22, 24, 41, 45–47, 75, 81, 133, 137, 139, 142, 147–48, 156, 158, 160, 164, 170, 175, 189, 190, 192, 193

minority, 3–4, 6, 9–11, 39, 44, 46, 54–55, 72, 77, 85, 98, 100, 114, 156, 169; minoritized, 4, 6, 10, 17, 24, 35, 38, 41, 43, 45
mission activity, 32, 36, 47, 64, 76, 122, 124, 127, 176
Moabites, 24, 137, 148–49, 166

national narrative, 125, 155, 157, 160, 168, 189
Noah, 4, 24, 31, 51, 58, 60, 71, 72, 74, 76, 79, 83–91, 106, 112, 125, 129, 137, 148

occupation, 11, 91
orientalism, 6, 23, 35, 53, 149, 164, 169

postcolonialism, 1–23, 35, 39, 41, 45, 52, 66, 80, 93–94, 98, 100, 109, 121, 127, 131, 147, 187, 190, 192–93
power, 1–2, 4–10, 12–13, 15–16, 18–19, 21–25, 32, 38–41, 44–45, 47, 52, 58–59, 61–63, 66, 75–76, 81, 84, 86, 89, 90–93, 98–103, 106–11, 113–15, 118–22, 125–27, 129, 131, 133, 138–41, 143–44, 146–49, 151–52, 155, 158–61, 164, 167–68, 170, 175, 182, 184, 187, 190–91, 193

qahal, 149
qaniti, 52
qayin, 52

Rachel, 79, 169, 176–78
racism, 54, 73, 79, 90, 105, 191
Rebekah, 132, 165–66
revelation, 11, 14, 21, 29, 40, 42–43, 52–53, 62, 65, 75, 84, 93, 97, 100, 102, 107, 111, 112, 119, 122, 142, 148, 152, 154, 157, 161, 188, 193

Sarah, 24, 79, 132–33, 151–52, 155–61, 176, 178
Satan, 3, 44–45, 49, 54, 65–66, 75, 89, 103, 120, 145

Index

sexuality (including homosexuality), 14, 24, 27n38, 29–30, 34, 38, 51–52, 67, 137–39, 142–46, 167

shiyt/shat, 64

sin, 44, 56, 61, 78, 87, 90, 92–93, 123–24, 149

sin (deity), 54

slavery, 3–4, 23, 36, 47, 56, 60, 62, 64, 67, 71–72, 74–80, 86, 92, 94, 114, 122, 131, 133, 144, 148, 155, 158, 167, 172, 175, 178–80, 183

Sodom, 124–25, 137–38, 140–49

supersessionism, 79, 86, 119

Tamar, 17, 176, 183–84

translation, 1, 3, 9, 16, 35, 52, 67, 83–84, 88, 92, 97, 99, 103, 105, 107, 113, 117, 121, 139, 158, 178, 190

Tubal-Cain, 63

unitarian universalism, 39, 145

yada,' 142, 146

Zillah, 63

Zilpah, 79, 178

About the Author

Jeremiah Cataldo is professor of history in the Frederik Meijer Honors College at Grand Valley State University. With a doctorate in the areas of biblical studies and history of ancient Israel, he has written extensively on biblical interpretation and the sociology of monotheism. His previous books include *What the Bible Says About Sex*, *A Social-Political History of Monotheism*, *Biblical Terror*, *A Theocratic Yehud*, and others.